BISMARCK AND HOOD

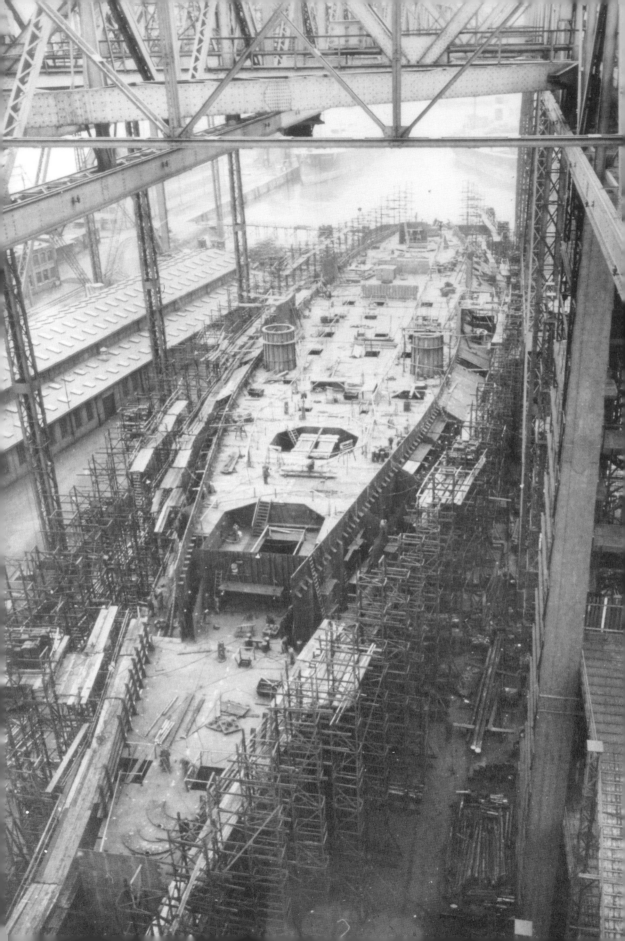

BISMARCK AND HOOD

THE BATTLE OF THE DENMARK STRAIT: A TECHNICAL ANALYSIS FOR A NEW PERSPECTIVE

MARCO SANTARINI

FONTHILL

Previous page: Battleship *Bismarck* under construction, Hamburg, 1938. (*Blohm & Voss*)

Left: Bismarck's *Panzersprenggranate* 38 cm L/4.4 together with a *Sprenggranate* 30.5 cm L/3.8. (*Podzun Pallas Verlag*)

Fonthill Media Limited
Fonthill Media LLC
www.fonthillmedia.com
office@fonthillmedia.com

First Published 2013

British Library Cataloguing in Publication Data:
A catalogue record for this book is available from the British Library

ISBN: 978-1-78155-231-5

Typeset in 10.5/13pt Minion Pro
Printed and bound in England

Connect with us
 facebook.com/fonthillmedia
twitter.com/fonthillmedia

Contents

Preface

The analysis by an author of another nationality of an event like the Battle of the Denmark Strait – fought with great valour on 24 May 1941 – is rather like casting a furtive glance at the interior of someone else's home. Besides, trying to write something new about such a thoroughly discussed subject might seem presumptuous. However, the large amount of data available makes it appealing to give further investigation to a few aspects of this battle that are still 'blurred' in spite of the many historical contributions. In particular, once the historian's instinctive aversion to the use of supposedly 'dull' technicalities is overcome, it is possible to achieve a quantitative analysis aimed at a better understanding of the most critical stages of this event. This can be attained by a more realistic interpretation of the facts, namely an interpretation capable, where necessary, of going beyond traditional accounts that are often firmly based on deep-rooted stereotypes rather than indisputable matters.

This is the author's aim – to present a new approach to the elements that are still unclear, in order to attain a potentially more credible and true-to-life perspective. The relevant aspects – strategic, operational, tactical, technical and terminal – are discussed one by one, progressively reviewing how the protagonists used the resources available to them and deployed their forces:

- Strategic – use of battleships by the *Kriegsmarine* in the Second World War.
- Operational – use of battleships by the *Kriegsmarine* during Operation *Rheinübung*, and the forces used by the British to counter them.
- Tactical – use of German and British heavy ships during the battle.
- Technical – use of heavy-calibre guns in the same engagement.
- Terminal – use of ammunition of heavy-calibre guns and its effects.

This study is based on a reconstruction of the events made possible by the wealth of information contained in the vast Bibliography, which also includes graphs of the main ballistic quantities of Krupp 380/47 guns aboard KMS *Bismarck*. The Appendices contain a detailed, mathematical description of the kinematic and ballistic model of the battle, which was then used to carry out the statistical analysis substantiating the final remarks.

Acknowledgements

The genesis of this book was my realisation that the literature on the Battle of the Denmark Strait, however abundant, includes no technical analysis of the event. So I set out to attempt an unbiased critical analysis of the battle based on real ballistic data and realistic technical estimates.

First of all, I wish to thank the staff of the *Historisches Archiv Krupp* for providing the graphs of the main ballistic quantities of Krupp 380/47 guns onboard the *Bismarck*. This source material was essential to the project.

A great contribution to the English version was given by Catharine Blore, who collaborated with the translator Paola Leoni. They both deserve my most grateful acknowledgement.

Special thanks must go to Philippe Caresse, the *Wilhelmshavener Zeitung*, and Blohm & Voss for providing photographs of the *Bismarck*. I am also very grateful to William Jurens, John Roberts and Peter Hodges, who kindly gave their consent for the use of their drawings, and to Frank Allen of the HMS *Hood* website. I also want to thank my publisher, Alan Sutton, for his interest and support.

Thanks must also go to my children, who have tolerated my obsession with naval gunnery.

Finally, I would like to express my gratitude to my wife for her editorial help, critical questions, and advice. This book is dedicated to her with all my love.

The views expressed in this book are mine alone and are not to be construed as those of the Italian Navy. All errors in fact or analysis remain my own.

Introduction

The epic quality of the Battle of the Denmark Strait on 24 May 1941 has produced such a deep impression on historians and ordinary people that the giant steel vessels and their crews are almost legend. Many elements together lend an aura of greatness and heroism to the event:

- The majestic power of the opposing ships. HMS *Hood* – the 'Mighty Hood' as she was called then – embodied the greatness of the Royal Navy. On the other hand, KMS *Bismarck* was the most advanced operational German battleship, as well as the heaviest in the world for displacement by the spring of 1941, although this was kept secret by the Third Reich.[1]
- The tactical situation recalled an ancient medieval duel between bold, armoured warriors riding towards each other with intent to kill, bound by the same fate of death and glory.
- The incredible similarities between the Battle of Jutland and the Battle of the Denmark Strait. The latter – in spite of the few units involved – seems like a sort of posthumous bloody appendix to the former. We can easily imagine *Korvettenkapitän* (KK) Adalbert Schneider being directly inspired by KK Georg von Hase (the celebrated First Artillery Officer of SMS *Derfflinger*) while he was 'magically' employing the battery of heavy-calibre guns on the *Bismarck*.
- The extreme shortness of the battle (less than 20 minutes) and the ravaging German firepower, whose effectiveness – already famous – became mythical and sometimes overestimated. In particular, the Royal Navy, after its nightmarish experience with the *Bismarck* in May 1941, was inclined to attribute disproportionate capabilities to her sister ship, the *Tirpitz*.

Aim of this study

Certainly, there is an abundance of literature on the subject of the Battle of the Denmark Strait. All the same, the accounts of the event are frequently schematic, traditional and sometimes even clichéd. The standard version insists on a few well-known key points: the absolute and immediate accuracy of the German fire; the thinly armoured protection of the *Hood*'s decks; and the technical problems affecting the guns on board the *Prince of Wales*. However, a different approach, together with an analysis of more technical

Battlecruiser *Hood*. (*Imperial War Museum, London*)

aspects, may raise a few reasonable doubts as to what really happened and justify a more thorough investigation. In this way, a technical analysis offers the opportunity to dispose of a few myths in order to gain a clearer understanding but, at the same time, imposes exacting constraints on the selection of the information available. With reference to the first aspect of the battle worthy of further investigation, for example, the author has chosen to consider only the hits that can be *definitely* attributed to one specific contender, as an exploratory study should, at least, rely on a few indisputable facts.

Aspects of the battle worthy of further investigation

First of all, the difference between the hits scored by the *Bismarck* against the *Hood* and those scored by the (hardly efficient) guns of the *Prince of Wales* against the German battleship is striking, even if both the distance and the time intervals were roughly similar: 1 or 2 hits out of 40 shots in the first instance (between 0556, when the Germans started to fire, and the moment when the *Hood* was sunk) and 3 hits out of 55 in the second (between 0553, when the British started to fire, and the moment when the *Hood* was sunk). This is an interesting difference, even if the above performances cannot be directly compared as belonging to different types of guns. There is also a marked difference between the effectiveness of fire displayed by the German battleship against the *Hood* and then against the *Prince of Wales* (although this time the hits were scored at mean distances and under kinematic-geometric conditions which were not comparable): 1 hit out of 40 shots and 3 out of 53 by 0609 (when the Germans stopped firing) respectively. It is therefore necessary to investigate the above differences to ascertain whether they were produced by chance or should be attributed to other, more likely, causes.

Second, the available data of exterior and terminal ballistics recorded for the *Bismarck*'s 380/47 shells and the distribution of the *Hood*'s armoured protection raise doubts about the trajectory (according to standard accounts) followed by the German shell responsible for the sinking of the British battlecruiser. Again, it may be worthwhile to investigate further.

Third, during the Battle of Jutland as many as three British battlecruisers had exploded, and yet could anyone reasonably expect that HMS *Hood* was to suffer a similar fate? And that only after five large-calibre salvoes fired against her? A quantitative analysis appears sensible.

Fourth, the problems affecting the working of the *Prince of Wales*' 356/45 guns, frequently highlighted by the British, did not actually prevent the battleship from firing a total of 55 shells against the *Bismarck* (3 hits); a similar amount was fired by the German vessel against the *Prince of Wales* herself, with a comparable number of hits. Furthermore, the fire from the *Prince of Wales* surely caused more damage than vice versa. However, historians have praised only the effectiveness of fire from the *Bismarck*, while that from the British battlecruiser has been hardly acknowledged. This issue, too, should be given careful thought.

Finally, when closing in on the enemy, and throughout the battle, the British made a few important tactical mistakes. At the same time, they were plagued by unfavourable events and technical failures, which had a negative effect on the final outcome. This is well known and has been thoroughly discussed. However, no one has ever tried to specify the relative weight of each of the above elements on the outcome of the battle. For this reason, the analysis proposed, based on Lanchester's Laws determining the effects of the 'concentration of force' in a fight, attempts to quantify the most fateful events afflicting the British.

An analysis and a synthesis

Certainly, absolute knowledge of what really happened cannot be acquired. All the same, it is possible to gain new insights. In fact, hypotheses can be made to explain a certain occurrence and its evolution over a period of time and then the results obtained through projections can be compared with historical elements. In the process, the initial hypotheses will be gradually refined with results increasingly closer to reality. In practice, the hypotheses concur to build a 'model', i.e. an algorithm expressing the inner connections (the laws governing the evolution of the situation) between the initial conditions and the effects recorded at the end of the event. The level of knowledge thus achieved will depend on the model's degree of refinement – the more the projections (calculated on the basis of the model) are in agreement with the actual events, the more realistic and reliable the model.

Obviously, more satisfactory results can usually be obtained when the event under investigation is simple, short-lived and well documented by plenty of information and data. The Battle of the Denmark Strait, with its extreme brevity and ample literature, appears totally suitable in this respect. However, the great amount of information available (not completely homogeneous and at times even contradictory) requires work on investigating its consistency, as reality allows just one description – a difficult task considering the multiplicity and diversity of sources and references.

Using a model also means resorting to calculation. This attempt at quantification, albeit technical and seemingly unattractive, is nonetheless particularly important because this is the only way the probability of the occurrence of the hypotheses can be worked out. Otherwise the hypotheses would never acquire enough credibility to be considered as possible alternatives to traditional interpretations and widespread beliefs.

In short, the model (or, more correctly, the set of models) proposed in this study is the instrument used to gain new insights into the Battle of the Denmark Strait and to put a more probable and realistic interpretation on this famous event.

1

The Strategic Context

1.1 Anglo-German naval rivalry between the *Belle Époque* and the First World War

Since its birth, the Imperial German Fleet had never represented either a threat or a term of comparison to major navies. However, in 1873, with the approval of the *Flottengründungsplan* (Fleet Foundation Plan) the work of the Command of the German Navy was finally rewarded with the awarding of funds for the construction of new vessels, which in turn gave impetus to the national shipbuilding industry. When Kaiser Wilhelm II ascended the throne (in 1888) the naval leaders continued to act with the full support of the Emperor, who had a great passion for all things maritime. In particular, Alfred von Tirpitz, then *Konteradmiral* (Rear Admiral), worked indefatigably to obtain Parliament's approval of the important Naval Law of 1897 and of the subsequent 1900 Act, which gave a significant boost to the building of new ships. These events contributed to the rapid development of the fierce Anglo-German naval rivalry that many historians consider to be one of the causes of the First World War.

Certainly, Wilhelm's navy could count on excellent materials and training. All the same, in 1897 the quantitative gap between the German Navy and the Royal Navy was still wide, with a strongly unbalanced force ratio of 1 to 5 in favour of the British. At that time Germany did not represent a real threat to the maritime power of Britain, whose main competitors at sea were France and Russia. In this context, the British Parliament had passed the Naval Defence Act in 1889, setting the 'two-power standard' criterion. The aim was to have a fleet with a force equal to the sum of the ships in active service belonging to the second and third navies. Towards the end of the nineteenth century, the French Navy followed the so-called *Jeune École* strategy advocated by Admiral Aube (who became Minister of the Navy in 1886) and strongly decreased battleship building, while great stimulus was given to the construction of a considerable number of large armoured cruisers designed for commerce raiding against merchant shipping. The French strategy led to the adoption by Britain of a new 'two keels for one' policy, which was far more costly than the previous one as two new ships had to be built for each one of the main competing navy.

The state's finances were drained by the Royal Navy in order to maintain British superiority. Paradoxically, a few years later (in 1904) the latter was endangered by a decision of the First Sea Lord, Admiral John Arbuthnot Fisher, who ordered the construction of a new kind of armoured vessel, HMS *Dreadnought*, outclassing any other existing ship.[2] The advent of the new and (in some ways) revolutionary battleship drastically reduced the value of previous vessels and their suitability for use as key elements of the fleet's fighting line. Actually, Fisher realised that the opportunities offered by the growing new trends in the fields of artillery and naval propulsion, if neglected, would enable any other navy to achieve technological supremacy over the Royal Navy, which, however powerful, was hindered by an extreme reluctance to abandon its traditions for a more innovative approach.[3]

Fisher was well aware that the greater efficiency of modern naval guns and the higher speed provided by a propulsion plant equipped with steam turbines acted as 'multipliers' deeply affecting the actual numbers of the force ratio.[4] With the significant imminent changes in the field of shipbuilding, the force estimate had to be qualitative as well as quantitative. However, Fisher's decision to 'mount the tiger' of technology before other nations realised its importance made it easier for the Imperial German Navy to catch up, as the British advantage was nullified *de facto* by the new terms of the competition. Given the lack of operational experience with the use of the new battleships at war,[5] the contest between the two navies resulted practically in a double-sided competition involving the national economies on the one hand, namely the funds that could be allocated to the purpose, and the relevant industry sectors on the other, especially heavy industry.

In 1912, (after the Agadir crisis of the previous year) Britain decided on a superiority of at least 60% to counter the growing German rivalry at sea, i.e. 16 battle units *v.* 10 (the number set in the German Naval Act). Qualitatively, Admiral Fisher's revolutionary concept, immediately adopted by the Imperial German Navy, involved the construction of two new-type battle units: the Dreadnought and the battlecruiser.[6]

Both types had a 'monocalibre' architecture (i.e. a high number of heavy guns with the same calibre, initially 305 mm) and a turbine propulsion plant. The main differences concerned the number of heavy guns, the power of the propulsion plant and the speed it provided, together with the thickness and the extent of the armour-plating as the tasks these ships were designed to perform were varied.[7] Dreadnought-type vessels, better armed and protected, were expected to fight against similar enemy units. Battlecruisers instead were the hard core of the searching forces – they acted as the 'cavalry' and the 'eyes' of the fleet. Their operational task was to sight the enemy, and to maintain contact until the arrival of superior forces, accepting or refusing battle by means of their higher speed. Battlecruisers would prove their vast superiority over enemy cruisers in operations of commerce warfare.[8]

In 1914, the force ratio (R) (limited to modern battle units for qualitative considerations) between the Royal Navy and the Imperial German Navy was 22 British ships against 16 (around R_{UK} 1.5 *v.* 1). The German Navy was still at a distinct disadvantage and yet it was sufficiently powerful according to Tirpitz's risk theory. In fact, Tirpitz believed that the German fleet had to be large enough to represent a substantial risk for Britain[9] – the very modern concept of deterrence.[10]

Contrary to what Tirpitz had anticipated, however, the British would indeed take the risk. During the first two years of war, on the basis of the force ratio the Germans plausibly searched for the most favourable conditions for a 'decisive battle'. On several occasions German heavy units made raids into the North Sea and bombed the English coasts, thus provoking a British reaction resulting in sea battles, the most important of which were at Dogger Bank (24 January 1915) and above all the Battle of Jutland, the largest battle without fighting aircraft in naval warfare history (31 May-1 June 1916).

At the Battle of Jutland the force ratio between the new capital ships was 38 to 27. The UK formation included Admiral Jellicoe's Grand Fleet with 24 battleships and 3 battlecruisers[11] plus Admiral Beatty's battlecruiser fleet with 7 battlecruisers and 4 Queen Elizabeth-class 'Super Dreadnought' battleships.[12] The Germans deployed the High Seas Fleet under Admiral Scheer with 22 battleships and a scouting force commanded by Admiral Hipper including 5 battlecruisers, hence R_{UK} was about 1.4 to 1.[13] Interestingly, the assessment of the force ratio includes not only battleships but also battlecruisers, which seems wrong considering the tasks originally envisaged for them.[14]

Beatty himself in a letter to his wife before the Battle of Jutland wrote that he commanded 'the best battle force in the world', showing that he had fatally misunderstood the role given to battlecruisers by design makers. It was during the Battle of Jutland, when these units fought against each other and against superior forces including battleships, that Beatty bitterly realised how mistaken he had been in their deployment.[15] Actually, this mistake was made at Jutland by both the British and the Germans who employed battlecruisers in the same way as fast battleships.

In 1941, Admiral Tovey, Commander of the Home Fleet, did likewise: he did not hesitate when it came to send HMS *Hood* against KMS *Bismarck*. He was sure that the old battlecruiser was perfectly capable of fighting even the most advanced German battleship. Moreover, this time the force ratio (theoretically) approached a very favourable 2 to 1. However, both at the Battle of Jutland and at the Battle of the Denmark Strait, the consequences of the mistaken deployment of battlecruisers by the Royal Navy were absolutely disastrous.

At the end of the First World War, the core of the glorious High Seas Fleet, the splendid result of Tirpitz's indefatigable efforts and the Kaiser's pride and joy, no longer existed. The years of inactivity subsequent to the Battle of Jutland had undermined morale and made it easy prey to the propaganda spread by the numerous Bolsheviks who were part of the crews. The outcome was the scuttling of the fleet interned at Scapa Flow on 21 June 1919 – in a surge of nationalistic spirit the seamen proudly followed the orders of Admiral von Reuter. The few remaining ships were given to the Allied navies as war reparations. The Treaty of Versailles also limited the German naval forces to a minimum of 15,000 men, 8 armoured ships (6 in service and 2 as a reserve) with a displacement of 10,000 tons and 280-mm calibre guns at most.[16]

1.2 The importance of the force ratio

General considerations

In the previous section the approximate value of the force ratio (R) between the antagonists has been mentioned several times:

$$R = \frac{F_{OWN}}{F_{ENEMY}}$$

The reason for the emphasis lies in the importance of this value whenever it comes to set the criteria behind the choice of the most effective employment of forces in a military conflict and in turn for each of the levels – strategic, operational, tactical and technical. Therefore, careful consideration will be given later in this study to the force ratio in the analysis of the operational employment of German large capital ships in the Second World War, and especially of the tactical operations during the Battle of the Denmark Strait. In this context, it is immediately evident that all possible situations affecting R are complementary when there are just two opponents. In fact, if a unitary value is assigned to the sum of the opposing forces, with the force ratio expressed by a fraction, then the value of antagonist *a* is the reciprocal of the value of antagonist *b*:

$$Fa + Fb = 1 \quad Ra = Fa/Fb = (1 - Fb)/Fb \quad Rb = Fb/Fa = Fb/(1 - Fb)$$

As a result, it is possible to extract a first general principle, i.e. the decisions concerning employment suitable for force *a* are usually complementary to those for *b*. This concept is represented in the schematic diagram of Fig. 1 at the end of this chapter.

The Principles of War and Lanchester's Laws
First of all, there is the need to obtain the most favourable value of R. To this end, since the nineteenth century western military culture has developed a few theoretical guidelines for the increase (or *concentration*) of one's own forces and the decrease of the enemy's before a battle. These guidelines are called the Principles of War and for the most part are derived directly from an idea of war based on the achievement of the highest level of force to employ in an open decisive battle, i.e. in that direct confrontation which is the essence of the *western* conduct of war.[17] There is neither a fixed number nor a standard formulation of these principles in the war-fighting doctrine of different countries. Moreover, there is no hierarchy among the principles – none is considered more or less important than the other, as they are all closely connected.

However, there is general agreement about the importance of the Force Concentration Principle, from which most of the other principles derive. Interestingly, this principle has long been discussed and has been the subject of important analytical studies.[18] In this regard, a significant contribution was given by Frederick Lanchester, a British engineer, who devised a series of mathematical formulae known as Lanchester's Laws. These laws are differential equations describing the variation in the attacker and defender strengths over a period of time. Each strength is subject to attrition by the other's and is defined by coefficients which quantify qualitative aspects, such as leaders' ability, personnel training, superior manoeuvring, materials performance and supply, etc. In particular, Lanchester proposed a mathematical law (Square Law) describing a time dependence (quadratic equation) of attacker and defender strengths and the final outcome of a combat. This law also highlighted the self-amplifying feature of force concentration (i.e. the inherent trend towards fast, quadratic increase following even a small initial difference in strength between the two antagonists).[19] Hence, the great importance of the ability to 'hit first', as Admiral Fisher constantly recommended. (He was First Sea Lord in 1914, and a supporter of the dawning fire-control modern technologies.)

Sun Tzu's quantitative criteria

Sun Tzu, the famous Chinese military strategist, saw the relationship between R and the most convenient use of one's own force and proposed a first approximate ratio to be considered at operational level in his famous treatise *The Art of War* (sixth century BC).[20] This relationship, which can be easily applied by analogy to the higher strategic level and the lower tactical, technical and terminal levels, has been variously interpreted by generals and admirals of all ages, who knew nothing of the theory developed in China but were well aware that it is crucial to identify the best move and to make it at just the right moment.[21]

After a quick analysis of Sun Tzu's values for R, producing the desired outcome, it is possible to conclude that his criteria were fairly prudent, i.e. they were intended to secure victory by a wide margin (see Fig. 6). However, the much higher value of force required to accept battle turns out to be impractical to implement for economic as well as temporal, technical and logistical reasons. This is why it is often necessary to consider R values lower than Sun Tzu's and resort to factors that can virtually *amplify* the available force in order to reach the *canonical* values. These factors are called *force multipliers* and are of differing natures. They are usually linked with the adoption of new technologies to achieve technical surprise and/or particular manoeuvres aimed at tactical surprise or the division of enemy forces.[22] During the Battle of the Denmark Strait, the British naval force was superior on paper but did not allow the margin suggested by Sun Tzu for responding to the unexpected.

1.3 The strategic context from 1935 to 1941: the reasons for commerce raiding

On 16 March 1935, Hitler unilaterally declared that the Versailles provisions prohibiting German rearmament were no longer in force. Consequently, Britain tried to reach an agreement to put a limit on the growth of the German Navy. This was achieved with the Anglo-German Naval Agreement of 18 June 1935, which recognised Germany's right to rebuild the fleet with the proviso that the total tonnage of German surface units would not exceed 35% in relation to the naval strength of the British Commonwealth. Accordingly, the command of the *Kriegsmarine* developed a construction programme extending the projects already started and in some measure exceeding the limits imposed by the Treaty of Versailles. The new programme took into account the trends in German foreign policy which saw France, Poland and Russia as potential enemies, i.e. countries without a powerful navy.

However, around mid-1938, Hitler openly started to consider the idea of a potential war with Britain. This was a significant change with far-reaching implications for

The launching of the *Bismarck*, Hamburg, 14 February 1939. (*Blohm & Voss*)

German naval forces. In fact, the need to include the Royal Navy in the number of possible enemies required a radical adjustment both of the strategic predictions concerning the employment of the *Kriegsmarine* in war and of construction as well as training programmes. Towards the end of 1938, a new programme was proposed that markedly potentiated the construction of military units well beyond the limit set by the 1935 agreement.

The so-called Plan Z – at a predicted cost of over 33 billion *Reichsmarks* – was officially approved on 29 January 1939. It was based on the assumption that the fleet would not be employed at war before January 1946,[23] and on the unrealistic hypothesis that Britain would not similarly start naval rearmament, even if the restrictions imposed by the Washington Naval Treaty (6 February 1922) had expired two years before. The span of time considered was medium to long term, and the final goal was to produce a great surface fleet capable of directly competing with the Royal Navy for control of maritime areas. According to the plan, the fleet was also to acquire in a shorter period of time commerce warfare capacity, which implied fighting convoy protection forces in favourable temporary and local conditions of superiority.

To this end, specific priorities for the new naval units were established. First of all, the new vessels had to operate in oceanic waters quite independently, hence submarines and surface units with armament, endurance and speed as required by commerce raiding.

Accordingly, most battle units should have been completed by 1943, whereas aircraft carriers –as a last priority – were to be built afterwards.

It is well known that, despite Hitler's assurance to *Großadmiral* Raeder, the date for the employment of the fleet in the war was anticipated to be 1943-44. Actually, in September 1939, construction was well behind schedule, while the operational requirements had changed again. The delay, especially regarding capital ships, resulted from the sheer impossibility of reducing the time necessary to build such ships to fit into the ever more urgent dates imposed by Hitler. For this reason, a major portion of Plan Z concerning large battleships was practically abandoned when war broke out or shortly thereafter, even if German naval engineers went on updating their projects nearly up to the end of the war, envisaging ships that were so large as to make their construction highly improbable.[24] Therefore, the Bismarck-class battleships were to be the last and most modern German capital ships used in war.[25]

This situation forced the *Seekriegsleitung* (Naval Warfare Command) to reduce expectations and alter the initial strategic objectives, giving up long-term sea control and reallocating all available resources on projects consistent with the new scenarios. The *Kriegsmarine* opted then for a strategy involving the use of the whole fleet for commerce raiding: an implication of the wider concept of 'sea denial', the purpose of which was to prevent the flow of vital supplies to the enemy.[26] It is worth noting that as early as the end of the nineteenth century, France had already centred its anti-British naval strategy on commerce raiding, following the ideas developed by the *Jeune École* school of strategic thought. The French naval theorists were well aware that the French economy could not face a long-term battleship building competition with Britain, and hence they wished for a fleet of different naval vessels, (cruisers and torpedo-boats) to threaten the British sea lines of communications and counteract the strength of the Royal Navy credibly. The *Kriegsmarine*'s choice instead was contingent on events or, more exactly, it was largely forced by Hitler's decision to anticipate the war with Britain. In fact, the force ratio between the two fleets at the beginning of the war made it impossible for the Germans to pursue and establish sea control through winning great battles:[27]

ROYAL NAVY (1939)			KRIEGSMARINE (1939)	
Battleships	12[28]		Battleships	2 (+3)[29]
Battlecruisers	3		Battlecruisers	0
Aircraft carriers	6[30]		Aircraft carriers	0

The overwhelming R_{UK} value of 6 to 1 made it impossible for the *Kriegsmarine* to consider engagement in direct confrontations with its opponent. It was therefore necessary for the German Navy to resort to the sea denial strategy and, in particular, to trade warfare, while the Royal Navy was in a position to impede the free use of the sea. Actually, given the lack of heavy units and patrol units available, this strategy was once again implemented through the 'distant blockade' already adopted in the First World War, i.e. the control of access routes to the North Atlantic from the North Sea.

A long time before, the *Kriegsmarine* had started to consider seriously the use of great surface units, to complement submarines, for anti-commerce warfare. This strategy had been formally proposed by Admiral Wolfgang Wegener in a book in which he criticised the naval strategy adopted by Germany during the First World War.[31] Wegener pointed to the lack of fleet action, stating that the engagement of large units in the control of communication routes would have been much more useful than the few raids on the eastern coasts of Britain or the resort to the concept of a power fleet which the German Navy had been compelled to adopt after the strategic defeat of the Battle of Jutland. In the first years of the Second World War, the *Kriegsmarine* therefore planned and carried out operations involving heavy units against enemy maritime trade. The war at sea was characterised by the epic deeds of the 'pocket battleships' and by the raids into the Atlantic of the 'terrible twins' (*Scharnhorst* and *Gneisenau*) together with the heavy cruiser *Admiral Hipper*.[32] Then came the famous episode with the battleship *Bismarck*.

In particular, the outcome of the Battle of the Denmark Strait highlighted the outstanding war fighting capabilities of Bismarck-class units which could have been safely countered only with preponderant forces. Battleship *Tirpitz*, the *Bismarck*'s twin, was always regarded with great anxiety by the Allies and the *Seekriegsleitung* exploited as a deterrent the credibility earned in her short life by the first unit of this class. However, the solitary end of the *Bismarck* on 27 May 1941 after repeated attacks by vastly overwhelming British naval forces induced the Germans to abandon commerce raiding in the Atlantic by heavy surface units.[33] Nonetheless, the *Kriegsmarine* continued to pursue a sea denial strategy, employing heavy units too, even if their actual contribution in terms of sunk tonnage was inadequate in relation to the losses suffered.

In 1943, a few large vessels (the *Scharnhorst*, *Admiral Hipper* and *Lützow*) were deployed in the Arctic for targeted disruption of trade, namely the interception of specific Allied convoys transporting military supplies to Russia. Moreover, the *Tirpitz* was sent to Norway where her mere presence in the fjords acting as a 'fleet in being' was a threat to Allied merchant shipping. The *Tirpitz* was highly effective in her action because of the terrible memories of the sinking of the *Hood*.[34] In fact, this episode significantly contributed to the almost legendary aura surrounding the ships of that class after the Battle of the Denmark Strait.

1.4 Technical aspects of shipbuilding

In this respect, the historic and technical importance of pocket battleships needs mentioning. Their relevance to the birth of modern fast battleships, including KMS *Bismarck*, was considerable. In fact, around the mid-1930s, there were three concomitant circumstances:

- A sustained evolutionary trend started by new operational requirements demanding fast battle units truly capable of producing equal or higher speed than the 'old' battlecruisers without sacrificing protection and armament.
- The development of new technologies enabling ships of the line to reach the performance targets set by major navies.
- The will to build larger battleships than in the past.

Bismarck's bow superstructures at the end of her fitting out. (*Philippe Caresse*)

In particular, naval engineering produced a strong increase in the power generated by steam plants with no added weight.[35] The power-to-weight ratio of 85 kg per shaft-horsepower (shp) of the *Dreadnought* (1906) became about 17.5 kg per shp of the *Bismarck* (1940). Without an increase in the displacement percentage devoted to propulsion at the expense of other components, it was then possible to provide a higher value of installed power and – consequently – higher speed.[36] Moreover, the *Kriegsmarine* was the world's first navy (1930) to adopt and put into service capital ships with a welded rather than riveted hull (Deutschland class). Thanks to this procedure, extended in Germany to many following vessels but belatedly adopted by other navies, the cost of greater structural rigidity was more than counterbalanced by a considerable saving in weight accompanied by a possible increase in the percentage devoted to protection, while the hull solidity remained unaffected.

These technological developments, together with greater displacement than the average ships of the First World War, were the essential prerequisites of modern fast battleships possessing both the firepower and protection of classic battleships and the speed of battlecruisers. Sacrificing protection for higher speed was no longer necessary. Even if the new-type unit first in the line was the Italian RN *Vittorio Veneto*, the concatenation of events leading to the birth of fast battleships was caused by the revolutionary design of the *Deutschland* in 1930. This German masterpiece of naval architecture was created out of the very limits set by the Versailles Treaty of 1919.[37] She outgunned the fastest ships of her time and outran all the largest armed vessels. Such a ship could be fought only with an innovative battleship faster than 28 knots and armed with over 280-mm calibre guns.

The French Navy was the first to accept the challenge. In 1931, it approved the construction of the battleship *Dunkerque*: 27,500 tons standard displacement, eight 330/52 guns (two quadruple forward turrets), a speed of 30 knots (130,000 hp) and a maximum 241-mm belt armour.[38] For armament and protection this vessel should not be classified as a fast battleship. However, after commissioning in 1937, she started an irresistible 'domino effect': all major navies produced many other modern armoured vessels, as listed in Table 1.[39] For comparison, Table 2 contains the characteristics of HMS *Hood*. Table 3 indicates the weight distribution for each ship fighting in the Battle of the Denmark Strait. Finally, Table 4 includes the major events marking the life of the warships that took part in the battle.

Table 1

Name	Navy	Full load disp. (metric tonnes)	Main guns (shell weight in kg)	Vertical max. armour (mm)	Prop. system power (hp)	Max. speed (kt)	In service
Scharnhorst	GE	39,000	9 x 280/52 (330)	350	160,000	31	1939
Vittorio Veneto [40]	IT	46,000	9 x 381/50 (885)	350 (70 + 280)	132,000	31	1940
Bismarck	GE	50,900	8 x 380/47 (800)	320	150,000	30	1940
Prince of Wales	UK	44,500	10 x 356/45 (720)	356	115,000	29	1941
North Carolina	USA	46,000	9 x 406/45 (1225)	310	120,000	28	1941
Richelieu	FR	48,000	8 x 380/45 (890) in 1944 381/44.9 (879)	350	150,000	32	1943

Table 2

Name	Navy	Full load disp. (metric tonnes)	Main guns (shell weight in kg)	Vertical max. armour (mm)	Prop. system power (hp)	Max. speed (kt)	In service
Hood	UK	49,134	8 x 381/42 (879)	305	144,000	31	1920

Table 3

Weight (metric tonnes)	KMS *Bismarck*	KMS *Prinz Eugen*	HMS *Hood*	HMS *Prince of Wales*
Hull	11,950	5,400	15,900	13,700
Armour	18,100	3,600	13,850	12,700
Armament	5,500	1,600	5,400	6,150
Prop. & aux.	4,850	1,600	6,050	2,800
Fittings	900	700	950	1,150
Ammunition	1,550	700	1,300	1,500
Food & spare parts	800	600	700	700
Standard disp.	43,650	14,200	44,150	38,700
Oil & lub.	3,100	2,000	2,500	3,000
Boiler water	500	250	450	350
Normal load disp.	47,250	16,450	47,100	42,050
Extra weight	3,650	2,150	2,034	2,450
Full load disp.	50,900	18,600	49,134	44,500

Table 4

		KMS *Bismarck*	KMS *Prinz Eugen*	HMS *Hood*	HMS *Prince of Wales*
Laid down		1/07/1936	23/04/1936	31/05/1916 1/9/1916	1/01/1937
Shipyard		Blohm & Voss Hamburg	Krupp Germania Kiel	John Brown Clydebank	Cammell Laird Birkenhead
Launched		14/02/1939	22/08/1938	22/08/1918	3/05/1939
Commissioned		24/08/1940	1/08/1940	29/03/1920	31/03/1941
Sunk	on	27/05/1941	15/11/1947	24/05/1941	10/12/1941
	Lat.	48° 10' N	9° N	63° 21' N	3° 34' N
	Long.	16° 08' W	168° E	31° 47' W	104° 28' E
	Depth	≈ 4,800 m	0	≈ 2,800 m	≈ 60 m
Wreck found	on	6/6/1989	///	20/7/2001	///
	by	R. Ballard	///	R. White D. L. Mearns	///
Remarks		The hull stands upright on the sea bottom	Damaged in atom bomb tests (Bikini Lagoon), stranded and sank near Kwajalein Atoll (Marshall Islands) when she was towed toward the open sea. The hull lies upside down on a coral barrier	Construction was interrupted after the Battle of Jutland and restarted in September 1916. The wreck is broken into three main parts	The wreck was first inspected in 1966

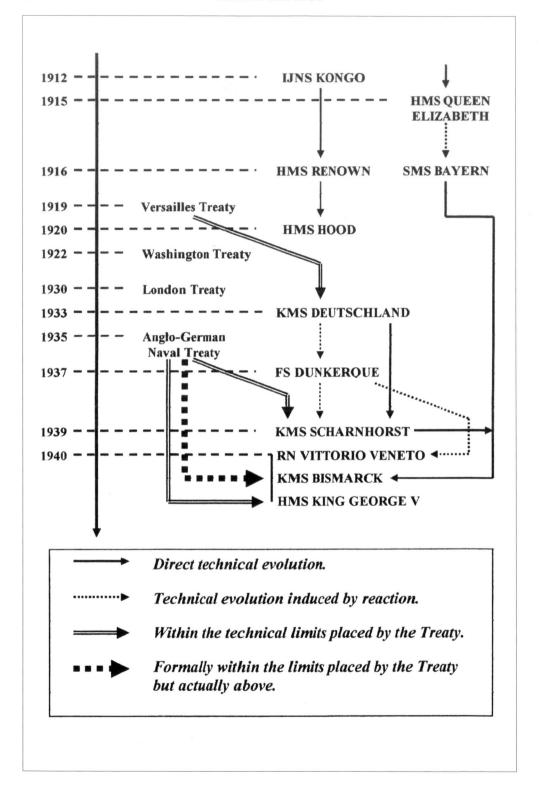

Fig 1: Evolution of the modern fast battleship.

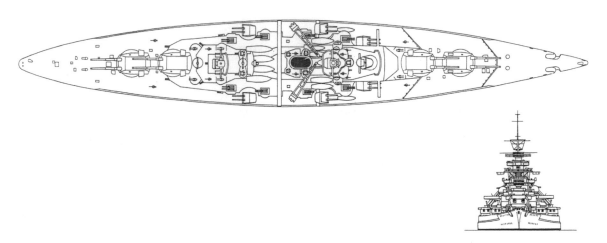

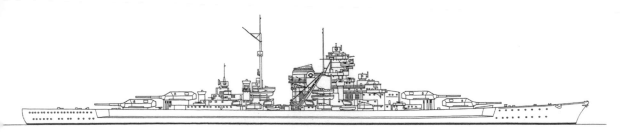

Fig 2: Battleship *Bismarck*'s external profile.

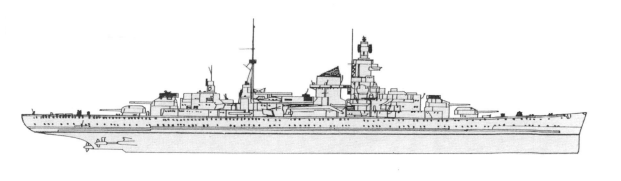

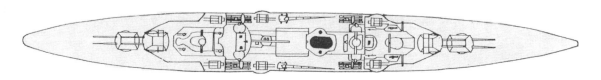

Fig 3: Heavy cruiser *Prinz Eugen*'s external profile.

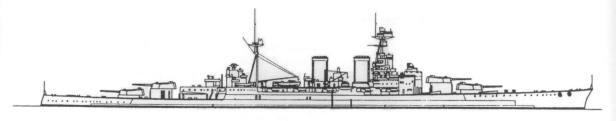

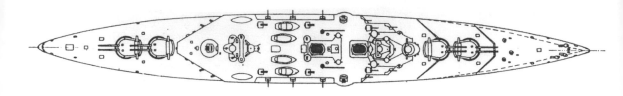

Fig 4: Battlecruiser *Hood*'s external profile before refit in 1940 when the 5.5-inch guns were removed.

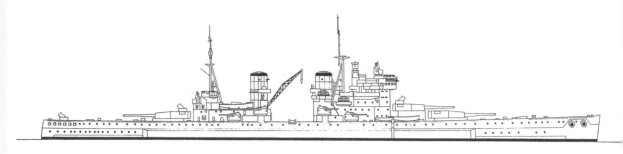

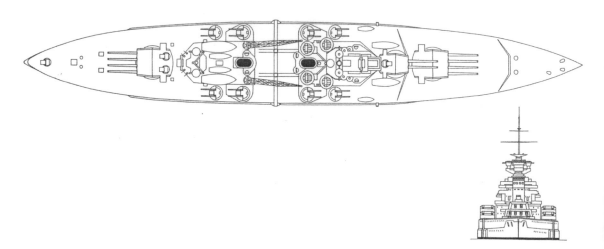

Fig 5: George V-class battleships.

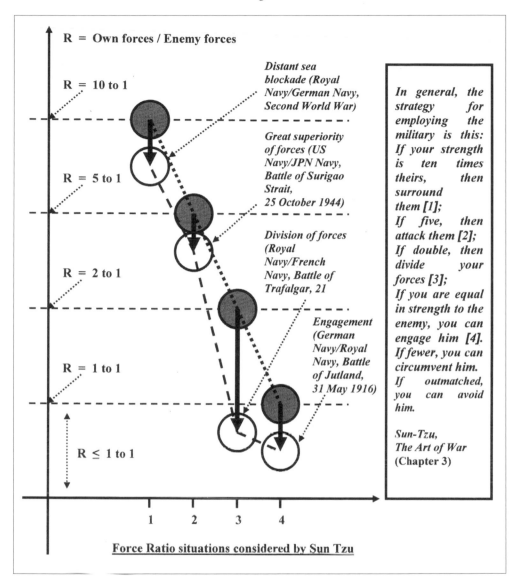

R = Own forces / Enemy forces

R = 10 to 1

Distant sea blockade (Royal Navy/German Navy, Second World War)

R = 5 to 1

Great superiority of forces (US Navy/JPN Navy, Battle of Surigao Strait, 25 October 1944)

R = 2 to 1

Division of forces (Royal Navy/French Navy, Battle of Trafalgar, 21

R = 1 to 1

Engagement (German Navy/Royal Navy, Battle of Jutland, 31 May 1916)

R ≤ 1 to 1

1   2   3   4

Force Ratio situations considered by Sun Tzu

In general, the strategy for employing the military is this: If your strength is ten times theirs, then surround them [1]; If five, then attack them [2]; If double, then divide your forces [3]; If you are equal in strength to the enemy, you can engage him [4]. If fewer, you can circumvent him. If outmatched, you can avoid him.

Sun-Tzu,
The Art of War
(Chapter 3)

Fig 6: Influence of the force ratio on operative decisions. Sun Tzu was probably the first strategist to give formal doctrinal indications of how to act in a confrontation with the enemy in order to achieve supremacy and ensure oneself the maximum freedom of action (the latter being necessary for offensive and defensive operations). Sun Tzu's proposed behaviour supports graduality as a function of the force ratio R. The graph is a comparison between Sun Tzu's prescriptions (grey circles) and what really happened (white circles), in terms of R in selected historical examples. The force ratio was almost always below Sun Tzu's indications. In fact, difficulty in reconciling doctrinal prescriptions with mission constraints and the forces actually available often made commanders at sea take a calculated risk.

2

The Operational Context

2.1 General remarks on Operation *Rheinübung*

The operational planning of the *Kriegsmarine* was based on strategic guidelines defined by the highest command envisaging the offensive use of the surface fleet for trade warfare. In fact, British trade was rightly regarded as vital to support the country's war effort and life itself. During the first years of war, the German Navy therefore carried out a series of operations involving the deployment of heavy units for commerce raiding.[1]

Rheinübung (Exercise Rhine) is the name given by the *Seekriegsleitung* to the Atlantic battleship operation planned to take place in the spring of 1941 with the object of attacking merchant ships, especially those proceeding towards Britain. This mission followed the positive experience gained in the previous successful raids in the Atlantic accomplished by the *Admiral Sheer* pocket battleship (27 October 1940-1 April 1941) and the battleships *Scharnhorst* and *Gneisenau* (23 January-22 March 1941). During the latter operation (Operation Berlin) under the command of Admiral Lütjens,[2] the two capital ships performed so effectively that they sank a total of about 116,000 gross register tons of enemy merchant ships.[3] It is worth noting that during that mission the employment of German capital ships had been heavily influenced by the presence in the area both of a few British vessels patrolling the Denmark Strait and of a battleship escorting a merchant convoy sailing in the Atlantic. However, on both occasions the German ships carefully eluded these forces and succeeded in sailing away unobserved, thus meeting the major requirements of commerce raiding: elude the enemy search and attack, fast and unexpectedly, only in conditions of clear force superiority.

In the hope of replicating the success of Operation Berlin, *Rheinübung* also envisaged the employment of the heavy units available in a commerce raiding mission, once again under the command of Lütjens. The aim, yet again, was to attack and destroy/interrupt enemy shipping lines in the Atlantic. The task of the forces participating in the operation was to penetrate the enemy's distant blockade undetected, break out into the Atlantic and start searching and destroying single convoys/merchant ships sailing to and from Britain.[4] In particular, the *Bismarck*'s task was to distract the escorting warships of the attacked convoy, allowing the other ships of the task force to get at and destroy the merchant vessels undisturbed. At the end of the operation, the German ships were to make for the safe ports of occupied France, which implied penetrating undamaged the British blockade again. The *Seekriegsleitung*'s orders for the operation included the pre-deployment of tankers and

Battleship *Bismarck* embarking materials in Scheerhafen, March 1941. (*Philippe Caresse*)

auxiliaries in the North Atlantic, far from the routes of the Allied convoys and the areas patrolled by the Royal Navy. This shift in the area of operations was necessary to provide technical and logistic support to the ships assigned to *Rheinübung*.

2.2 British operations to block access to the central Atlantic

Given the naval force ratio in 1939, the best option for the *Kriegsmarine* was commerce raiding to destroy British trade, whereas the clear superiority of the Royal Navy over its opponent enabled it to implement strategies of containment. These strategies included sea blockade operations in order to impede German access to the high seas. For the implementation of this blockade of German units stationed in the ports controlled by the Axis forces in the Baltic Sea and in the North Sea, the Royal Navy adopted the same general guidelines followed in the First World War.

The hypothesis of a close sea blockade (as against France during the Napoleonic Wars), placing warships near the blockaded ports with sufficient strength for success, was necessarily discarded in favour of a distant blockade because of the threat posed by the possible presence of enemy U-boats as well as the lack of an adequate number of suitable units. The distant blockade entailed patrolling (with air and naval forces) all possible routes to the central Atlantic between Greenland and the English Channel and ensuring that the core of heavy surface vessels (consisting of battleships and aircraft carriers) stationed at Scapa Flow intervened only if the need arose.

The British naval base of Scapa Flow was of the utmost importance because of its location in the Orkney Islands (off the north coast of Scotland), which made it convenient for the areas to be patrolled – even if a few hundred miles away. It was well known since the First World War as a major naval base for anti-German warfare, and also for the scuttling, on 21 June 1919, of the *Hochseeflotte* (High Seas Fleet) interned there.

Scapa Flow's geographical position and distance from patrol areas called for fast ships. All the R- and Nelson-class battleships whose speed was inadequate were therefore excluded from missions to counter breakout attempts. Furthermore, a number of the capital ships had to be deployed in the Mediterranean for the specific needs of that theatre of war, thus reducing the number of those actually available to prevent German heavy ships from sailing the Atlantic. HMS *Hood* was among them, together with the new *King George V* and the 'old' but still dreaded battlecruisers *Repulse* and *Renown*.[5] Actually, in spring 1941 both vessels were assigned to convoy escort operations in the Atlantic and the Mediterranean respectively.

As for aircraft carriers, in May 1941 just a few of this type were able to contribute to the sea blockade because of the sinking of HMS *Courageous*, torpedoed by U-boats in September 1939, and HMS *Glorious*, destroyed by the *Scharnhorst* and *Gneisenau* during the Norwegian Campaign (8 June 1940). In addition, HMS *Illustrious* was undergoing repairs in the USA, while HMS *Furious* and HMS *Formidable* operated in the Mediterranean. HMS *Eagle* was deployed in the South Atlantic, and HMS *Hermes* in the Persian Gulf.

In practice, only HMS *Victorious* and HMS *Ark Royal* could be employed for the distant blockade of the German ports. Planning the best possible use of the few major ships available was therefore absolutely necessary. In particular, it was imperative that they were not employed in interception operations where inaccurate information could jeopardise success and therefore render their employment useless in operations doomed to failure. For this reason, only the certain passage of enemy forces across the patrol area would make the naval group designated to the control of the high seas leave Scapa Flow.

However, this intrinsically implied delayed intervention. That is why it appeared convenient to act on the safe side and keep a second naval task force at Scapa Flow for another attempt to intercept and engage the enemy in case of failure of the first group. This was the rationale behind the division into two groups of the already scarce major ships available for the blockade, with the resulting decrease in the 'force' projected by each group.

From the above, it is clear that the extension of the maritime areas to patrol, added to the limited number of heavy and fast surface vessels, made it difficult for the Royal Navy to carry out, with the necessary force concentration, the containment of the German units within the Baltic Sea and the North Sea. Actually, this difficulty typically pertains to reactive defence where the power to exercise the initiative is left to the enemy. In this context, the communication of 'ship ready for combat' given by the Captain of the newest (and reasonably fast) *Prince of Wales* was surely met with favour and relief by Admiral Tovey, Commander-in-Chief of the Home Fleet.

2.3 The German forces and the opposing British units

In spring 1941, the 'terrible twins' were plagued by various types of problems which kept both of them in the French port of Brest.[6] These were initially meant to accompany the *Bismarck*. However, the necessity for repairs first caused a postponement of the operation of one month. Then it became necessary to abandon the initial plan and to fall back on the only available heavy cruiser, the *Prinz Eugen* (the first of its class derived from the previous Admiral Hipper class). In the end, the task force assigned to *Rheinübung* under the command of Lütjens[7] was solely made up of the brand-new battleship *Bismarck* commanded by *Kapitän zur See* (KzS) Ernst Lindemann (a specialist in naval artillery)[8] and by the equally new heavy cruiser *Prinz Eugen* commanded by KzS Helmuth Brinkmann.[9] Therefore the German High Command also had problems of force concentration at operational level, during the preparation of *Rheinübung*. However, the resulting limitations were considered acceptable in view of making proper use of surprise tactics – namely, select the most convenient time, location and target when it came to attack the British shipping lines.

The British side had as its protagonists in the early phase of the operation the heavy cruisers *Suffolk* (Kent class, County type) and *Norfolk* (Dorsetshire class, County type) under the command of Rear Admiral Wake-Walker. A second task force included the battlecruiser *Hood* (the only one in her class) commanded by Capt. Ralph Kerr[10] and the battleship *Prince of Wales* (King George V class) commanded by Capt. John C. Leach, a specialist in naval artillery.[11] This more powerful force was subject to the orders of Vice Admiral Lancelot Holland (also a specialist in naval artillery) aboard HMS *Hood*.

Above: Heavy cruiser *Prinz Eugen* in Kiel, 1940. (*Bundesarchiv, Bild 146-1989-027-20/Lagemann*)

Below: Battlecruiser *Hood*, 1933. (*Imperial War Museum, London*)

2.4 Planning *Rheinübung*: critical aspects

Evasion

The key element *par excellence*, evasion is fundamental to the success of all commerce raiding operations. It derives from the need to elude enemy surveillance and hence avoid being discovered while:

- attempting to break the blockade in order to reach an area of operations;
- searching and singling out possible targets;
- lying in wait for merchant ships to destroy or capture;
- leaving the area after the attack;
- breaking the blockade again in order to return to port at the end of an operation.

Evasion of enemy surveillance is extremely important in every phase listed above to avoid enemy counteractions, ranging from the deployment of superior forces to the scattering of its merchant ships. In fact, the problems posed by surface commerce raiding arise from the very reason behind the decision by smaller navies to pursue this particular strategy: a *highly unbalanced* force ratio. In this situation, the stronger opponent can be attacked only when its total superiority (considering all its forces wherever they might be deployed) is not expressed when and where the weaker opponent wants to sail and act.[12] In practice, the enemy should be prevented from concentrating in the relevant tactical area a task force superior to that of the commerce raiders. In this way, the latter will circumvent a heavy engagement. Concentration requires early discovery and accurate recognition. It is therefore absolutely essential to evade enemy surveillance and continue to evade it for as long as possible in order to prevent potential targets that have realised they are in danger from taking flight before getting within effective shooting range of commerce raiders.

Other critical aspects

A few critical aspects concern kinematics, especially speed and endurance, which are instrumental in attempting to:

- break the enemy blockade more easily;
- explore wider areas in search of possible targets;
- sail away more rapidly at the end of an attack.

Furthermore, the use of embarked aircraft for reconnaissance and the availability of organic sensors could play an important role in convoy interception. For greater endurance instead, an adequate number of tankers should be appropriately pre-deployed in the tactical area (these ships too will have to break the enemy blockade and consequently be exposed to attack by hostile forces).

It is worth noting that in the interwar period, especially after 1928, the German Navy had made great efforts to exercise and improve fuelling at sea, a key factor given the limited number of ports available in wartime. From 1937 to 1940, the Dithmarschen-class supply ships were also launched, the most innovative of their time for load capacity, armament, speed and endurance.[13]

Finally, an equally critical need for ships employed as commerce raiders is high reliability (not plagued by frequent breakdowns) and low vulnerability to enemy attack. Technical failures of combat or other systems are likely to jeopardise the continuation of an operation. In fact, the pre-deployment of supply ships and the high preparation of crew members could hardly counter the effects of substantial technical problems. This requirement makes the capital ship an ideal candidate. It was usually provided with the very best of existing technology, which in this case – German technology – could boast efficiency and reliability. In addition, the vessels selected for the operation were equipped with powerful active defence systems as well as strong and extensive passive protection. However, these ships were 'high value' and so their employment in risky commerce raiding operations was intrinsically non-economical.[14] In spite of this, in the first two years of the Second World War the conduct of war at sea by Germany was particularly aggressive and envisaged their extensive use also. The small *Kriegsmarine* had to prove itself in the eyes of the *Führer* to be as successful as the *Wehrmacht* and the *Luftwaffe*.

2.5 Remarks on the first part of *Rheinübung*

Leaving aside the well-known detailed account of events, it is worth noting that the first important operational decision made by Lütjens concerned the choice of route for the *Bismarck* and *Prinz Eugen* to break out into the Atlantic undetected. The Commander of the German group knew that their sailing from Gotenhafen (the former Polish town of Gdynia) to Norway had been followed by British reconnaissance aircraft.[15] On 20 May, the two capital ships had also been sighted by the Swedish aircraft-carrying cruiser *Gotland* while passing through the Kattegat.[16] In attempting to elude enemy surveillance during the critical phase of transfer from Norway to the operational area, it was therefore vital to take the course offering the best chance for success. The route to the North Atlantic involved steaming through one of the following passages:

- the English Channel;
- the Shetland Islands-Orkney Islands passage;
- the Faroe Islands-Shetland Islands passage;
- the Iceland-Faroe Islands passage;
- the Denmark Strait between Greenland and Iceland.[17]

The first option was considered excessively risky as it meant passing rigorous enemy surveillance, with the fleet based in Portsmouth.[18] Similar considerations applied to the next three hypotheses because of the proximity to the naval base of Scapa Flow in the Orkney Islands evoking sad memories for the German Navy. Lütjens therefore decided to try the northernmost passage close to the seasonal ice limits extending further off the coast of Greenland. After all, this route had proven to be a good choice for Operation Berlin. The Denmark Strait (around 320 km at its narrowest) in May offered an ice-free navigable stretch as wide as 50 km at the most.

During Operation *Rheinübung*, bad weather favoured concealment from British surveillance, yet the German task force remained undetected for short periods only, especially in the first part of the operation (from 21 to 24 May). Bad weather provided protection from air reconnaissance during the voyage from Norway to the north-east approaches to the Denmark Strait.[19] At around 2000 on 23 May, the German ships were detected by the cruisers *Norfolk* and *Suffolk* (the latter was equipped with a type-284 radar with a range of around 10 nautical miles) patrolling the area under command of Rear Admiral Wake-Walker.[20] In the meantime, Admiral Sir John Tovey, due to lack of information, delayed the departure of the bulk of the force under his command.[21] However, he thought that most probably the Germans would try, once again, to break out into the Atlantic via the northernmost passage. Therefore he ordered the group formed by the *Hood* and the *Prince of Wales* to leave Scapa Flow for that area at midnight on 21 May. The rest of his ships were to remain in the base until 2245 on 22 May. In this way they could be concentrated in the area where the breakout attempt was sure to take place. In fact, Tovey, in spite of the substantial superiority of the Royal Navy over the *Kriegsmarine*, did not have sufficient forces at his disposal to control all access routes into the central Atlantic under conditions of local superiority such as to bring about a successful outcome in case of confrontation.

Between 0010 and 0247 on 24 May, Wake-Walker's cruisers lost both visual and radar contact with the German group, which induced Holland to change the interception route initially chosen and to steer his naval group north, towards the last known enemy position, thus tightly adhering to the standard tactical procedures. This change of course would contribute to actually worsening the geometry of the British ships when they came into ballistic contact with the German group. It is therefore possible to claim that the insufficient evasion of British surveillance during the first phase of *Rheinübung* jeopardised the chances of success of the operation entrusted to Lütjens by preventing him from fully meeting an essential requirement of commerce warfare.

However, the discovery and the pursuit (shadowing) by Wake-Walker's cruisers did not preclude all chances of *Rheinübung*'s success. Actually, weather conditions were such as to favour the loss of contact, which indeed repeatedly happened later, albeit not definitively. As the breakout of the British blockade had still some likelihood of a favourable outcome, Lütjens decided to continue with the operation. Furthermore, the loss of contact, however occasional (due to bad weather, to the long hours of darkness, and to the unexceptional range of *Suffolk*'s radar) had two important tactical effects to the advantage of the *Bismarck* group:

- Tovey did not clearly realise the course followed during the breakout attempt; hence he did not immediately concentrate the whole of his force in the Denmark Strait.
- Holland was denied the opportunity of achieving the best geometry of interception that would have allowed him much more favourable conditions for the ballistic contact than those that actually occurred.[22]

Holland's task was to intercept the German naval group and engage it in a decisive artillery battle. In fact, the theoretical superiority of the *Hood* and the *Prince of Wales* together was high (although not overwhelming), with a total broadside weight of over 14 tons *v.* 7.4 tons of the Germans. In addition, it is true that the *Prince of Wales* had only recently been commissioned.[23] However, it was the first war mission for the *Bismarck*, too.

Finally, the *Hood*, as previously mentioned, was the most renowned British heavy

Battleship *Prince of Wales*, 20 April 1941. (*Imperial War Museum, London*)

unit and – undeservedly – continued to be considered the most powerful, despite her age and her 'flawed' design (heavy guns and high speed but scarce armour). On the other hand, the *Prince of Wales* was regarded as practically unsinkable at the time of her construction.[24] The presence of the *Hood* group came as an unpleasant surprise for the Germans: it meant that it was impossible to break the blockade undisturbed.

2.6 The Battle of the Denmark Strait and its effects on *Rheinübung*

Outcome

Certainly, the German crews knew that they could rely on good training as well as excellent materials and machinery. All the same, the tactical outcome of the Battle of the Denmark Strait with the sinking of the *Hood* and the withdrawal of the *Prince of Wales* was a totally unexpected success. The reverse was true for the British, whose consternation at this event was profound. However, the operational situation for the German naval group had become critical after the battle. Not only were Lütjens' ships still pursued by Wake-Walker's cruisers[25] but the *Bismarck* herself suffered considerable damage. In particular, she had been hit by three 356/45 shells fired by the *Prince of Wales*.

The first hit at 0556, forward of the transverse bulkhead in the forecastle, passing completely through the ship from port to starboard.[26] It failed to explode but left a one-and-a-half metre hole in the exit side. This shell caused the most serious damage suffered by the German battleship, namely to compartments XX and XXI and the forward pumping station. Consequently, speed had to be reduced by 2 knots to prevent the bulkhead behind compartment XX (shored up while the action was still going on) from giving way under the pressure of water flooding in through the shell's entrance and exit holes in the hull. As much as 2,000 tons of sea water flowed into the forecastle. As a result, the *Bismarck* initially went down 3 degrees by the bow and had a 9 degree list to port, which was later compensated for. The attempt to repair the pumps failed and 1,000 tons of fuel in the forward tanks became inaccessible.

The second shell fell short at 0558 and, after covering a short distance underwater, hit the bottom hull amidships below the armoured belt (extending for 2.2 m under the waterline). The projectile pierced the hull and exploded about 5 m farther on against the 45-mm-thick torpedo bulkhead. It caused the flooding of the forward port generator room and power station No. 4 (compartment XIV) and shattered the bulkheads between that room and the adjacent ones.[27] Some fuel tanks stored in the double bottom were also damaged.

The third shell hit at about 0600, causing minor damage to the fore post of one of the service boats before splashing into the water without exploding.

Operational effects

It is true that in the Battle of the Denmark Strait the Germans had scored a brilliant (and unexpected) tactical victory. All the same, the forces commanded by Lütjens had not broken out into the Atlantic undetected and had been pursued by the Royal Navy. In addition, while the *Prinz Eugen* had come out practically undamaged (in spite of the large-calibre shells falling near her), the *Bismarck* had reported considerable damage affecting her maximum speed and endurance. None of the survivors was able to report what happened on the bridge at the end of the battle. It is possible only to guess that Lütjens, as was his custom, did not share with anyone the thinking behind his decisions, which were initially not to go after the *Prince of Wales* and later to reject all suggestions of making emergency repairs on the damaged forecastle. The latter involved reducing speed, and hence further delay in getting the ship to port. It is not certain whether between 0630 and 0730 on 24 May, Lütjens had already decided to give up commerce raiding or was still pondering the possibility of fulfilling the mission assigned to him. Basically, three alternatives were possible, two of which involved abandoning the operation:

- to discontinue the operation and return to Norway (about 1,100 nautical miles to Bergen);
- to discontinue the operation and make for a French port (about 2,000 nautical miles to St Nazaire);
- to continue the operation at any cost.

The *Bismarck* at anchor in the Grimstadfjord, 21 May 1941. (*Philippe Caresse*)

He probably rejected the first option immediately, assuming that considerable enemy forces could be deployed on that course. However, nobody knows the reason why he decided to make for St Nazaire.[28] In spite of the great distance, perhaps what made the idea most inviting was the vast expanse of water further south, the possible support from U-boats and, at that season, more hours of darkness than in the north. Anyway, the shortage of fuel due to the effects of the first 356/45 hit and the missed replenishment in Bergen was a great concern.

The outcome of the *Bismarck*'s increasingly desperate attempt to reach St Nazaire from 24 to 27 May 1941 is well known. However, it is worth noting that the significant tactical success scored by the German battleship had caused great consternation throughout Britain and had also magnified the *Bismarck*'s potential in the British imagination: only a Leviathan could have swept away the 'Mighty Hood', the pride of the Royal Navy and Britain itself, in just a few minutes.[29]

Consequently, the British were immediately strongly determined to destroy the *Bismarck* at all costs. Thwarting the sortie attempt would not have been enough to heal wounded national pride! Paradoxically, it was the German battleship's striking success

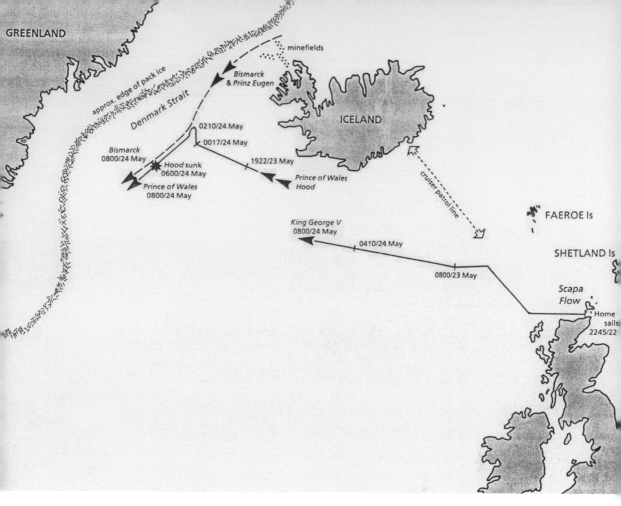

Fig 7: The pursuit of the *Bismarck* from 22 May to 24 May 1941.

that greatly increased the counterattack initiative, giving rise to such a build-up of force as to make the final outcome of the immediately launched pursuit a certainty. In practice, the sinking of the *Hood* had just denied the most essential requirement of commerce raiding – evasion of enemy surveillance and force concentration. At the same time, it had aroused and focused Britain's attention, and the country was now desperate to avenge the insult as soon as possible.[30]

In short, it is true that the Battle of the Denmark Strait had a favourable tactical outcome for the German Navy. Yet this success also in fact indicated the failure to break out into the Atlantic undetected; hence the failure of the whole *Rheinübung*. Never again would the Germans try a similar operation.

3

Tactical Aspects

3.1 British interception manoeuvres

Vice Admiral Holland's mission was to prevent the *Bismarck* group from breaking the British distant blockade in that part of the Atlantic Ocean called the Denmark Strait, stretching from Greenland to Iceland (both under the Danish Crown at that time). To achieve this result, the British commander had to actively look for conditions that would make a decisive battle unavoidable and the damage caused to the German vessels would have prevented the continuation of the enemy mission. The first necessary step was the interception of enemy ships to subsequently enable the tactically most favourable ballistic contact: namely, the situation giving, at tactical level, the highest force concentration over the opponent.

To this purpose, the rules of classic naval warfare of that time suggested the so-called 'crossing the T' manoeuvre.[1] The British ships were to face the enemy at a distance of at least 25 km on a convergent course so that the angle of intersection would have been wide enough (possibly a right angle) to enable all the big guns to fire for effect with a total salvo weight about twice that of the German ships.[2] If the British vessels had steamed in front of the enemy line, compatibly with the seasonal line of the Greenland icepack, their position would have been slightly more favourable to optical rangefinding, too (although by then the British rangefinding method relied mostly on the radar). In fact, in this situation the *Hood*'s group would have been in front of the German ships steaming on a south-westerly course, hence to the east of the Royal Navy group. In the early morning light their silhouette would have stood out more distinctly from the horizon. It is also plausible to presume that Holland wished to approach the enemy so as to avoid 'turn' manoeuvres during the battle which, however necessary with the classic 'crossing the T' to keep ahead of the enemy, would have disturbed and temporarily interrupted British firing.[3]

It is therefore likely that Holland wanted (at least initially) to approach the enemy from the south-east on a convergent course, enabling him to train all his main ordnance on the enemy. However, Holland's ships failed to reach this favourable geometry of interception mainly because of the significant delay accrued from 0010 to 0210 on 24 May following Wake-Walker's loss of contact. In this time span, Holland erroneously decided to change course and turn to the north. This mistake and its effect on interception could not be corrected given the insufficient speed of the heavy ships under his command (actually 28 knots max.). When the *Suffolk* regained contact, Holland realised his mistake and tried to close the range without losing too much bearing, i.e. ending up with an even worse geometry of interception in the attempt to make ballistic contact. However, much to his dismay, at 0535 the German group was sighted abaft the beam on a bearing of 335°, at a distance of about 17 nautical miles – an unfavourable position for the final approach. In fact, the course to follow in order to avoid a further loss of bearing (practically a 'collision course', the only one keeping the enemy bearing constant)[4] did not allow full deployment of the main armament, by denying the use of the after turrets which were unable to train on the target. As S. W. Roskill rightly observes, 'The British squadron did not possess a sufficient margin of speed to win back the lost bearing.'[5]

This influenced the course of the battle, denying the use in the first decisive minutes (between 0553 and 0600) of 45% of the heavy ordnance on board: four out of eight 381/42 guns and four out of ten 356/45 guns. This limitation prevented the force concentration necessary to put in action from the very beginning, at tactical level, the theoretical existing British superiority. The British group was also plagued by other negative events that further reduced the force exerted against the enemy's 'centre of gravity' – the *Bismarck*:

- A mistake concerning the target to engage, so that only the *Prince of Wales* fired against the German battleship. The so-called 'family likeness' characterising the outline of all modern German heavy ships confused the British. In addition the British tactical procedure then in force prescribed that each ship in the line had to fire against the corresponding enemy ship.
- Serious technical problems affecting the *Prince of Wales*' 356/45 guns (Capt. Leach himself had contributed to the development of this gun type during his service at the Admiralty). Consequently, between 0553 and 0602, the average number of 356/45 projectiles per salvo was only three out of six, which were otherwise to be fired by the same number of guns mounted in the two forward turrets (the only ones that could be brought to bear). As many as 15 shells were not fired (due to mechanical and/or electrical problems at the guns and/or propelling charge defects) out of the theoretical 74 that could have been fired in that time span. Hence, only 59 projectiles were fired by the *Prince of Wales*, the last four of them by the turret astern in 'local control' (thus with poor accuracy) after the ship turned to port; just 55 were therefore fired by 0602, the time of the eighteenth salvo. HMS *King George V* had also had problems with the tune-up of her heavy guns during the period of sea trials and practice preceding commissioning. Those problems had not been completely overcome by 27 May 1941, when at the final battle against the *Bismarck*, HMS *Rodney*'s nine 406/45 guns fired 380 projectiles, while *King George V*'s ten 356/45 guns fired only 339, meaning that each large-calibre gun of the second fired about 20% fewer shells than the guns of the older battleship. If the ratio between the theoretically and the actually fired shells is considered as a rough efficiency indicator of the *Prince of Wales*' 356/45 guns, it is possible to quantify (on the basis of the outcome of the battle):

Efficiency = 55 shells / (18 salvoes x 6 theoretical shells until 0602) ≈ 50.9%

To go back to the British approaching manoeuvres, Roger Chesneau in his book *Hood: Life and Death of a Battlecruiser* interestingly observes that Vice Admiral Holland:

[…] was desperate to close the range as rapidly as possible, to lessen the chances of his ship being struck by plunging fire, but he could not aim his bows directly at the enemy, for to do so would enable the latter to draw ahead of him, requiring continuous, gradual changes of course to port by the Battlecruiser Squadron […] until the range was short enough to risk turning *Hood* on a course parallel to that of the target […] he had chosen to close the range more gradually, in a series of 'steps', as it were. The problem was that a rapid closing of the range was not compatible with bringing the full weight of his guns to bear: only his forward turrets would be able to fire at the enemy for the time being.[6]

As suggested by this extract, the (alleged) fear of Holland had its origins in the huge terrible explosions – imprinted indelibly on the British memory – that in a few minutes had destroyed as many as three large ships at the Battle of Jutland: HMS *Indefatigable*, HMS *Queen Mary* and HMS *Invincible*.[7] Surely, the comparison between the Battle of the Denmark Strait and the Battle of Jutland is particularly intriguing when one considers that, on 31 May 1916, HMS *Invincible* was the flagship of Vice Admiral Hood, who died that very day in his sinking ship. Given that fateful circumstance, and in his memory, the barely laid down battlecruiser known as *Construction 460* at John Brown's shipyard on Clydebank was named after him.[8]

The interpretation of the event given by the passage above is the one suggested and accepted by all literature on this subject emphasising the *merely defensive* rationale behind Holland's decision on the final closing manoeuvre. However, this does not seem too realistic. Actually, the British commander, if well aware of the inadequate protection of his flagship, was nonetheless equally aware of the need to perform his mission to the best of his abilities, which called for extremely resolute action against the German attempt to force the blockade. That is why he aimed for a decisive ballistic result with the consequent impossibility for the enemy to continue with the breakout attempt. A high hit probability, hopefully with a success scored before the enemy, could be achieved only at comparatively short ranges. After all, Holland was commanding the only group in contact with the enemy and as such was the one in charge of the scene of action. He had to make every effort to prevent the enemy from breaking into the central Atlantic before it somehow managed to flee and disappear into the vast expanses of the ocean, possibly helped by bad weather.

In retrospect, and with the benefit of hindsight, it is possible to observe how close to success Holland was. If KK Adalbert Schneider, first gunnery officer of the German battleship, had prolonged the adjusting phase by only a few minutes repeating the 'ladder' procedure to make sure that the main battery was on target,[9] the British group would have probably completed undamaged the second turning to port of 20° (ordered a few seconds before 0600) thus bringing to bear all the ordnance onboard. Even with the *Prince of Wales*' guns firing a few at a time (because of breakdowns) and taking into account the time wasted by the *Hood* (when she initially fired against the *Prinz Eugen*), in all likelihood the higher salvo weight of the British ships would have been enough to gain victory.[10]

One should not forget Lt Cdr McMullen's superb performance during the first part of the battle (he was the first gunnery officer on the *Prince of Wales*). However, KK

Schneider's audacity was rewarded by fate. He bet on the accuracy of his second salvo and, throwing caution to the wind, immediately ordered 'full salvoes good rapid', displaying his own great tactical awareness. The following success was so complete and so unpredictable as to leave the Germans themselves in utter disbelief. Not only had the *Hood* been promptly hit by the *Bismarck*'s guns, she had also exploded and sunk a few minutes later with all her crew except for three men – an ensign and two sailors – out of 1,419. This event was almost unprecedented, apart from a few sporadic, dramatic and well-known examples such as the previously mentioned sinking of three British battlecruisers at the Battle of Jutland 25 years before and the explosion of the French armoured ship *Bretagne* in the Algerian port of Mers-el-Kebir (on 3 July 1940 during the controversial Operation Catapult) with the contribution of HMS *Hood* herself then under the orders of Admiral Somerville.[11]

3.2 Fighting manoeuvres of the British units

A few aspects worthy of consideration emerge after a thorough examination of British manoeuvres:

- Of course, Lütjens wished for a replay of his trouble-free previous sortie into the central Atlantic at the beginning of Operation Berlin, but the arrival at the scene of action of Royal Navy heavy units could not have been totally unexpected. In addition, the constant shadowing by the cruisers *Norfolk* and *Suffolk* of Wake-Walker could not have given much hope of evading the blockade. Therefore, it can be argued that the British did not achieve tactical surprise. In fact, the great disappointment and the strong emotion aroused by the discovery of Holland's group, and above all by the presence of the 'Mighty Hood', may have slightly delayed the opening of fire, but the *Kriegsmarine* units were not caught unprepared. Nor was technical surprise a factor, as none of the British ships was fitted with systems of such advanced technology and performance as to ensure clear-cut superiority over the enemy, even with the participation of the recently commissioned *Prince of Wales*, although the same was true also for German ships.[12] By contrast, HMS *Hood*'s old-fashioned design (especially regarding thickness and distribution of vertical and horizontal armoured protection) had never been technically amended, despite the numerous refits she was given over the previous twenty years. Finally, although the Royal Navy was well aware of these limitations, it repeated the operational mistake made at the Battle of Jutland of using battlecruisers as fast battleships regardless of their limited protection. Beatty's error, and perhaps Fisher's, should not have been repeated after the lesson of 31 May 1916! In retrospect, one could say that the lesson was learnt the hard way and yet not fully understood, as it did not lead to the development and the adoption during the ship's life of effective solutions for the last and most important battlecruiser built for the Royal Navy.[13]
- Looking at the course of the battle, it appears as if the British Admiral saw the fight as a mere duel between the two main opposing groups. Seemingly, he failed to consider adequately the presence in the area of Wake-Walker's two heavy cruisers,

which conversely would have been able to intervene, thanks to their maximum speed between 31 and 32 knots, if ordered to do so in time.[14] Clearly, the ballistic contribution of these units would not have been particularly significant, but the use of their torpedoes could have yielded more relevant results. In addition, their very involvement in the battle would probably have caused a different distribution of German fire, as well as kinematic manoeuvres (possibly anti-torpedo evasive manoeuvres) with consequent disturbance to Krupp heavy gun laying. In practice, a more direct involvement of both cruisers could have created an effective diversion, compelling the enemy to divide its force – preventing, or at least disturbing, the correct concentration of fire against HMS *Hood*.[15] In this connection, it is of interest to note that the nominal 2 to 1 tactical superiority of the British group at the beginning of the battle[16] nonetheless required, for the sake of caution, 'a multiplier of its own force' that could have been represented by the diversion mentioned above.[17] However, this requirement was not followed by Holland, who was perhaps guilty of overconfidence in the performance of his group. On that occasion, Wake-Walker's conduct too was not particularly outstanding. In this regard, the author shares the opinion expressed by Ludovic Kennedy in his book *Pursuit: The Chase and Sinking of the Bismarck*. He maintains that it would have been useful if the *Norfolk* and *Suffolk* had closed in on the *Bismarck* and engaged her astern, thus drawing fire on them, but Holland did not give any order to Wake-Walker and the opportunity was lost. Certainly, the ultimate responsibility for this mistake falls to the British commander who was in charge of the scene of action. Even so, it was also a result of the poor initiative shown by Wake-Walker.[18]

- Holland kept the *Hood* in the lead of the British formation. This decision was meant to give his flagship more freedom to fire and manoeuvre, but being the traditional position of the commanding unit in a battle it did not help in deceiving the enemy. In this way, the old and defectively protected *Hood* found herself in the more dangerous position (Plate 3). In this regard, Kennedy writes (see ref. 31) that just before the battle Tovey considered suggesting to Holland that he should move the *Prince of Wales* to the head of the line so that the better protected ship would draw the enemy's fire. However, he decided not to give this order as he '[…] did not feel such interference with such a senior officer justified'. Undoubtedly, Holland's positioning of his ships was not ideal. However, it lends evidence to the conviction that the British commander's decisions were not solely or chiefly affected by defensive considerations.

- Another important element concerns the battle formation adopted by Holland. The *Hood* and *Prince of Wales* were stationed about 4 cables away from each other, equal to 810 yards (nearly 740 m) – really close considering the deployment and speed of the two giant British ships.[19] Not only did this involve a risk of collision during imperfect manoeuvres at high speed but it was not in the least justified: gunfire had to be concentrated on the enemy and not the ships mounting the guns![20] By contrast, the adoption of a highly closed order was useless and actually made German firing easier:[21] after the *Hood*'s explosion there was no need to adjust the firing data but only to lightly correct the gun training against the *Prince of Wales* (Plate 4).

- Furthermore, the British Admiral's handling of his group was rather inflexible. The following extracts further illustrate this point:

The British squadron, moreover, went into battle in close order and was manoeuvred throughout by the Admiral. Individual Captains thus had no freedom to adjust their courses to the best advantage of their own ships. (See ref. 16, p. 402)

The method of handling his squadron may, however, have owed a good deal to the fact that the 1939 issue of the Admiralty's 'Fighting Instructions' which were then in force, not only laid down the tactics to be employed by heavy ships in very rigid terms, but in terms which were redolent of an earlier age – the age of great battle fleets – such as fought at Jutland. (See ref. 17, p. 132)

The following extract from 1939 *Fighting Instructions* may well have been in Admiral Holland's mind: 'Prior to deployment the Admiral will control the movements of the Battle

Battle of the Denmark Strait: a British heavy-calibre shell hits the sea between the *Bismarck* and the *Prinz Eugen*. (*Bundesarchiv, Bild 146-1990-081-10A/Lagemann*)

Fleet as a whole. He will dispose the guiders of divisions on a line of bearing at right angles to the bearing of the enemy battle fleet …'. The rigid wording of those instructions may usefully be compared with Nelson's Trafalgar Memorandum. (See ref. 17, footnote on p. 132)

The greatest tactical difficulty faced by the Admirals of the opposing forces at the Battle of Jutland concerned the need for knowledge – accurate and updated – of the enemy's position. With a field of action so vast and so many squadrons involved, the need to know, at the very least, the position of one's own forces justified the adoption of a rigid handling of manoeuvres. The rather simple tactical situation at the Battle of the Denmark Strait, however, allowed for a much more flexible leadership, giving individual captains a certain degree of discretion necessary for the best use of artillery. The Germans did it, while the *Hood* group unnecessarily proceeded … in close order.

3.3 Manoeuvres of the German group

After leaving Bergen at 1930 on 21 May, the naval force of Lütjens rapidly made for the eastern approaches to the Denmark Strait, the *Bismarck* in the lead at 24 knots followed by the *Prinz Eugen* about 2,000 yards away. They entered the vast sea passage between Iceland and Greenland at 0800 on 23 May. Weather conditions were bad but propitious for the undetected passage and the attempt to break the British blockade. However, this was not achieved and, contrary to German hopes, at 1922 on that very day the German task force steering southward was sighted by the cruiser *Suffolk* patrolling the area together with her 'nearly' sister ship *Norfolk*, both under the command of Wake-Walker. Any chance of achieving surprise by a furtive breakout into the Atlantic had therefore vanished.

At about 2030, to discourage the cruisers from shadowing further, Lütjens gave the order to reverse course to close the range and fire a few salvoes against the pursuers. Three 380 salvoes were fired at the *Norfolk* about 10,000 yards away. The shells fell very close and flooded the target with water and fragments, but no hits were scored. Nor did they weaken British determination while the violent jolts caused by firing put the *Bismarck*'s forward radar out of action. Lütjens then ordered the *Prinz Eugen* to take the lead: her radar was to secure the formation adequate coverage forward. It is not for us to know if this decision was also possibly inspired by the wish to deceive the enemy, given the similar silhouettes of the two German heavy units.[22]

At around midnight on 23 May, the two shadowing cruisers lost both radar and visual contact because of a violent snowstorm. After an erroneous assessment of the kinematic situation, Holland made his units turn northwards at 0010 on 24 May and keep that course until 0210 when he ordered 'course 200°' thus resuming the south-westerly direction, and yet continuing to move slowly away from the German group heading 220°. Later on, at 0247, the *Suffolk* fortuitously regained contact. Realising his error, Holland altered course appropriately and increased speed up to the maximum of 28 knots. However, the accrued delay was to play a major role in bringing about unfavourable geometric conditions during the first minutes of the battle. At 0500 hydrophones aboard

Heavy cruiser *Prinz Eugen*, 1940–1942. (*Bundesarchiv, DVM 10 Bild 23-63-10/G. Urbahns*)

Battle of the Denmark Strait: the *Bismarck* releases a full salvo, 24 May 1941. (*Bundesarchiv, Bild 146-1990-061-27/Lagemann*)

the *Prinz Eugen* detected the sounds of distant fast-moving propellers and a little later, roughly around the same time, the two naval groups sighted one another.[23]

In the early morning of 24 May, while the German task force was speeding on a south-westerly course at 28 knots, the failure of the attempt to elude the enemy was clearly evident. By then it was equally obvious that engagement with the Royal Navy forces implementing the naval blockade in that area was unavoidable. To the Germans the imminent fight was an unwelcome necessity. Not only had they failed in their attempt to avoid detection; they also had to do battle with a theoretically far more powerful enemy. However, the contact geometry favoured the *Bismarck* group, which was able to train all its guns on the target. Paradoxically, the side which would have preferred to avoid battle, in order to best carry out its mission, was forced to engage in combat (albeit under better tactical conditions), while those who had to resort to an all-out engagement to stop the enemy were forced to do so in an unfavourable situation.

Throughout almost the whole confrontation the German task force maintained its south-westerly course (namely that required by its mission), as if the encounter with the British group was only a 'slight hitch'. Furthermore, the German ships enjoyed far more freedom of manoeuvre than their British counterparts (at least in the crucial phase of the battle). After the sinking of the *Hood*, Lindemann apparently tried to persuade Lütjens to pursue and destroy the hard-hit *Prince of Wales*, which was withdrawing rapidly. However, Lütjens decided to hold the breakout's south-westerly course without further delay. He probably hoped, at least initially, to be able to carry out his mission of commerce warfare anyway.

3.4 Remarks on the choice of targets and artillery fire

Holland chose to concentrate the fire of his task force on the leading German ship, erroneously taking it to be the *Bismarck*. Obviously, he had not realised that the *Bismarck* was now following the *Prinz Eugen* (they had changed places many hours before the battle). The order to shift target was eventually given, but it was not immediately followed by the *Hood* herself. The Germans concentrated fire on the ship at the head, HMS *Hood*, whose unmistakable profile with her extra-long forecastle deck and her graceful silhouette, although old-fashioned by then, was promptly recognised.[24] The decision to fire against the famous battlecruiser was surely influenced by her greater importance and war fighting value. The *Hood* was the very epitome of British naval power; however, her great popularity was to be fatal for her.

What if the *Hood* and the *Prince of Wales* had changed places? Would that have been enough to deceive the Germans so that the *Bismarck* would have engaged a different target? After all, the brand-new battleship commanded by Leach (which the Germans mistook for the *King George V*, the flagship of Admiral Tovey) could have been the flagship in her own right. This is not an idle question, albeit a hypothetical and unanswerable one. In fact, had the *Bismarck* concentrated fire on the *Prince of Wales*, this battleship thanks to her sturdy protection (the maximum thickness of her armour was greater than that of the *Bismarck*) would not have sunk rapidly and deprived the British task force of its alleged nominal superiority, which was what happened with the loss of the *Hood*.

Returning to the facts, the decision to fire against the *Hood* complied with the fundamental principle of force concentration. Both British heavy units represented a serious threat of the same level. Nevertheless, the correctly presumed enemy's centre of gravity was immediately engaged with the maximum firepower available.[25] The decision not to divide the fire of the 380/47 battery between the two British capital ships made the adjusting phase more effective, too.[26] However, shortly before 0600 (i.e. before the explosion and the subsequent rapid sinking of the *Hood*) the *Prinz Eugen*, which since 0556 had already fired six 203/60 salvoes against the British flagship, was ordered to redirect her fire onto the *Prince of Wales*.[27] Perhaps this order was given mainly for more accurate observation of the impact points of the projectiles fired by the German battleship, whose salvo frequency was lower (about half as much) than the rate of the heavy cruiser, which implied when both units fired at the same time the presence of water pillars produced by the 380/47 projectiles and twice as many produced by the 203/60 shells.[28] However, the contribution made by the *Prinz Eugen* was surprisingly significant, as she quickly scored a hit on the *Hood* (still during the adjusting phase with her second salvo).

After the explosion of the 203/60 shell in the ready-use lockers of the UP ammunition (unrotated projectiles, anti-aircraft ammunition used by the Royal Navy in the early years of the Second World War), the resulting fire quickly spread fore and aft of amidships. The *Hood*'s three survivors recounted that this fire rapidly became uncontrollable, damaging the ship's superstructure significantly. This testimony prompted a few analysts to offer the suggestive – and somehow 'desecrating' – hypothesis that this wildfire was responsible for the loss of the vessel.[29] However, both boards of inquiry set up by the Royal Navy after the disaster excluded such a possibility and were decidedly inclined to blame the effects of a 380/47 projectile striking the after ammunition room or its immediate vicinity, perhaps the adjacent AA 102/45 magazine which exploded and in turn caused the after 381/42 magazine to blow up.

Regarding this point, one should note that the likelihood of causing the abovementioned fire was increased by the mistake (in retrospect, a very useful mistake!) made by the first gunnery officer of the *Prinz Eugen*, who initially thought he had to fight against light units and provided blasting instead of piercing shells: the first were less capable of penetrating the thick protection of an armoured ship, but they had a superior intrinsic pyrophoric capacity as they contained a much higher quantity of explosive. The fire caused by the *Prinz Eugen* also made German rangefinding far easier as, thanks to stereoscopic Zeiss technology, it could profit from images with blurred outlines too, if sufficiently illuminated (in this instance by extended flames).

At all events, after the first few minutes of the battle (less than four) the Germans preferred the better observation of large-calibre shell impact points to the bigger firepower given by fire concentration. After all, the 203/60 ballistic contribution was limited, little less than one ton per salvo *v.* the virtual 6.4 tons per salvo of the *Bismarck*; in practice less than 16% (with limited piercing capacity) of the total broadside weight per salvo of the German task force.[30] In fact, even her piercing shells could not perforate

Battle of the Denmark Strait: the *Hood* blows up at 0601 on 24 May 1941. (*Bundesarchiv, Bild 146-1998-035-05/Lagemann*)

anything thicker than the armour plates usually fitted to heavy cruisers. The *Prinz Eugen*'s tactical contribution was far greater. Thanks to the British misidentification, it was important to divert the *Hood*'s fire from the German battleship during the first crucial minutes of the battle. The *Hood* failed to engage the *Bismarck*, while the *Prince of Wales* was left undisturbed from 0553 to 0601 and could take her time adjusting fire on the German battleship, on which she scored as many as three hits.

It is now worth examining the damage caused by the opposing units. The *Prince of Wales* opened fire at 0553 and at 0556 struck the *Bismarck* for the first time with a projectile of the sixth salvo fired at a distance of approximately 18,600 m. The other two hits struck at 0558 and 0600. It has to be noted that, in spite of the several mechanical failures dogging her brand-new 356/45 guns, the battleship's rate of fire, inclusive of the interval for the observation of the falling pattern and the ensuing corrections, was excellent: two salvoes per minute, albeit with a rather low number of shots per salvo. Moreover, only 20 shells or so were fired before the first hit, a very good result when actually only five out of her six forward guns were operational.[31] The other two hits on the *Bismarck* followed approximately every 2 minutes, with a further use of about 21 shells: three hits with about forty 356/45 shells fired altogether.

By contrast, the German battleship opened fire at 0556 and struck the *Hood* with her fifth salvo at a present range of about 15,500 m (firing range of about 15,200 m) at around

0600 (40 shells altogether). She was able to train all her guns on the enemy, and this is what she actually did. After the *Hood's* blowing-up, fire was concentrated on the *Prince of Wales*, with as many as seven hits scored between 0602 and 0610 (another fifty-three 380/47 shells were fired by the *Bismarck* from 0601 to 0609).[32] The damage sustained by the British battleship is briefly described below:[33]

- At 0602, the first 380/47 shell struck the bridge (unprotected in the King George V-class vessels), crossing it transversely from starboard to port and killing everyone except the Captain and the Chief Yeoman of Signals.
- At nearly the same time, another shell, whose calibre experts are divided over,[34] penetrated (without exploding) the support of the forward medium-calibre gun director (the High Angle Control System, HACS) of starboard dual-purpose (anti-aircraft and anti-surface targets) 133/50 guns, temporarily jamming it. All the electrical leads between the port director and the same side medium-calibre guns were cut. Finally, the shell struck and heavily damaged the Admiral's charthouse.
- At about 0603, a 380/47 shell from the *Bismarck* struck the mid-ship starboard crane and was deflected upwards, bursting against the base of the after funnel and heavily damaging, among other things, the Walrus plane located near the catapult. As a result, the Walrus was jettisoned over the side.
- At about 0604, a 203/60 shell hit the boat deck. It failed to explode and after passing through some internal bulkheads, fell to the deck where the crew threw it overboard.
- Probably shortly after 0604, the last 380/47 hit fell short and failed to explode on impact with the water at about 24 m from the *Prince of Wales'* starboard side at the height of the back funnel. The shell travelled underwater and penetrated the hull with an angle of entry of about 45°, 8.5 m below the waterline (underneath the armoured belt which extended for 3 m below the waterline). The projectile penetrated about 3.6 m into the ship, causing local damage and limited flooding in the area between the lower and the upper platform deck. When the ship was dry-docked for repairs after the battle, this shell was discovered practically intact (but without the nose cap) against the undamaged 51-mm-thick torpedo bulkhead, after penetrating the keel, an oil tank (with a total estimated resistance equal to a 25-mm-thick plate) and two 10-mm-thick bulkheads.
- Between 0606 and 0608, a 203/60 shell struck the hull slightly below the waterline astern of Y turret, penetrating about 3.5 m into the ship and exploding defectively, thus causing only limited flooding of the area.
- The last 203/60 shell struck the hard-hit British battleship at 0610. It fell short, but with a slight underwater trajectory penetrated the hull on the starboard side, about 1.5 m below the waterline near the rudder stock. The shell detonation caused local dishing of armour plating and minor flooding.

At 0613, as a result of the damage sustained, the *Prince of Wales'* commanding officer, Capt. Leach, decided to break off the engagement and turn rapidly away to the south-east.

3.5 Further remarks

As is well known, the British battleship withdrawal was highly criticised by the First Sea Lord Sir Dudley Pound, who insisted, with Churchill's support, on having Leach court-martialled. This emotional and wholly unjustified behaviour was fiercely opposed by the Commander-in-Chief of the Home Fleet, Admiral Tovey. He rightly recognised that the decision to break off the action had been wise, if difficult.

Certainly, the total damage caused to the *Prince of Wales* during the battle cannot be classed as serious from a material point of view. All the same, the battleship was unable to continue the ballistic engagement with her average rate of fire, i.e. three shots per salvo, imposed by the numerous mechanical failures dogging the 356/45 guns. Only at about 0800 on 24 May (about 2 hours after disengagement) were the mechanical problems that had arisen during firing solved by Vickers-Armstrongs civilian technicians, who were on board to complete the working-up. At all events, the heavy guns required a definitive tune-up at anchor.

Tovey's position was so resolute that Leach was even awarded the DSO (Distinguished Service Order). When he heroically died in the sinking of his ship later that year, the shadow over the decisions he made during the Battle of the Denmark Strait was dispelled once and for all.[35]

In retrospect, some respectful criticisms might be made of the performance of the above British commanders concerning the following:

- *The bold but unrealistic decision taken by Leach to declare the* Prince of Wales *fully operational on 21 May 1941.*[36] In fact, he was well aware that a considerable portion of the crew had not received sufficient training and that the unit as a whole still needed working-up. It is likely that Leach's strong desire to make a contribution to the operations, added to the hope that the crew's commitment and the sturdy passive defences of his ship could counterbalance the existing deficiencies, accounted for his optimistic decision. After all, the King George V-class ships were then considered unsinkable, at least in Britain, thanks to the extent and thickness of their armour. The mechanical defects in the 356/45 guns early in the battle were to prove Leach's decision highly premature. His controversial (but in retrospect totally right) decision to break off the engagement was also prompted by the shock of witnessing the explosion and the immediate sinking of the *Hood* at 0601, as well as the death-and-havoc-wreaking transit of a 380/47 shell through the *Prince of Wales'* compass platform at 0602.

- *Tovey's decision to take the above 'combat-ready' declaration at face value and immediately employ the* Prince of Wales *to intercept the naval group of Lütjens around midnight on the very day that the British battleship was ordered to steam off.* Tovey could have moved his flag on to another unit, making HMS *King George V*, surely more ready than her sister ship, available to join the *Hood* in the operation. However, uncertainty about the German route, together with considerable overconfidence in the global performance of the famous *Hood*, made him optimistically choose the newer vessel.

As for the tactical course of the battle, if it is only right to express admiration for the expertise with which the first and the second gunnery officers of the *Prinz Eugen*, *Fregattenkapitän* Jasper and *Korvettenkapitän* Schmalenbach, accurately adjusted fire and laid the battery, the same should also be said of Lt Cdr Colin McMullen on the *Prince of Wales*. In spite of the evident troubles caused by the numerous breakdowns affecting the 356/45 guns, he managed with great skill to hit the *Bismarck* three times, employing a total of just 55 shells – an average of one hit every 18.33 shots. The German battleship, by contrast, with her guns working perfectly, scored a total of four to five hits out of 93 shots – an average of one hit every 20-25 shots approximately.[37] Furthermore, the *Prince of Wales* scored the first hit 3 minutes after opening fire and after firing six partial salvoes with a total of about 20 projectiles, while it took the *Bismarck*, with her five full

Battle of the Denmark Strait: the *Bismarck* fires one of her last full salvoes. (*Bundesarchiv, 146-1984-055-13/Lagemann*)

salvoes, 4 minutes and 40 projectiles.[38] However, all existing literature stresses the serious mechanical defects in the *Prince of Wales'* heavy gun turrets and the superb performance of the *Bismarck's* artillery! Hence the following observations for the sake of fairness:

- It is true that the *Prince of Wales'* heavy guns were far from efficient, but her fire accuracy was not lower than the *Bismarck's*.
- Considering the results gained by the British battleship, the *Bismarck* was slower in adjusting and correcting her fire against the *Hood*.

Yet no great emphasis has ever been placed on the excellent performance of the *Prince of Wales*, which caused the *Bismarck* much greater damage than that suffered by the British battleship herself. Two different reasons may account for this incongruity. On the one hand, the sinking of the 'Mighty Hood', disappearing after an apocalyptic explosion, was so unexpected and so tragic as to capture the attention and imagination of everyone, both specialists and non-specialists. The British were sure – and probably *needed* to believe it – that the ship capable of causing such a catastrophe involving the loss of the Royal Navy's most powerful ship, Britain's pride and glory, *must* possess absolutely extraordinary war capabilities. In particular, the *Bismarck's* guns grew to huge proportions in the British collective imagination and her firing would be remembered for its legendary efficiency. On the other hand, by excessively exalting the effectiveness of fire of the *Prince of Wales* it would have reinforced doubts in the minds of those who were strongly dissatisfied with the outcome of the battle over Leach's hard and objectively valid decision to break off the engagement.

The *Bismarck's* firing performance is worthy of further investigation in the light both of what has been observed above and what emerges from a direct comparison of the results achieved against the *Hood* and successively against the *Prince of Wales*. In fact, there is an apparent incongruity between the statements exalting the *Bismarck's* gunnery performance and the technical data still available. An analysis addressing this issue will be attempted in the next chapter.

3.6 A different scenario?

As stated in the Introduction to this book, the author chose to consider only *definite* hits in the belief that the probability study had to rely on *indisputable data* (i.e. the first hit on the *Hood* scored by the *Prinz Eugen* at around 0557 and the second, fatal, hit on the *Hood* scored by the *Bismarck* at around 0600). However, in the last decade some sources have reported that one or more hits were scored on the British battlecruiser in the minutes between 0557 and 0600.[39]

These reconstructions are based on the testimonies of the three survivors (Bob Tilburn, William Dundas and Ted Briggs) and on the report of Flt Lt R. J. Vaughn, who in his Sunderland saw the *Hood* on fire in two places, aft amidships and at the base of the bridge. In particular, Ted Briggs stated: '[…] a shell I think went through the spotting top […] and there were bodies falling down on the wing sail bridge'. Falling bodies were also seen by Dundas from the loopholes in the conning tower. A shell going 'through the spotting top' is supposedly a first hit by the *Bismarck* with the third salvo, even if none of the three survivors actually witnessed the event. The hit has been inferred from the difficulty in contacting the first gunnery officer from the bridge, as reported by Briggs. Was Moultry dead or simply disconcerted by the order to redirect *Hood's* firing and too busy to answer the bridge? After all, *Hood's* guns boomed till the end. In any event, what is more important is that this 'hit' cannot be unquestionably attributed to the *Bismarck*. In fact, until 0559 or so, the *Prinz Eugen* had been firing on the *Hood* and her firing had been well on target since her second salvo; hence another hit by the *Prinz Eugen* cannot be excluded. As for the falling bodies, given the *Hood's* aspect angle, this hit would have made metal pieces and bodies fall at her port stern, probably into the sea and out of Dundas' field of view.

In the following minutes, the *Hood* would have suffered another hit. According to Tilburn, a shell landed inside the bridge structure killing 200 men. However, Briggs up in the compass platform just above the bridge heard only cries of 'Fire'. He did not feel the shock wave of the explosion – but the impact of an 800 kg shell could not pass unnoticed. Conversely, a hit scored by the *Prinz Eugen* before redirecting fire against the *Prince of Wales* appears more plausible. Moreover, the possibility cannot altogether be excluded that the carnage witnessed by the survivors and the explosion reported by Flt Lt Vaughn were caused by the *Prinz Eugen's* first hit setting off the pom-pom, 4-inch and the UP ammunition, with a fire spreading fore and aft and possibly reaching the bridge structure (hence the cries of 'Fire').

In conclusion, the uncertainty surrounding these hits, by the way '[...] corroborated in no other known source [...]'[40] and unobserved by both the British – the *Prince of Wales* was sailing only 800 yards away from the *Hood* – and the Germans, has induced the author to base his analysis of the *Bismarck's* firing on the only one sure fact: the *Bismarck's* hit or, possibly, two hits with the fifth salvo.

3.7 'Virtual' analysis of the battle

A method of investigation based on Lanchester's Quadratic Law enables us to test alternative hypothesis, i.e. to discuss the possible realistic outcomes of the battle if the events had been different from what actually happened. This kind of historical analysis (sometimes suggestively referred to as 'virtual history') considers only plausible events, namely those that are not contrary to the laws of physics and/or to the constraints imposed by the historical context. These constraints derive mainly from the level of technology reached by the opposing countries in the period under consideration. Virtual history therefore examines a range of possible alternative events, quantifying the probability of occurrence of each one. Such an approach often leads to the discovery that reality can be quite bizarre at times as it is open to the occurrence of a highly unlikely situation. In this way, one can begin to question well-established beliefs, at the same time showing the true weight of seemingly marginal events or decisions on the final outcome. Virtual history, within certain limits at least, can be considered a useful instrument of investigation and discussion.

Here the empirical calculation method proposed in 1905 by Lt Fiske (US Navy) is preferred because it is simpler and more intuitive to Lanchester's more 'elegant' and rigorous mathematical approach.[41] The time is then marked by the succession of salvoes fired by the opponents. Moreover, each salvo is assumed to contribute to the progressive 'erosion' of enemy force. By also taking into account the force of a naval unit (what in Anglo-Saxon countries is referred to as 'staying power') defined with the empirical and arbitrary procedure – partially modified – proposed in 1930 by Cdr Giuseppe Fioravanzo (Italian Navy), it is possible to quantify the *initial force* of both naval groups fighting the Battle of the Denmark Strait.[42] Finally, applying the method described by Fiske, the decreasing trend in the force level of each group is examined and that in the alternative situations considered for a quantitative investigation of the influence on the final outcome of the series of events marking the battle. In particular, five events (A, B, C, D, E) concerning the British (Table 5) are considered together with eight out of 32 possible alternative tactical situations (Table 6). The five events plus the eight selected tactical situations are especially interesting for a virtual analysis of the battle which considered both the real and the theoretical fighting conditions. The first included the 3-minute initial German delay in opening fire, the target shift (from the *Hood* to the *Prince of Wales*) by the *Prinz Eugen* at 0559, and the *Prince of Wales* firing at the *Bismarck* throughout the battle. The second assumed, for example, that had the *Hood* not exploded, she would have redirected her target from the *Prinz Eugen* to the *Bismarck* 10 minutes after the beginning of the battle.

The 'erosion' of enemy force was assumed to be the product of the technical features of the guns and the 'staying power' of the firing ship, as long as the ships were afloat. The combination of actual and theoretical conditions was allowed to determine the possible outcome of the battle in a series of tactical situations different from reality.

Table 5

Events	Possible alternatives	Description
A	A1	Only a few of the *Hood*'s and the *Prince of Wales*' guns are able to bear from 0553 to 0600
	A0	The above event does not occur
B	B1	Reduced efficiency of the *Prince of Wales*' 356/45 guns after 0553
	B0	The above event does not occur
C	C1	Missed initial engagement of the *Bismarck* by the *Hood*
	C0	The above event does not occur
D	D1	Wake-Walker's cruisers do not attack the German group during the battle
	D0	The above event does not occur
E	E1	Explosion and rapid sinking of the *Hood* at 0601
	E0	The above event does not occur

Table 6

Tactical Situation	Description
1 = A0 * B0 * C0 * D0 * E0	Zero unfavourable events occur to the British forces
2 = A1 * B0 * C0 * D0 * E0	Only event A occurs
3 = A0 * B1 * C0 * D0 * E0	Only event B occurs
4 = A0 * B0 * C1 * D0 * E0	Only event C occurs
5 = A0 * B0 * C0 * D1 * E0	Only event D occurs
6 = A0 * B0 * C0 * D0 * E1	Only event E occurs
31 = A1 * B1 * C1 * D1 * E0	All unfavourable events occur except event E
32 = A1 * B1 * C1 * D1 * E1	All unfavourable events occur to the British forces *(What actually happened)*

Plate 5 illustrates both graphically and numerically the final results of the virtual analysis. Admittedly, this quantitative approach has its own limits due to the empiric and arbitrary assessment of the initial 'staying power' and force-erosion capability of gunfire. Nonetheless, the analyses performed indicate the following:

- Only the tactical situations marked by event E0 (explosion of the *Hood* does not occur) lead to victory for the British. Of them all, situation 1 is the most favourable to Britain, while situation 31 is the most arduous as it involves the highest percentage of British force lost. By contrast, all situations marked by event E1 (explosion of the *Hood* occurs) contribute to a German victory, with situation 32 being the most favourable to Germany and situation 6 the most difficult. It is also worth noting that even if E0 situations are as many as E1 situations (16 for each type), the probability of occurrence associated with them is far from equal. In fact, the probability of occurrence of events A, B, C and D can be assumed at 50% each (at least on first approximation),[43] whereas event E1 (that is the *Bismarck*'s probability of kill, Pk, calculated on the basis of estimates summed up in Chapter 5) is far lower. Pk is 10.6% at its highest, and that assumes the certain penetration of the *Hood*'s armour and the perfect working of German artillery fuses as well as overestimating the probability of hitting the magazines. Then, if hypothetically we assume by excess, i.e. about 50% more,

$$P(E1) = 0.15 \qquad (Pk = 15\%)$$

as events A, B, C, D and E are compatible with one another and independent so that it is possible to apply the Theorem of Compound Probabilities, we have:

❖ Each one of the 16 situations marked by event E0 with a probability of occurrence (Po) equal to:

$$Po = P(A) * P(B) * P(C) * P(D) * P(E0) =$$

$$= 0.5 * 0.5 * 0.5 * 0.5 * (1 - Pk) =$$

$$= 0.5 * 0.5 * 0.5 * 0.5 * 0.85 = 0.053125$$

❖ Each one of the 16 situations marked by event E1 with a Po equal to:

$$Po = P(A) * P(B) * P(C) * P(D) * P(E1) =$$

$$= 0.5 * 0.5 * 0.5 * 0.5 * (Pk) =$$

$$= 0.5 * 0.5 * 0.5 * 0.5 * 0.15 = 0.009375$$

Therefore, the range of situations possible but incompatible with one another would be divided into two groups:

❖ 16 situations with event E0 and a total[44] Po of 85% (0.053125 * 16)

❖ 16 situations with event E1 and a total Po of 15% (0.009375 * 16)

It is then clear that theoretically/virtually the probability of success favoured the British; i.e. on paper a German tactical victory was highly unlikely: about 1 to 6.

- If the British naval group had not been plagued by other negative events apart from the loss of the *Hood* early in the battle and had kept on fighting until the end (situation 6), it would have secured a substantial reduction of the enemy force, even if at the expense of the entire group. Then it would have been difficult for both German ships to reach France, even without a further engagement. As a matter of fact, a German tactical success would have been a Pyrrhic victory with a very low residual force for the Germans.

    This fact, added to the numerous mechanical breakdowns that affected the British battleship, surely makes her disengagement at 0613 appropriate. Had Leach decided otherwise, the *Prince of Wales* could have been lost or damaged beyond repair. On the other hand, the analysis of situation 31 indicates that the British would have gained a tactical victory even with the occurrence of all negative events except the early explosion and sinking of the *Hood*.[45] It is therefore possible to conclude that it was the sudden and basically unexpected destruction of the *Hood* that was the main cause of the outcome of the battle, so calamitous for the British. Although the architectural vulnerabilities of British battlecruisers had become manifest during the First World War and especially on the occasion of their involvement in the Battle of Jutland, the explosion of the *Hood*'s magazine can be considered a low-probability event that becomes even more statistically marginal if the circumstances of the lethal hit are considered.

- The number of mishaps following the gravity of the sinking of the *Hood* are listed here in order of importance:

❖ Numerous mechanical breakdowns affecting the *Prince of Wales'* 356/45 guns (situation 3), which heavily influenced the firing performance of the British unit, practically halving the broadside weight and curtailing the extent of the damage to the *Bismarck's* effectiveness. In the light of the aforesaid, the error concerning the combat-readiness of the brand-new battleship appears in all its magnitude.

❖ The failure to actively employ Wake-Walker's heavy cruisers (situation 5), which could have usefully diverted or at least disturbed German firing, with the additional possibility of a torpedo attack on the *Bismarck*.

❖ (With almost the same level of importance) the failure of the *Hood* to engage the *Bismarck* (situation 4) and the unfavourable geometry of interception denying the British naval group the use of all its firepower (situation 2). Actually, the latter limitation, traditionally regarded as highly important by historians, lasted just a few minutes, from 0553 to 0600. If, in that very short time, the rapid and unexpected sinking of the *Hood* had not taken place, in all probability the gun-training circumstances affecting British early fire might have been barely mentioned.

• To return to reality, all the events potentially capable of influencing the course of the battle were unfavourable to the British (situation 32). In fact, events A, B and C drastically reduced the number of large-calibre projectiles fired against the *Bismarck*, falling from the theoretical ≈ 28 per minute (the *Hood's* ≈ 8 per minute 381/42 shots and the *Prince of Wales'* ≈ 20 per minute 356/45 shots) to ≈ 6 per minute. Under these propitious conditions, the first gunnery officer of the German battleship was probably able to concentrate best on his difficult task during the first crucial minutes of the engagement. The *Hood's* unexpected explosion determined the fate of the battle (together with the breakdowns in the 356/45 guns of the *Prince of Wales*). The damage inflicted on the German group was not beyond repair, although the 356/45 shell hitting the *Bismarck* forward, together with the difficulty of evading British surveillance, made it impossible for her to continue Operation *Rheinübung* according to plan, which meant the failure of the commerce raiding operation and, at the same time, Britain's *operational* victory. However, had Lütjens ordered the pursuit of the *Prince of Wales* (slower and hence unable to disengage effectively and to use her 356/45 battery to the full), she would have been very seriously damaged and perhaps sunk. Wake-Walker's cruisers that had remained by themselves during the battle were unlikely to come to her aid and, in retrospect, other British forces would have never reached the area in time. Hitler's regret may therefore be justified. To Raeder he furiously said that 'after finishing off the Hood she [*Bismarck*] should have dealt with the Prince of Wales too, and not run away'.[46] However, when Lütjens decided not to go after the *Prince of Wales* the serious consequences of the hit suffered forward had not then been realised. So he gave priority to the pursuit of his principal mission – a rapid breakout into the central Atlantic to destroy convoys delivering vital supplies to Britain.

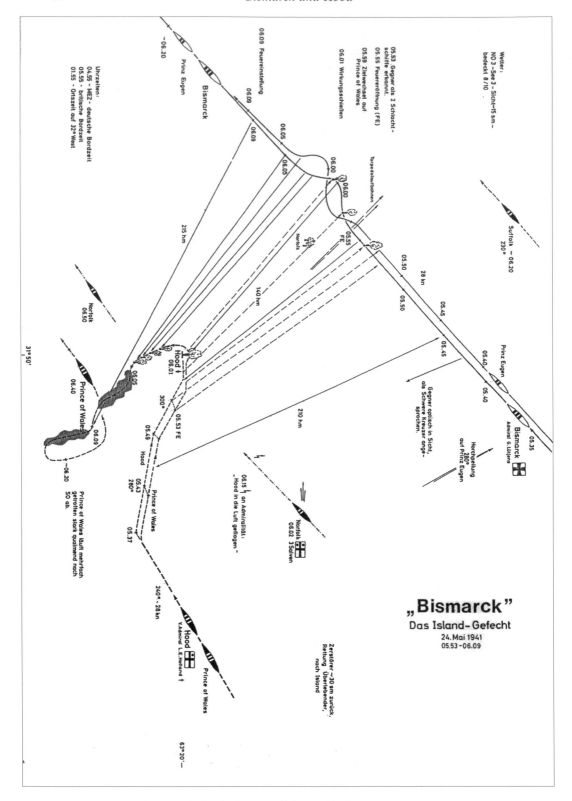

Fig 8: Battle map from 'Schlachtschiff Bismarck' by U. Elfrath.

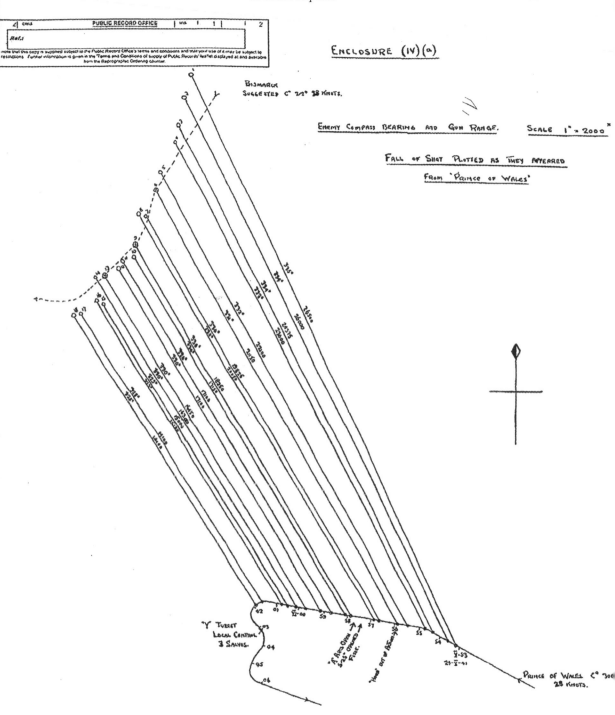

Fig 9: Fall of shot plotted as they appeared from the *Prince of Wales*. (*Public Record Office, London*)

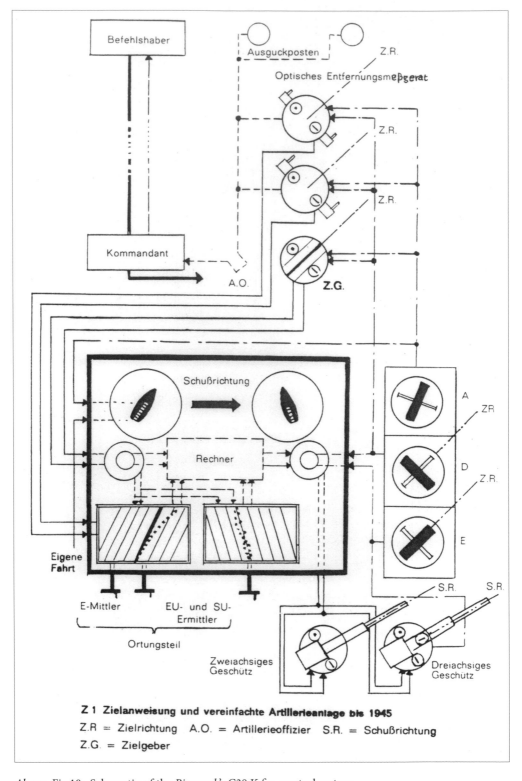

Above: Fig 10: Schematic of the *Bismarck*'s C38 K fire-control system.

Opposite: Fig 11: Schematic of a Mk V Dreyer Table, *c.* 1930. (*source BR 938*)

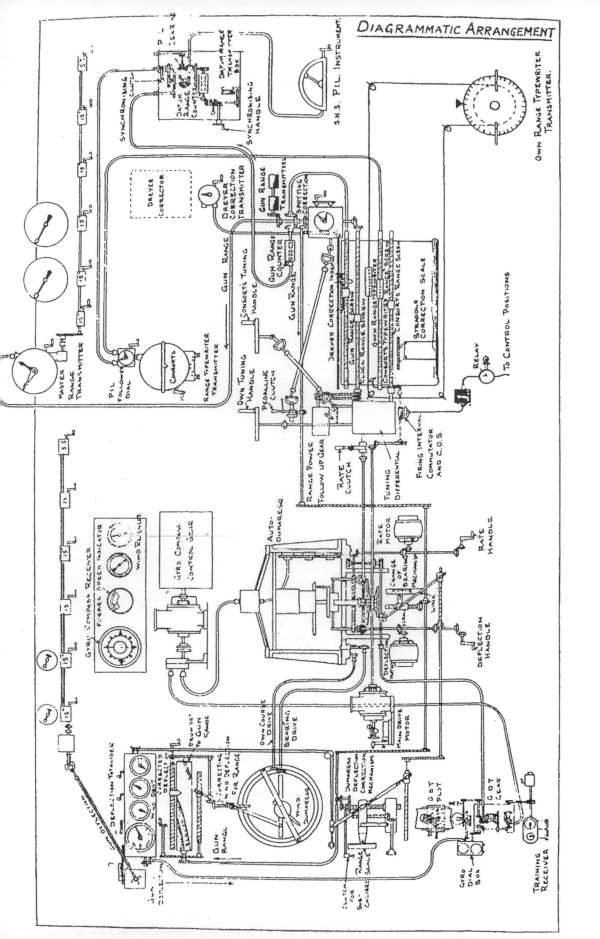

DIAGRAMMATIC ARRANGEMENT

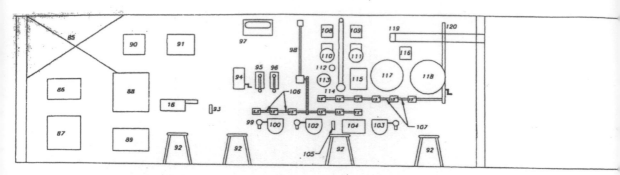

ELEVATION A

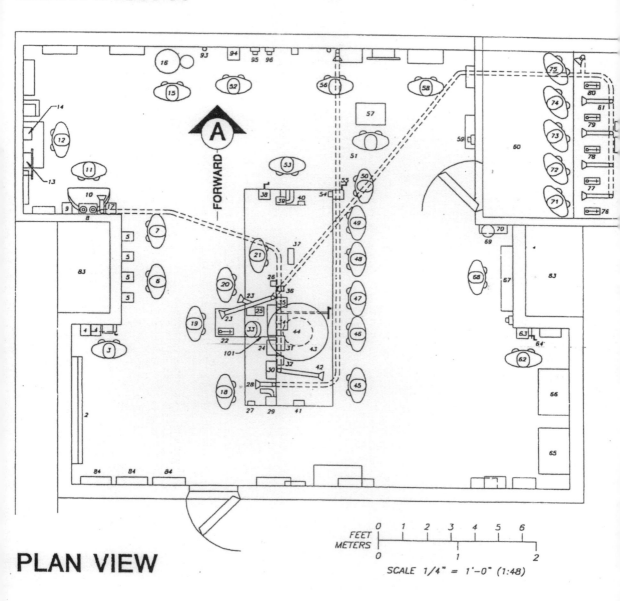

PLAN VIEW

SCALE 1/4" = 1'-0" (1:48)

Legend for Figure

Air Space
Low Power Panels
Consort's Range Plotter Operator
Range Receivers from link positions
Rangefinder Range Receivers
R/F Range Plotter
R/F Range Reader
Adding Dial
Gun Range receiver, exposed positions.
P.I.L. Instrument
P.I.L. Operator
Dreyer Calculator Operator
(illegible) Receiver
Rate Receiver
Sector Clock Operator
Sector Clock
Distance of Datum Ship Receiver
Deflection Calculator Operator
Tel (G) W/T Remote Control Operator
Concentration Officer
Table Tuner
(G) W/T Key
2" Voicepipe to W/T Cabinet
Wind Speed Indicator
Datum Range Receiver
Plug Box for Phone G.58
Deflection Handle
2" Voicepipe to Range Phone Operator
Electromegaphone Receiver
Wind Direction Receiver
Elphinstone's Speed Indicator
Evershed Duplex O.F.I.
Deflection Repeat Receiver (B)
Gyro Compass Receiver
Inclination Receiver
Plugs for Phone G.35
Datum Range Transmitter & Counter
Range Spotting Corrector Handle
Electromegaphone to Spotting Handle
Plugs for Phone G.25

41. Target Visible Lamps
42. 2" Voicepipe to P.I.L. Operator
43. Table Dumaresq
44. Evershed Bearing Receiver (over)
45. G.D.T. Operator
46. Dumaresq Operator
47. Suggestion Dumaresq Operator
48. Table Officer
49. Diary Keeper
50. Mean R/F Range Operator
51. Time Of Flight Operator
52. Order Operator
53. Spotting Corrector Operator
54. Plug for Phone G.43
55. Mean R/F Range Transmitter
56. Range Phone & Fire Gong Operator
57. Fall of Shot Instrument
58. Master Range Operator
59. Telephone G.28
60. W/T Cabinet
61. 2" Voice Pipe
62. Torpedo Instrument Operator
63. Inclination Instrument Operator
64. Compass Bearing Transmitter
65. Training and Slewing Motor Transmitter
66. Elevation Motor Transmitter
67. Fire Control Exchange
68. Telephone Exchange Operator
69. Navyphone to Ship's Exchange
70. Grouping Switch for Electric Megaphones
71. Tel AQ@ Buzzer
72. Tel Aircraft W/T
73. Tel (G) W/T
74. Tel AP@ Buzzer
75. Sig Remote Aldis
76. AQ@ Buzzer Key
77. Aircraft W/T Remote Control Key
78. AG@ W/T Key
79. AP@ Buzzer Key
80. Remote Aldis Key
81. Deflection Repeat Receiver (Y)
82. Datum Range Receiver
83. Dredger Hoist

84. Junction Box
85. Space for Gastight Vent Handwheels
86. J.B. 39
87. J.B. 36
88. J.B. 27
89. J.B. 28
90. J.B. 40
91. J.B 54 (5.5 Group)
92. Stool
93. Push For Sector Lamp
94. Order Transmitter
95. Phone to AY@ Space
96. Phone to AB@ Space
97. Evershed O.F.I. (Z58)
98. Deflection Drive from Table
99. Plug Box
100. Phone G.8
101. Slping Plate
102. Phone AD9 or 10
103. Phone G.18
104. Fire Gong Push Box
105. 5.5" Fire Gong Push
106. Deflection Transmitters
107. Range Transmitters
108. G.R. Lamp Box for Port 5.5" Guns
109. G.R. Lamp Box for Stbd 5.5" Guns
110. Combined Range and Deflection Receivers for 5.5" Guns (Port)
111. Combined Range and Deflection Receivers for 5.5" Guns (Stbd)
112. Sector Lamp
113. 15" Deflection Repeat Receiver (Exposed Positions)
114. 2" Voicepipe to Deflection Calculator Operator
115. 15" Gun Ready Lamp Box
116. Gun Range Receiver (Armored Positions)
117. 15" Range Repeat from Exposed Positions
118. Master Range Transmitter
119. Vent to W/T Cabinet
120. From Range Spotting Corrector

Figs 12 and 13 (legend): Mk V Dreyer Table and Transmitting Station aboard HMS *Hood*, *c.* 1930, courtesy of William Jurens, taken from 'The Dumaresq and the Dreyer' by W. Schliehauf (*Warship International* Nos 1-3, 2001).

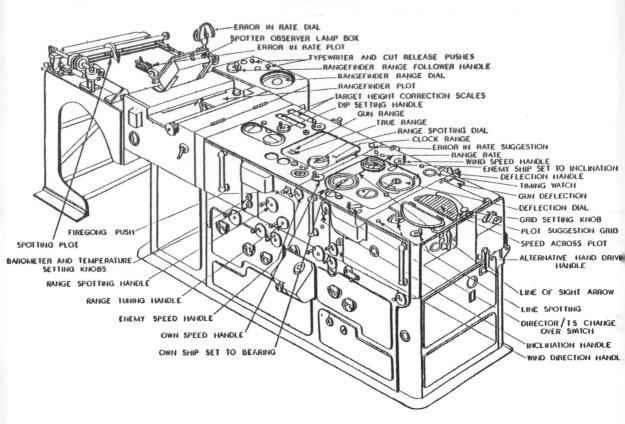

ERROR IN RATE DIAL
SPOTTER OBSERVER LAMP BOX
ERROR IN RATE PLOT
TYPEWRITER AND CUT RELEASE PUSHES
RANGEFINDER RANGE FOLLOWER HANDLE
RANGEFINDER RANGE DIAL
RANGEFINDER PLOT
TARGET HEIGHT CORRECTION SCALES
DIP SETTING HANDLE
GUN RANGE
TRUE RANGE
RANGE SPOTTING DIAL
CLOCK RANGE
ERROR IN RATE SUGGESTION
RANGE RATE
WIND SPEED HANDLE
ENEMY SHIP SET TO INCLINATION
DEFLECTION HANDLE
TIMING WATCH
GUN DEFLECTION
DEFLECTION DIAL
GRID SETTING KNOB
PLOT SUGGESTION GRID
SPEED ACROSS PLOT
ALTERNATIVE HAND DRIVE HANDLE
LINE OF SIGHT ARROW
LINE SPOTTING
DIRECTOR / TS CHANGE OVER SWITCH
INCLINATION HANDLE
WIND DIRECTION HANDL

FIREGONG PUSH
SPOTTING PLOT
BAROMETER AND TEMPERATURE SETTING KNOBS
RANGE SPOTTING HANDLE
RANGE TUNING HANDLE
ENEMY SPEED HANDLE
OWN SPEED HANDLE
OWN SHIP SET TO BEARING

Fig 14: Admiralty Fire Control Table (AFCT) aboard the *Prince of Wales*.

GERMAN 15in TWIN MOUNTING (*BISMARCK*)

1 Local gunsight telescope
2 Main cage cable sheaves
3 Breech mortice
4 Exhaust fean trunking
5 Rangefinder
6 Rammer
7 Shell on shell tray
8 Armoured barbette
9 Training base support trunk
10 Machinery compartment
11 Auxiliary ammunition hoist trunk
12 Overhead cordite rail
13 Overhead shell rail
14 Shell handing room
15 Shell ring rollers
16 Revolving shell ring
17 Cordite ring rollers
18 Revolving cordite ring
19 Cordite handing room
20 Main ammunition trunk
21 High pressure air cylinder
22 Hydraulic pump unit
23 Elevating gear
24 Training base ball bearing
25 Toothed elevating arc

Legend for Figure 15.

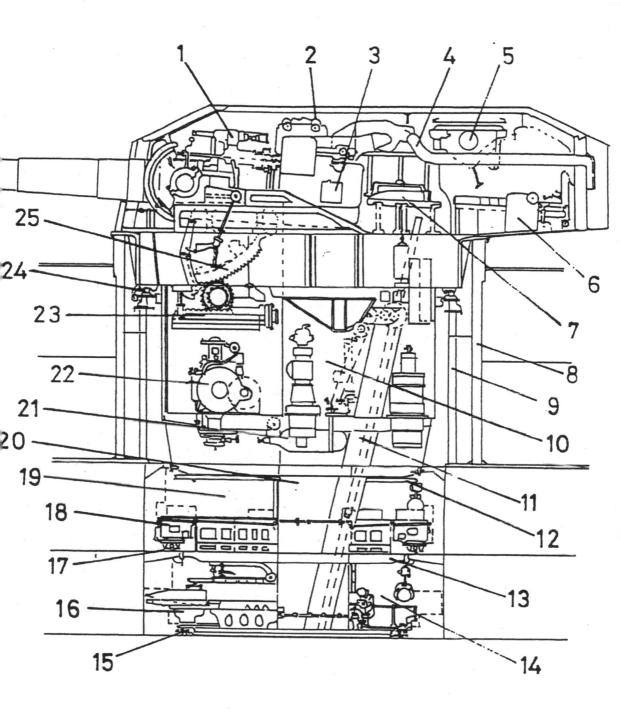

Fig 15: The *Bismarck*'s 15-inch twin mounting, courtesy of Peter Hodges, *The Big Gun: Battleship Main Armament 1860–1945.*

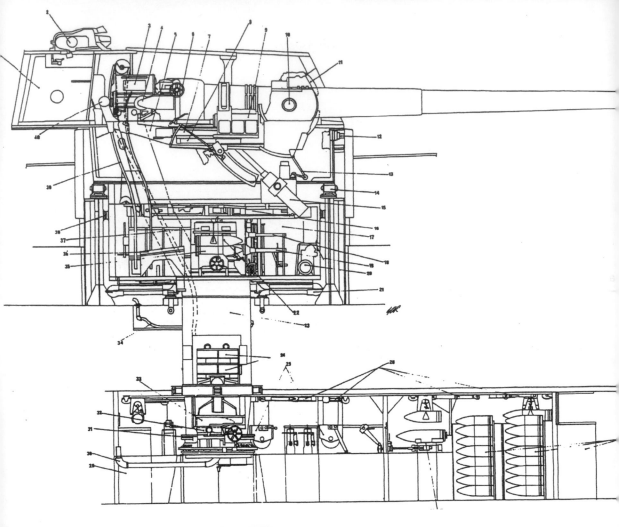

BRITISH 15in Mk II TWIN MOUNTING

1 Officers' cabinet
2 Rangefinder
3 Gunloading cage
4 Breech (open)
5 Loading arm (attached to gun slide)
6 Breech operating hand wheel
7 Run-out cylinder
8 Chain rammer casing
9 Gun cradle and recoil cylinder
10 Trunnion
11 Splinter shield to gunport
12 Turret training locking-bolt
13 'Walking pipes' (hydraulic power to elevating structure)
14 Roller path
15 Elevating cylinder
16 Ammunition hoist lifting gear
17 Working chamber
18 Cordite rammers (hoist to cage)
19 Shell rammer (hoist to cage)
20 Electric pump
21 'Walking pipes' (hydraulic power from fixed to revolving structure)
22 Shell suspended from radial transport rail (ready-use)
23 Trunk (containing shell and cordite hoists)
24 Cordite hoppers
25 Shell traversing winches
26 Hydraulic shell lifting and traversing gear
27 Shell bins
28 Shell traversing bogie
29 Shell bin
30 Electric cables
31 Shell bogie ring
32 Revolving shell bogie
33 Shell on bogie
34 Flexible voicepipe (fixed to revolving strucure)
35 Shell waiting position
36 Shell waiting tray (ready-use)
37 Cordite waiting position
38 Training rack
39 Gunloading cage rails
40 Rammer motor
(Note: Drawing shows 'Y' turret HMS *Hood*, with 30° elevation. Shell room is reversed — ie, forward end of shell room is facing aft — for compactness on drawing.)

Fig 16: The *Hood*'s 15-inch Mk 2 twin mounting, courtesy of John Roberts, taken from *The Big Gun: Battleship Main Armament 1860–1945* by Peter Hodges.

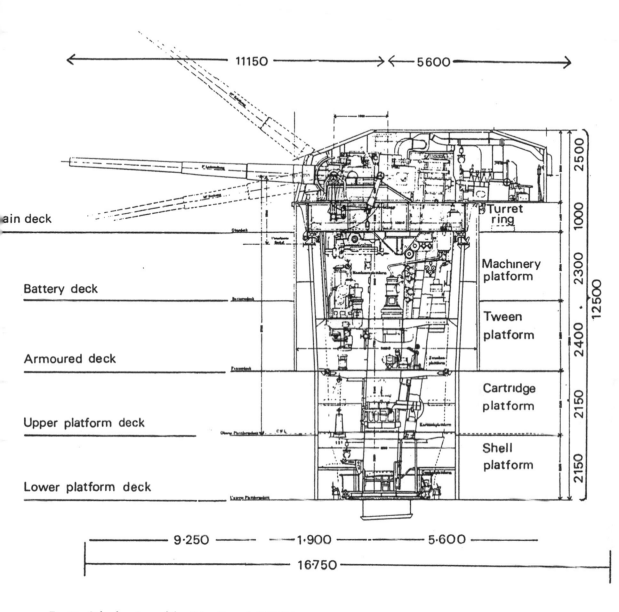

Fig 17: Side elevation of the *Prinz Eugen*'s 203/60 turret.

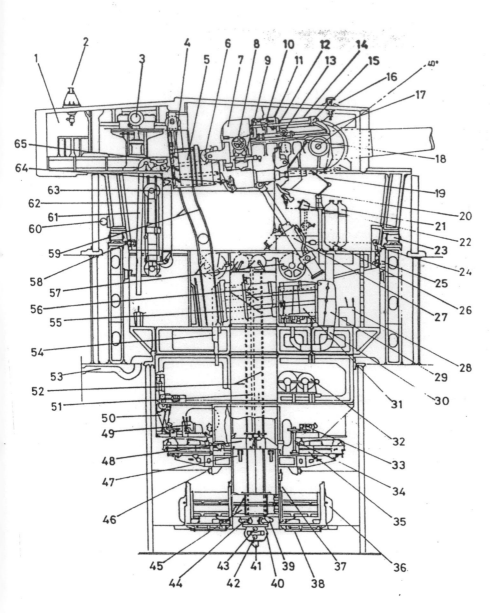

1 Navigating compartment ('A' mounting only)
2 Navigator's periscope
3 Rangefinder
4 Flash door linkage
5 Gunloading cage
6 Breech-screw (open)
7 Upper balance weight
8 Manual breech-operating hand wheel
9 Power breech-operating cylinder
10 Automatic recuperator gland pressure intensifier
11 Recuperator cylinder
12 Right-hand recuperator tie-rod
13 Power elevation control wheel
14 Recuperator ram
15 Recuperator ram crosshead
16 Look-out periscope
17 Mantlet plate
18 Telescopic air-blast and hydraulic supply sliding pipes to breech mechanism
19 Hydraulic 'walking pipes' to elevating mass
20 Elevation cut-off cam
21 High-pressure air cylinders
22 Elevation buffer
23 Training roller
24 Training clip
25 Safety firing cam rail
26 Cut-off linkage from safety firing cams
27 Elevation cylinder
28 Rammer and traverser control console
29 Rammer, 'traverser to gunloading cage'
30 Retracted chain-rammer casing
31 Traverser
32 Training gear
33 'On-mounting' shell-ring hydraulic motor
34 Shell-ring power drive
35 Revolving shell-ring

36 Cordite rammers
37 Cordite hopper flash door
38 Rammer/flash door linkages
39 On-mounting pressure supply
40 Centre-pivot swivel connection
41 High-pressure air supply
42 Off-mounting pressure connection
43 Off-mounting exhaust connection
44 On-mounting exhaust line
45 Cordite cage
46 Trunk guide rollers
47 Spring-loaded shell cage stops
48 Shell cage
49 On-mounting rammer, shell-ring traverse and locking-bolt control console
50 Retracted chain rammer casing
51 Cage lifting cables
52 Ammunition lift rails
53 Electric cables to 'winding platforms
54 Retracted chain rammer casing
55 Rammer, 'ammunition cage to traverser'
56 Bridge trays
57 Ammunition cage winche
58 Vertical guide roller
59 Gunloading cage rails
60 Training buffer
61 Gunloading rammer casir
62 Gunloading cage lifting press
63 Link rod from elevation control hand wheel
64 Breech thread protection tray operating linkage
65 Gunloading rammer

Figs 18 and 19 (legend): The *Prince of Wales'* 14-inch Mk III quadruple turret, courtesy of Peter Hodges, *The Big Gun: Battleship Main Armament 1860–1945*.

4

Technical Analysis of
KMS *Bismarck*'s Fire

When you can measure what you are speaking about, and express it in numbers, you know something about it; but when you cannot measure it, when you cannot express it in numbers, your knowledge is of a meagre and unsatisfactory kind.

Sir William Thomson (Lord Kelvin)

4.1 General remarks

At a technical level force concentration is generally achieved by hitting the chosen target with projectiles fired by one or more weapon systems with the aim of delivering damage and preventing the continuation of the target's mission. The result of this contest clearly depends on the ratio between the characteristics and performance of the opposing weapon systems, including sensors and countermeasures, calculation instruments, weapons, protection, defence and damage control systems as well as the target's kinematic performance and size, which in turn are the overall product of the technological level achieved by the participants. Basically, this ratio expresses the value of the force ratio at a technical level:

$$R_{TECH} = \frac{F_{WEAPON\ SYSTEM}}{F_{TARGET}}$$

In order to maximise R_{TECH} value, the following is necessary:
   a.   the highest number of projectiles intercepting the target;
   b.   the highest amount of energy transferred to the target by each projectile intercepting successfully.

The projectile's level of lethality must also be appropriate to the target's size and sturdiness: cartridges for game bird shooting are not suitable for bringing down a rhinoceros![1] This last point pertains to the force ratio at terminal level, with F_{TARGET} indicating the part of the target hit by the projectile:

$$R_{TERM} = \frac{F_{AMMUN}}{F_{TARGET}}$$

The fulfilment of requirement 'a' above calls for reducing systematic and accidental firing errors to a minimum – i.e. weapon systems must have a high hit probability (HP). Furthermore, terminal lethality requires that a given weapon system will actually destroy a target after hitting it – i.e. has a high probability of kill (Pk). The values referring to both probabilities (HP and Pk) have immediate technical logistic consequences in so far as they contribute to define the following:

- amount of hits required to achieve the desired Pk, at all distances allowed by the weapon system;
- amount of shots required to achieve at least the above hits, at all distances allowed by the weapon system;
- time required to achieve at least the above hits, at all distances allowed by the weapon system.

Therefore the technical investigation of the Battle of the Denmark Strait comes down to the analysis of the aspects concerning both the HP and the Pk of the *Bismarck*'s 380/47 battery. Moreover, this investigation must necessarily include some considerations about the *Prinz Eugen*'s firing.

As mentioned in the Introduction to this work, official sources as well as countless narratives of the battle have always emphasised the exceptional accuracy and effectiveness of German gunfire. It is necessary to point out that the term 'accuracy' is used in its most general and comprehensive sense, thus including both correctness with systematic errors[2] and precision with accidental errors.[3] However, an unbiased investigation of the subject appears necessary given the non-uniformity of the results achieved by the *Bismarck*'s firing in the two combats included in the battle: the first against HMS *Hood* and the second against HMS *Prince of Wales*.

4.2 Shots and hits against HMS *Hood*

The British task force started firing at about 0553, while the Germans opened fire 3 minutes later, as if the surprise and disappointment of such an 'unpleasant' encounter was petrifying Lütjens. However, towards 0556, immediately after the permission to fire, the *Prinz Eugen*'s 230/60 guns boomed, followed by the *Bismarck*'s 380/47 guns. As is well known, both vessels concentrated fire on the *Hood*.

At 0557, the *Prinz Eugen* struck the British flagship on the boat deck near the mainmast with one shell of the second adjustment salvo – an incredible hit at a distance of over 20 km – and at 0559, the German cruiser was ordered to redirect fire to the *Prince of Wales*. At 0600, the *Bismarck* fired her fifth full 380/47 salvo. About 23 seconds later, one 38 cm shell (alternative 1) or two (alternative 2) hit the *Hood*. As can be observed from the sketch drawn by Capt. Leach for the Royal Navy's boards of inquiry that investigated the event, the capital ship was quickly enveloped in flames and smoke.

Although the *Bismarck's* future range was about 15,200 m, the German gunnery officers looking through their Zeiss gun directors had a clear view of the strike. They were absolutely astonished, however, when at about 0601 an apocalyptic explosion ripped the 'Mighty Hood' in two, causing her to sink shortly afterwards (by 0602.30-0603). Then, as von Müllenheim-Rechberg remembers, 'When the Hood had gone, our heavy guns were ordered to "Shift to left target".[4] By the expression 'had gone', the author might be referring either to the moment when the explosion took place or when the ship went down. In any event, the order to switch target was given by KK Schneider at about 0601 and was probably executed by the Transmitting Station and by the ordnance of the German battleship shortly thereafter. As the *Bismarck's* 380/47 battery was firing rapidly, the sixth salvo at 0601 was probably still fired on the already hit British battlecruiser, which had greatly reduced speed after the explosion of the aft magazine and came to a standstill towards 0601, when the hull was broken in two. Therefore the *Bismarck's* salvo of 0601 most likely fell in the water off the wreck's bow – i.e. missing the target.

In the meantime, by 0601 the *Prince of Wales* had not yet covered the distance separating her from the *Hood* in her death throes, which is why she was to port of the German battleship ordnance and astern of her flagship. On the other hand, after the second 20° turn to port ordered by Holland, the British battleship was proceeding on a course a mere 5° off that of her flagship steaming ahead about 740 m away. Without a countermanoeuvre towards 0601, the *Prince of Wales* would have passed very close to the rapidly sinking hull of the slaughtered British battlecruiser. The risk of collision was high and Leach had to order an abrupt hard-a-starboard turn followed shortly thereafter by a similar turn to port in order to avoid the wreckage off her stern (Plate 6). This reconstruction of the events accords with the most accredited British accounts, as confirmed by the following extracts:

> Captain Leach in the *Prince of Wales* had to swing his ship rapidly to starboard to avoid the wreck of the *Hood*. Up till then he had been firing at the *Bismarck* virtually undisturbed, but the latter quickly and accurately shifted the fire [...].[5]

> Now *Prince of Wales*, turning to port to obey Holland's orders, had to go hard a-starboard to avoid the wreckage ahead, and Jasper, through *Prinz Eugen's* main rangefinder, saw on the far side of *Prince of Wales* a weird thing – the whole forward section of *Hood*, rearing up from the water like the spire of a cathedral, towering above the upper deck of *Prince of Wales*, as she steamed by [...] Then *Prince of Wales* passed, both parts of *Hood* slid quickly beneath the waves [...] and now *Bismarck* had to make only the smallest of adjustments to find the range too.[6]

It therefore appears justified to maintain that the first 380/47 salvo fired on the British battleship was the seventh since the beginning of the battle and was fired at about 0602. As an alternative to the above interpretation (hypothesis 'A') there is, however, the less likely possibility (hypothesis 'B') that the 380/47 salvo at 0601 was fired on the

Prince of Wales directly. Three (alternative 1) or four hits (alternative 2) were scored by the *Bismarck* on the *Prince of Wales*. Taking into account what has been previously discussed, the two scenarios concerning the evolution of events from 0556 to 0601 can be summarised in the following tables:

Table 7

Hypothesis 'A'						
Target HMS *Hood*						
	KMS *Bismarck*'s fire			KMS *Prinz Eugen*'s fire		
Time	Salvo	Rounds fired	Notes	Salvo	Rounds fired	Notes
0556	1st	8	off-target adjustment salvo	1st	8	on-target adjustment salvo
0557	2nd	8	on-target adjustment salvo	2nd	8	on-target adjustment salvo
0558	3rd	8	rapid salvo for effect	3rd-4th	16	rapid salvo for effect
0559	4th	8	rapid salvo for effect	5th-6th	16	rapid salvo for effect
0600	5th	8	rapid salvo for effect	///	///	///
0601	6th	8	off-target rapid salvo	///	///	///
Total rounds fired	48	///	///	48	///	
Total rounds fired on target		32	///	///	48	///
Average rate of fire	1 salvo/min	8 r/min	///	1.5 salvo/min	12 r/min	///
Hits *v.* rounds fired on target	1/ 4 salvoes (altern. 1) or 2/4 salvoes (altern. 2)	1/32 (altern. 1) or 2/32 (altern. 2)	observed hit probability: 3.125% (altern. 1) or 6.25% (altern. 2)	1/6 salvoes	1/48	observed hit probability: 2.08%

Table 8

Hypothesis 'B'						
Target HMS *Hood*						
	KMS *Bismarck*'s **fire**			**KMS** *Prinz Eugen*'s **fire**		
Time	Salvo	Rounds fired	Notes	Salvo	Rounds fired	Notes
0556	1st	8	off-target adjustment salvo	1st	8	on-target adjustment salvo
0557	2nd	8	on-target adjustment salvo	2nd	8	on-target adjustment salvo
0558	3rd	8	rapid salvo for effect	3rd-4th	16	rapid salvo for effect
0559	4th	8	rapid salvo for effect	5th-6th	16	rapid salvo for effect
0600	5th	8	rapid salvo for effect	///	///	///
Total rounds fired		40	///	///	48	///
Total rounds fired on target		32	///	///	48	///
Average rate of fire	1 salvo/min	8 r/min	///	1.5 salvo/min	12 r/min	///
Hits v. rounds fired on target	1/4 salvoes (altern. 1) or 2/4 salvoes (altern. 2)	1/32 (altern. 1) or 2/32 (altern. 2)	observed hit probability: 3.125% (altern. 1) or 6.25% (altern. 2)	1/6 salvoes	1/48	observed hit probability: 2.08%

It is also worth noting that the *Prinz Eugen*'s salvo fired at 0557 and the *Bismarck*'s salvo fired at 0600 hit the *Hood* beyond a shadow of a doubt, while, as mentioned before, there is no definite evidence of the isolated impact of other 38 cm shells before the fifth salvo.[7] However, two shells of the fifth salvo hitting at the same time could have been registered as only one. Both situations will be investigated through a statistical analysis.

4.3 Shots and hits against HMS *Prince of Wales*

The *Bismarck* and *Prinz Eugen* respectively fired another 45 (according to hypothesis 'A') or 53 (according to hypothesis 'B') 380/47 rounds and 131 203/60 rounds at the *Prince of Wales*. However, the British battleship laid down a smoke screen to cover her withdrawal at 0606. For this reason, German fire became intermittent and inaccurate from that time onward, ceasing altogether at 0609 following the order issued by Lütjens when the range increased to 22,000 m. In the light of the above considerations, the salvoes fired against the *Prince of Wales* can be represented as in the following tables:

Table 9

Hypothesis 'A'						
Target HMS *Prince of Wales*						
	KMS *Bismarck*'s fire			KMS *Prinz Eugen*'s fire		
Time	Salvo	Rounds fired	Notes	Salvo	Rounds fired	Notes
0600	///	///	fire still against *Hood*	7th	8	on-target adjustment salvo
0601	///	///	fire still against *Hood*	8th	8	on-target adjustment salvo
0602	7th	8	rapid salvo for effect	9th-10th	16	rapid salvo for effect
0603	8th	8	rapid salvo for effect	11th-12th	16	rapid salvo for effect
0604	9th	8	rapid salvo for effect	13th-14th	16	rapid salvo for effect
0605	10th	8	rapid salvo for effect	15th-16th	16	rapid salvo for effect
0606	11th	8	rapid salvo for effect	17th-18th	16	rapid salvo for effect
0607	12th	2	off-target (?) incomplete salvo	19th-20th	16	off-target (?) rapid salvo for effect
0608	13th	2	off-target (?) incomplete salvo	21st-22nd	16	off-target (?) rapid salvo for effect
0609	14th	1	off-target (?) incomplete salvo	23rd	3	off-target (?) incomplete salvo
Total rounds fired	45	///	///	///	131	///
Total rounds fired on target		40	///	///	128 (?)	///
Average rate of fire	0.70312 salvo/min	5.625 r/min	///	1.6375 salvo/min	13.1 r/min	///
Hits v. rounds fired on target	3/8 salvoes (altern. 1) or 4/8 salvoes (altern. 2)	3/40 (altern. 1) or 4/40 (altern. 2)	observed hit probability: 7.5% (altern. 1) or 10% (altern. 2)	4/17 salvoes (altern. 1) or 3/17 salvoes (altern. 2)	4/128 (altern. 1) or 3/128 (altern. 2)	observed hit probability: 3.125% (altern. 1) or 2.34% (altern. 2)

Table 10

Hypothesis 'B'						
Target HMS *Prince of Wales*						
	KMS *Bismarck*'s fire			KMS *Prinz Eugen*'s fire		
Time	Salvo	Rounds fired	Notes	Salvo	Rounds fired	Notes
0600	///	///	fire still against *Hood*	7th	8	on-target adjustment salvo
0601	6th	8	rapid salvo for effect	8th	8	on-target adjustment salvo
0602	7th	8	rapid salvo for effect	9th-10th	16	rapid salvo for effect
0603	8th	8	rapid salvo for effect	11th-12th	16	rapid salvo for effect
0604	9th	8	rapid salvo for effect	13th-14th	16	rapid salvo for effect
0605	10th	8	rapid salvo for effect	15th-16th	16	rapid salvo for effect
0606	11th	8	rapid salvo for effect	17th-18th	16	rapid salvo for effect
0607	12th	2	off-target (?) incomplete salvo	19th-20th	16	off-target (?) rapid salvo for effect
0608	13th	2	off-target (?) incomplete salvo	21st-22nd	16	off-target (?) rapid salvo for effect
0609	14th	1	off-target (?) incomplete salvo	23rd	3	off-target (?) incomplete salvo
Total rounds fired		53	///	///	131	///
Total rounds fired on target		48	///	///	128 (?)	///
Average rate of fire	0.70312 salvo/min	5.625 r/min	///	1.6375 salvo/min	13.1 r/min	///
Hits v. rounds fired on target	3/9 salvoes (altern. 1) or 4/9 salvoes (altern. 2)	3/48 (altern. 1) or 4/48 (altern. 2)	observed hit probability: 6.25% (altern. 1) or 8.33% (altern. 2)	4/17 salvoes (altern. 1) or 3/17 salvoes (altern. 2)	4/128 (altern. 1) or 3/128 (altern. 2)	observed hit probability: 3.125% (altern. 1) or 2.34% (altern. 2)

4.4 Remarks on the *Bismarck*'s accuracy of fire

In section 4.1 it was indicated that it might be appropriate to investigate why the *Bismarck*'s fire on the *Hood* and the *Prince of Wales* did not display the same degree of accuracy expressed by the noticeably different number of hits scored respectively. A careful examination reveals that, out of the rounds fired at *Hood,* the first adjustment salvo[8] at 0556 was 'short',[9] unquestionably affected by a substantial systematic error. The *Bismarck*'s first gunnery officer took note of that and, according to von Müllenheim-Rechberg (the *Bismarck*'s fourth gunnery officer), he 'corrected the range and deflection, then ordered a 400-meter bracket. The long salvo he described as "over", the base salvo as "straddling", and immediately ordered, "Full salvoes good rapid". This testimony indicates that the second 380/47 adjustment salvo was already registered as 'on target', even if the ladder procedure (at the time regularly adopted in the *Kriegsmarine*) deliberately made it highly dispersed.[10]

The sixth salvo at 0601 did not involve the *Hood*, as the British battlecruiser had reduced her speed practically to zero and the *Bismarck*'s C38 K firing computer could not have processed the new data in time because of hysteresis – a typical phenomenon of analogical electro-mechanical calculators – (hypothesis 'A'), or because fire had already been redirected on the *Prince of Wales* (hypothesis 'B'). It is therefore logical to assume that the centre of the impact point pattern of this salvo was very far from the target centre, hence these rounds did not help to increase the probability of kill. Consequently, only 32 were the on-target 380/47 projectiles fired on the *Hood*.

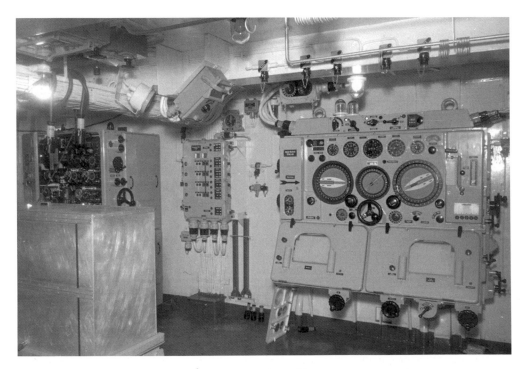

Bismarck's fire-control computer C38 K. (*Bundesarchiv, Bild 193-13-1-05A/o.Ang.*)

From the above scenario it is reasonable to assume a hit frequency for the *Bismarck* against the *Hood* equal to one or possibly two hits (of the fifth salvo) out of 32 rounds fired between 0557 and 0600. At 0601, the *Prince of Wales* was '[...] at approximately the same range and on the same course as the *Hood* had been. Consequently, Schneider could continue the action without adjusting the firing data.'[11] This extract clearly indicates that when fire was redirected on the *Prince of Wales* there was no need to repeat the adjustment procedure. In the second engagement, the German battleship scored three or four hits out of 40 or 48 shots fired for effect from 0602 to 0606. Only five 380/47 shots followed until 0609. However, by then the smoke screen laid by the withdrawing ship had caused low visibility, which made aiming difficult and reduced any chance of success. In this scenario, it is therefore possible to assume the onset of a systematic error, although difficult to quantify, as the target was no longer distinguishable. For this reason, the rounds fired after 0606 were not considered in the calculations.

A lack of uniformity in the *Bismarck's* accuracy of fire emerges from this mere preliminary analysis of the two phases of the battle. However, this analysis is intended to provide only a rough idea, as it does not consider the different ranges and geometrical-kinematic conditions existing in the two encounters as well as the ballistic properties of German guns. In a word, it does not take into account the probability of kill of the 380/47 guns in the events under investigation.

4.5 A statistical analysis of the effects produced by the *Bismarck's* fire

In order to carry out a more accurate analysis, it is first necessary to check the statistical significance of the difference observed. In fact, if this difference can solely be ascribed to random fluctuations (being in essence only apparent) then it is possible to agree with the interpretation historians have always attached to the event, considering it implicitly compatible with the *Bismarck's* fire on the *Hood* being perfectly and immediately on-target. Otherwise, it is necessary to investigate the possible underlying causes of it.

In short, the aim of the following statistical analysis is to examine a threefold hypothesis:

a. the *Bismarck's* perfectly-on-target firing on the *Hood* or, conversely,
b. the possible occurrence of systematic errors variously affecting the salvoes fired on the *Hood*;
c. the *Bismarck's* on-target firing on the *Prince of Wales*, by applying the same law of variation (as a function of the firing range) of the 380/47 guns' dispersion.

The investigation can be performed in accordance with procedures of statistical hypothesis verification, a form of statistical inference. In this instance, it is to be determined if the sample including the *Bismarck's* 380/47 rounds fired on a given target belongs to the population of theoretically infinite rounds fired exactly on target. Thus, if we consider hypothetically that during the Battle of the Denmark Strait the situation which actually occurred was that generally supported by historians, namely that the 380/47 fire was perfectly on target (i.e. the centre of the area covered by firing exactly overlapped the geometric centre of the target engaged) then it is possible to calculate the single shot hit probability (SSHP) relating to this situation. By subsequently examining the observed hit frequency (F_O), where the samples are the actual salvoes fired against the chosen target, the statistical 'chi-square' test (χ^2) may be used to check if the observed frequencies are consistent with the previously calculated probability. Namely, the chi-square test verifies whether or not the above samples (salvoes) belong to the population of the shells fired exactly on target (i.e. without systematic error). If they do, the on-target hypothesis can be confirmed; otherwise it can be refuted. The results thus achieved were subsequently tested with the Monte Carlo method.

4.6 Determining observed hit frequency and SSHP values

It is possible to consider the following values for the observed hit frequency (F_O), albeit with the uncertainties mentioned in the previous paragraphs:

Table 11

Hypothesis 'A'						
Target	Time	Salvo	Shots fired	Effective shots fired	Observed hit frequency F_O	
					altern. 1	altern. 2
HMS *Hood*	0556	1st	8	0	0	0
	0557	2nd	8	8	0	0
	0558	3rd	8	8	0	0
	0559	4th	8	8	0	0
	0600	5th	8	8	1	2
	0601	6th	8	0	0	0
Total 1			48	32	1	2
HMS *Prince of Wales*	0602	7th	8	8	1	2
	0603	8th	8	8	0	0
	0604	9th	8	8	1	1
	0605	10th	8	8	1	1
	0606	11th	8	8	0	0
	0607	12th	2	0	0	0
	0608	13th	2	0	0	0
	0609	14th	1	0	0	0
Total 2			45	40	3	4
Total 3			93	72	4	6

Table 12

Hypothesis 'B'						
Target	Time	Salvo	Shots fired	Effective shots fired	Observed hit frequency F_O	
					altern. 1	altern. 2
HMS *Hood*	0556	1st	8	0	0	0
	0557	2nd	8	8	0	0
	0558	3rd	8	8	0	0
	0559	4th	8	8	0	0
	0600	5th	8	8	1	2
Total 1			40	32	1	2
HMS *Prince of Wales*	0601	6th	8	0	0	0
	0602	7th	8	8	1	2
	0603	8th	8	8	0	0
	0604	9th	8	8	1	1
	0605	10th	8	8	1	1
	0606	11th	8	8	0	0
	0607	12th	2	0	0	0
	0608	13th	2	0	0	0
	0609	14th	1	0	0	0
Total 2			53	40	3	4
Total 3			93	72	4	6

It is important to note that only as a total can the fired salvoes be statistically classified as a 'large' sample, in that they are higher in number than the acceptable minimum (sampling number equal to 30). Each single salvo, by contrast, with 8 rounds, is just a 'small' sample.

Working out F_O values does not involve much difficulty. On the other hand, the method used to find SSHP values is more complex but rather interesting as it gives the opportunity to explore tactical and technical aspects of great significance in the past pertaining to the use of heavy naval ordnance in battle. In short, determining the values of the probability above involves the following:

- Postulating a *normal distribution* of impact points both on the longitudinal axis of the range (x) and on the transverse axis (y) of deflection. The point of intersection of the two axes is the centre of the battery beaten zone (Plate 7), while the statistical variables x and y are represented by the Cartesian coordinates of the impact points of each round fired for effect. Basically, the distribution of these coordinates expresses the firing dispersion: the narrower the dispersion, the higher the precision of the weapon-shell duo. Otherwise, there is high dispersion and low precision.
- Defining the conditions under which we will have a perfectly aimed on-target firing, i.e. when the centre of the battery beaten zone coincides with the target

geometrical centre, which implies the absence of systematic errors. From now on, we will assume the above as the null hypothesis (H_0).

- Considering the three-dimensional probability density function (pdf)[12] dependent on the aforementioned statistical variables x and y: pdf = f (x; y).
- Calculating the field integral equation for the pdf on the area called hitting space (HS).[13] The integral gives the value of the volume under the pdf curve on the HS. This volume expresses the hit probability SSHP:

$$\text{SSHP} = \iint \text{pdf } dx \, dy$$

Furthermore, it is necessary to consider that the dispersion of the impact points usually depends on the target range; hence the need to determine a good approximation of the latter for each one of the fired salvoes. To this purpose a kinematic model of the manoeuvres performed by both naval groups has been developed and included in Appendix A.

The model concerning the dimensions assigned to the HS of the *Hood* and the *Prince of Wales* is discussed in Appendix B. In this respect, it is interesting to acknowledge the great technical – and tactical – importance of the target aspect angle β (or *course inclination angle* under which the 'line of fire' meets the target longitudinal axis) for the hit probability. In fact, the HS (hence the SSHP) is the widest achievable for β = 90° or 270°, whereas it is at its smallest for β = 0° or 180°. Another equally important technical element is the shell's falling angle (ω); namely, the flatter the trajectory the wider the hitting zone (with equal target's height above water) and as a consequence the HS.

The dispersion along the x and y axes of the shells' impact points as a function of the firing distance is contained in the firing tables (or range tables), which provide detailed numerical data of the variation of exterior ballistics main parameters at different ranges for a given calibre and shell after trials in an artillery firing range.[14] Dispersion along the considered axes of shells' impact points from a battery firing during operations at sea is usually wider than that of a single gun in an artillery firing range. The procedure applied in the estimation of the fire dispersion of the *Bismarck*'s 380/47 battery is explained in Appendix C. As for the magnitude of this quantity, it is interesting to highlight the great technical importance of the alignment of the group of guns making up the battery, and the reciprocal interference among the trajectories of the shells simultaneously fired by the guns belonging to the same turret.

The tables in the Appendices give the results of the calculation of the SSHP as well as the test of consistency between the expected hit frequency (F_E)[15] and the frequency actually observed (F_O), together with the estimated confidence/significance level of the test itself.

Appendix D includes a short discussion of the fundamentals and the procedure employed for the above test carried out by applying the chi-square test.

4.7 Results of the statistical analysis

a. Engagement with HMS *Hood*

Results of the chi-square test

The chi-square test used to assess the outcome of the *Bismarck's* fire is based on the estimated dispersion of the 380/47 battery beaten zone and on the estimated HS size attributed to each actual target under the existing geometric-ballistic conditions. For the first estimate mentioned, the values of dispersion given by the Firing Tables for the weapons of the above battery were used as a factual basis. Then a basket of typically occurring errors (inter-alignment errors between guns, differences in muzzle velocity between guns, reciprocal interference between guns, etc.) was assumed in order to assess the total battery dispersion.

The estimation of the HS dimensions was based mainly on geometric considerations, also taking into account the kinetic energy of projectiles falling a little short, and their capability to hit. For this reason, this estimate does not imply a significant margin of error. On the other hand, the uncertainty is quite high for the abovementioned basket of typical *accidental* errors As a consequence, it is not possible to achieve totally reliable values for the *Bismarck's* firing dispersion at sea, and the study was performed considering a realistic range of variations. Obviously, the procedure adopted to estimate the standard deviation of the *Bismarck's* complete battery dispersion (on the basis of the errors basket) was applied to the engagements with both the *Hood* and the *Prince of Wales*. Furthermore, it is fair to assume that during the encounter with the *Prince of Wales* the German battleship's fire was perfectly (or almost perfectly) on target. Therefore the above standard deviation must be able to achieve a result related to the firing against the *Prince of Wales* that negates the possibility of rejecting the null hypothesis, thus confirming that against the British battleship the *Bismarck's* firing was exactly on target.

The results of the chi-square tests make it impossible to reach a point of absolute certainty that would clear up doubts (levels of confidence over 95%). Nonetheless, the levels obtained are high enough to doubt strongly the correctness of the null hypothesis of perfectly-on-target gunfire on the *Hood*. Out of 32 rounds fired for effect and within the considered range of variation of the *Bismarck's* firing dispersion at sea, the level of confidence is 85%. Conversely, the corresponding χ^2 values to refute the hypothesis of perfectly-on-target gunfire on the *Prince of Wales* remain low. Out of 40 rounds fired for effect, the confidence is about 17%. Statistical analysis usually considers confidence levels between 95 and 99%. However, lower levels have often led to important conclusions or decisions. In 2010, scientists declared that the remains of the famous Italian painter, Caravaggio, had been found on the basis of DNA test results showing a probability of 85% and in 2013, the actress Angelina Jolie, took the drastic decision (bilateral mastectomy) when she was told that she had an 87% probability to develop breast cancer.

The relatively low number of 380/47 rounds fired for effect by the *Bismarck* on the *Hood* and their estimated SSHP value do not allow us to absolutely refute the hypothesis of perfectly-on-target gunfire. However, the high level of confidence associated with the rejection of the null hypothesis, which is far higher than that scored by the opposite hypothesis, indicates the possible/probable occurrence of a significant systematic error affecting the *Bismarck*'s fire (concomitant with the casual fluctuations) that may have affected the second (the adjustment), the third and the fourth salvo. The fifth salvo, including the fatal hit (or hits), was probably on target (or accompanied by a less significant error) thanks to the continuous gunnery corrections made by KK Schneider.

In this regard, the then *Kapitänleutnant* Burkard von Müllenheim-Rechberg recalls in his book, 'I continued to hear Schneider's calm voice making gunnery corrections and observations.'[16] This means that Schneider continued to make corrections despite his earlier belief that the salvoes were effectively on target. Actually, no corrections would have been necessary had the centre of impact points covered the target well and if the fire-control system was steady on target. That was definitely not the case, as the *Bismarck*'s first gunnery officer was well aware that any adjustments made when the firing is already on target are usually counterproductive. This is the reason why the standard procedure dictates that corrections are to be applied only when the gaps registered through observation are significant, hence indicating a probable range error. This consideration appears to provide further evidence in support of the hypothesis of a systematic error.

Hits

According to the analysis performed and assuming that the *Bismarck*'s fire was perfectly on target, the scoring of *exactly* one single hit against the *Hood* out of 32 fired rounds exhibits a quite low probability of occurrence (about 10% without a *hit in the fifth salvo only* constraint). The hypothesis of two or more hits out of 32 rounds is instead associated with a much higher probability (about 87%; again when the *hit in the fifth salvo only* constraint is not imposed).[17] Therefore, under the ballistic, kinematic and geometric conditions existing between 0556 and 0600, if one assumes that the *Bismarck*'s fire was perfectly on target, it would be reasonable to expect a significantly higher number of hits by the German battleship (also in salvoes different from the fifth). On the other hand, the possibility of unobserved hits included in the second, third and fourth salvoes looks remote because not sufficiently supported by the testimonies of all the witnesses.[18]

While that possibility would support the null hypothesis, the hypothesis of two or more hits within the fifth salvo (concomitant and unobserved) has been tested and does not significantly reduce the confidence of the hypothesis involving a systematic error affecting 380/47 firing. The two 380/47 simultaneous striking shells scenario appears interesting also in view of the explosion of the forward ammunition magazine (located about 100 m from the aft magazine), which was probably responsible for ejecting the ship's heavy conning tower 2 km away from the main debris fields, as indicated by the 2001 expedition surveying the wreck.

b. Engagement with HMS *Prince of Wales*

Results of the chi-square test

The chi-square test applied to the encounter with the *Prince of Wales* demonstrates that the salvoes fired by the *Bismarck* were definitely on target (at least until 0606). According to the available data, the null hypothesis is not in question (whether with 40 or with 48 380/47 rounds on target). As mentioned in section a. above, in fact the level of confidence rejecting the hypothesis of perfectly-on-target firing against the *Prince of Wales* remains low (although not below the customary acceptance threshold of 5%). In short, the results of the analysis support the widely accepted and, in this instance, the most realistic hypothesis of the *Bismarck's* fire being almost perfectly on target.

Hits

Most historians believe that four out of the seven hits scored by the German vessels altogether against the *Prince of Wales* from 0602 to 0609 were fired by the *Bismarck*. However, the official British document *HM Ships Damaged or Sunk by Enemy Action* (1952 edition) is not definite on the calibre of the second shell impacting on the British battleship in rapid succession after the first hit.[19] Actually, Raven and Tarrant[20] credit the *Prinz Eugen* with this hit, even if the size of the holes ripped in the ship's plating by the penetration of the German shell does not look sufficiently convincing. In view of the existing doubts, the statistical analysis has to consider both alternatives:

Alternative 1:   three 380/47 hits + four 203/60 hits

Alternative 2:   four 380/47 hits + three 203/60 hits

As official data of dispersion calculated for Krupp 20.3 cm SK C/34 guns on the *Prinz Eugen* is not available, it will be necessary to assume for the purpose of this analysis that the average hit probability of each fired round is equal to the observed hit frequency. It is then possible to make the calculation considering the total number of rounds fired for effect (according to hypothesis A [40 rounds] or B [48 rounds]) and the total number of hits (according to alternatives 1 or 2 above). Then the probability of getting exactly three or four hits in the total number of rounds fired is calculated for each German ship (binomial distribution probability). A direct comparison of the results obtained should provide some indication towards attributing the right calibre to the second hit.

However, the probability of occurrence is not significantly higher in either of the two alternatives as one can clearly deduce from a comparison of the results in the following Tables 13 and 14.[21] Therefore the analysis performed is not conclusive because it cannot dispel the uncertainty surrounding the calibre of the second shell that struck the *Prince of Wales*. As a consequence, the statistical analysis of the *Bismarck's* firing on the British battleship requires that both alternatives be investigated. Of course, a fourth hit scored by the *Bismarck* would further support the hypothesis of her perfectly-on-target firing against the *Prince of Wales*.

Table 13

Hypothesis 'A'			
40 shells fired by *Bismarck v. Prince of Wales* 128 shells fired by *Prinz Eugen v. Prince of Wales*			
Altern. 1: 3 hits scored by *Bismarck* and 4 by *Prinz Eugen*			
Bismarck hits	*Bismarck* hit frequency	*Prinz Eugen* hits	*Prinz Eugen* hit frequency
3	3/40 = 0.075	4	4/128 = 0.0313
exactly 3 hits out of 40 shells fired P3/40 = 0.233		exactly 4 hits out of 128 shells fired P4/128 = 0.198	
concomitant occurrence of both events: P3/40 * P4/128 = 0.046134			
Altern. 2: 4 hits scored by *Bismarck* and 3 by *Prinz Eugen*			
Bismarck hits	*Bismarck* hit frequency	*Prinz Eugen* hits	*Prinz Eugen* hit frequency
4	4/40 = 0.1	3	3/128 = 0.0234
exactly 4 hits out of 40 shells fired P4/40 = 0.206		exactly 3 hits out of 128 shells fired P3/128 = 0.227	
concomitant occurrence of both events: P4/40 * P3/128 = 0.046762			

Table 14

Hypothesis 'B'			
48 shells fired by *Bismarck v. Prince of Wales* 128 shells fired by *Prinz Eugen v. Prince of Wales*			
Altern. 1: 3 hits scored by *Bismarck* and 4 by *Prinz Eugen*			
Bismarck hits	*Bismarck* hit frequency	*Prinz Eugen* hits	*Prinz Eugen* hit frequency
3	3/48 = 0.0625	4	4/128 = 0.0313
exactly 3 hits out of 48 shells fired P3/48 = 0.231		exactly 4 hits out of 128 shells fired P4/128 = 0.198	
concomitant occurrence of both events: P3/48 * P4/128 = 0.045738			
Altern. 2: 4 hits scored by *Bismarck* and 3 by *Prinz Eugen*			
Bismarck hits	*Bismarck* hit frequency	*Prinz Eugen* hits	*Prinz Eugen* hit frequency
4	4/48 = 0.0833	3	3/128 = 0.0234
exactly 4 hits out of 48 shells fired P4/48 = 0.204		exactly 3 hits out of 128 shells fired P3/128 = 0.227	
concomitant occurrence of both events: P4/48 * P3/128 = 0.046308			

Finally, it is worth noting the great importance of the rate of fire for the hit probability. Actually, in this respect a rapid rate of fire has about the same relevance as low fire

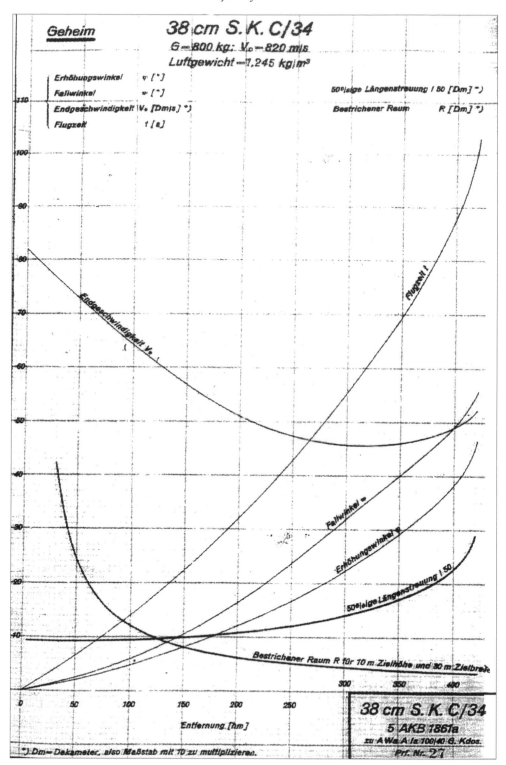

Fig 20: Ballistic curves for the 38 cm SK C/34 gun (*Endgeschwindigkeit*, terminal velocity; *Flugzeit*, shell flight time; *Fallwinkel*, angle of impact; *Erhöhungswinkel*, angle of elevation; 50%ige *Längenstreuung*, probable range error). (*Historisches Archiv Krupp*)

dispersion (in the absence of systematic errors). The mathematical formula expressing the relationship between the single shot hit probability, SSHP, (depending on fire dispersion for a given target) and the number of rounds fired, n, (depending on the rate of fire and the number of guns in a battery) is:

$$CHP = 1 - (1 - SSHP)^n$$

where CHP is the cumulated probability of hitting the target with at least one shell out of 'n' rounds fired.

As a general rule, just to have weapons displaying moderate dispersion of impact points of shots is not enough. The latter needs to be associated with a high rate of fire and, of course, an adequate supply of ammunition. Conversely, exceedingly low dispersion may negatively affect the initial adjustment phase as the correct range will become more difficult to determine.

In conclusion, with reference to the threefold initial hypothesis (section 4.5) the technical analysis provided the following results (Plate 8):

a.   Probably the *Bismarck*'s fire on the *Hood was not perfectly on target* (85% average confidence level rejecting the null hypothesis).

b.   This confidence level does not provide absolute certainty, but it substantiates the idea that the *Bismarck*'s perfectly-on-target firing, if any, *was not immediate* but was confined to the fifth 380/47 salvo and, at the same time, confirms the likely occurrence of systematic errors in the second, third and fourth salvo.

c.   According to the calculations, the hypothesis of the *Bismarck*'s perfectly-on-target firing on the *Prince of Wales* can be rejected with a statistical confidence of 17% average only. With such a low confidence level in favour of rejection, *this hypothesis is accepted.*

As for the different scenario shortly discussed in section 3.6, there seems to be no concrete evidence supporting the hypothesis of a hit on the *Hood* in the 2nd, 3rd or 4th salvo, nevertheless a complete chi-square analysis was performed to investigate this event, too. The analysis produced the following results:

- one hit in the *Bismarck*'s 2nd, 3rd or 4th salvo plus one hit in the 5th salvo, a systematic error is still probable (80% in favour of H0 correct rejection with kkk ≈ 1.22);

- one hit in the *Bismarck*'s 2nd, 3rd or 4th salvo plus two hits in the 5th salvo, or two hits in salvoes two to four, a systematic error is unlikely.

In any event, the results of the Bismarck's firing on the *Prince of Wales* remain substantially unaffected (the level of confidence passes from 17% to 25%).

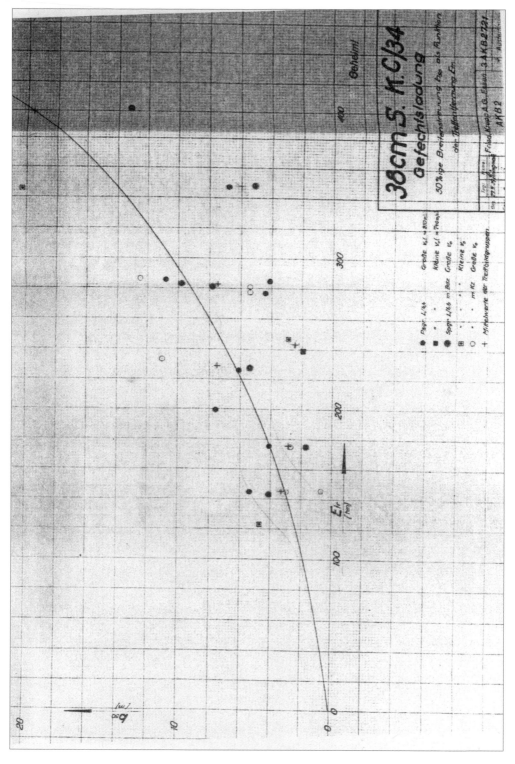

Fig 21: Krupp 38 cm SK C/34 gun firing dispersion, probable deflection error. (*Historisches Archiv Krupp*)

5

Aspects of Terminal Ballistics

5.1 Preliminary remarks

With a battle in the offing, the British commander deemed it necessary to reduce the fighting distance as rapidly as possible. According to traditional interpretations, this need derived from his awareness of the danger posed by plunging fire, i.e. enemy shells that, as a result of the firing distance, might have struck his flagship with a high falling angle and hence impacted on and *presumably*[1] penetrated the *Hood*'s weak horizontal protection of her most vital compartments, among which was the ammunition magazine. Most authors agree on this issue:

> She was hit by a shell or shells which probably penetrated the 3-inch armour over her after magazine and she blew up and sank. (See ref. 4, p. 73)

> Admiral Holland must also have considered whether it would be to his advantage to fight the enemy at long or short ranges. He had no information regarding the ranges at which the *Bismarck* would be most vulnerable to the gunfire of his own ships, but he did know that the *Prince of Wales* should be safe from vital hits by heavy shells from maximum range down to about 13,000 yards, and that the *Hood* should become progressively more immune from such hits as the range approached 12,000 yards and the enemy shells' trajectories flattened. At long ranges the *Hood*, which lacked heavy horizontal armour, would be very vulnerable to plunging fire by heavy shells. (See ref. 16, p. 398)

> Only three of her crew of 1,419 officers and men survived, and the probability is that one or more of her main magazines was penetrated by plunging shells, against which her armour protection was quite inadequate. (See ref. 17, p. 132)

> Plunging shells had exploded her magazines, and the 'might, majesty, dominion and power' which the ship represented had gone the same way as three others of her ill-fated type at Jutland, a quarter of a century before. (See ref. 23, p. 274)

> *Hood*'s weak deck armour – that hostage to fortune – had been penetrated by one of *Bismarck*'s armour-piercing shells […] (See ref. 14, p. 55)

After Jutland considerable amounts of additional high tensile plating were added to the decks of British capital ships. This was particularly marked in the modified design for *Hood* which had more protective plating over her magazines than any other ship in the fleet. The trials carried out with the new APC shell against the *Hood* target, therefore, had particular significance.[2] They showed that *Hood*'s magazines were vulnerable to long range gunfire, and that at 25,000 yards a 15-inch APC shell could penetrate all the decks, and burst in her magazines. (See ref. 15, p. 84)

Conventional wisdom is that [...] a 15-inch shell from *Bismarck* plunged through her thin deck armour and penetrated the 4-inch magazine, which then blew up igniting the main magazine. (See ref. 21, p. 80)

[...] *Hood* was hidden by a curtain of shell splashes. But at least one shell of that broadside made no splash: it came plunging down like a rocket, hit the old ship fair and square between centre and stern, sliced its way through steel and wood, pierced the deck that should have been strengthened and never was, penetrated to the ship's vitals deep below the water-line, exploded, touched off the 4-inch magazine which in turn touched off the after 15 inch magazine. (See ref. 31, p. 86)

Holland was desperate to close the range as rapidly as possible, to lessen the chances of his ship being struck by plunging fire. (See ref. 29, pp. 155-156)

[...] he [Vice Admiral Holland] was doubtless anxious to close the range as fast as possible so as to lessen the chances of a dipping shell striking his ship's decks. (Ibid., pp. 173-174)

Granted that 'The truth will probably never be known' as Roger Chesneau rightly concludes (ibid., p. 175), referring to what really caused the sinking of the *Hood* and the 'dynamics' of the sinking itself, the above extracts prompt the following observations:

- As stated by some historians, the *Bismarck*'s shells impacted on the *Hood* with a 'nearly vertical' falling angle. This claim is totally unsubstantiated. The shells' falling angle (ω), determined on the basis of the firing tables of the 380/47 guns, at the firing ranges considered in the present study (which are usually agreed on by most), was always between 10° and 14°. These values are not exactly high and are quite far from the vertical/perpendicular incidence mentioned in some literature.
- The most significant element pointed out by many authors is the highly defensive approach supposedly adopted by Holland when it came to decide the tactical manoeuvres for the final closing on the enemy. However, that does not do justice to the British commander, as mentioned before. Actually, it appears unlikely that his main reason for closing the distance so much in the initial phase of the engagement was to keep his ship 'safe and sound'. In July 1940, he had been chosen by the Admiralty to replace Tovey at the insistence of Admiral Cunningham, who wanted a 'more aggressive' Admiral leading his cruisers! Certainly, in his attempts to intercept the German group and in the earliest phase of the battle he made a few significant mistakes. Nonetheless, it seems more realistic that Holland was more worried by a possible loss of contact than by the vulnerability of his flagship's weak horizontal

protection. The best way to ward off the risk was to close the distance in order to achieve a higher hit probability. In fact, Nelson's famous lesson – 'Close the enemy' – was still valid if applied to the employment of conventional naval artillery. Although Holland's tactical conduct throughout the battle was undoubtedly faulty, we cannot be absolutely certain of his motives and, as the above remarks suggest, it would be unfair to sully his memory with an interpretation of the events so at odds with the traditions of the Royal Navy. Furthermore, it was clearly evident that such a frantic race to cut the distance was pointless even if Holland had considered the hypothesis that the ballistic characteristics attributed to the German 380/47 gun, possibly unknown in Britain, were roughly those of the British 381/42.[3] On top of that, at close distance this manoeuvre would have made the decks impenetrable, but at the cost of exposing a considerable length of the *Hood's* side, which was equally insufficiently protected, to enemy fire. Finally, owing to the increase in weight as a result of the alterations made after the First World War, by 1941 half of the 305-mm armour belt was under the waterline. To what purpose would he worry about the decks when the side was equally vulnerable? Had he really favoured a defensive approach, he would have opted for a higher rather than a shorter fighting distance. These considerations compel one to conclude that the usual interpretation offered to explain Holland's closing manoeuvre seems hardly convincing. The opposite appears more credible; namely that Holland's resolute closing manoeuvre was not inspired by tactical defensive restraint but by offensive bravery.[4] At a short distance, Holland would have achieved a higher hit probability and hence increase the likelihood of preventing the enemy from breaking into the Atlantic – i.e. he would have fulfilled the mission assigned to him. Of course, there was the very real risk that the opponent might achieve a serious hit before the British task force could deploy all its firepower due to the unfavourable geometry of interception. Holland decided to take this risk and face his destiny.

- Finally, the emphasis sometimes laid on the *Bismarck's* shells does not seem to be completely appropriate. Certainly, these projectiles were large. Each 380/47 shell (*Panzersprenggranate* L/4.4) had a calibre of 380 mm, a length of 1,672 mm and a total weight of 800 kg, of which a mere 2.35% (18.8 kg) was the explosive. With these characteristics, a hit would not pass unnoticed, especially when the impact velocity was higher than Mach 1.5 (at 15,200 m). Nonetheless, the *Hood's* 381/42 shells were bigger (even if the calibre was about the same). The latter weighed 879 kg, about 9% more than their German counterparts!

5.2 Investigation of terminal aspects

Terminal aspects are highly significant in relation to Holland's closing manoeuvre and appear to support the author's 'against-the-tide' interpretation.[5] Roskill illustrates the dilemma that might have tormented Holland.[6] Namely that the most favourable fighting distance for the *Prince of Wales* seemed to be greater than 13,000 yards (11,900 m), whereas the *Hood's* optimum engagement distance was thought to be around 12,000 yards (11,000 m). However, if the *Prince of Wales* was considered at risk when the distance from the opponent was under 13,000 yards, that was due to the possibility of large-calibre shells hitting the armoured belt (14 inches, 356 mm, thick) and penetrating it. Strangely enough, this fear did not also include the *Hood*, whose armoured belt had a maximum thickness of 305 mm, rapidly tapering to significantly thinner values. In fact, incredibly, for this battlecruiser the recommended distance from the enemy was almost, 12,000 yards! This interpretation hardly seems credible. It might be the result of the more or less automatic association prevailing in the Royal Navy after the Battle of Jutland of a battlecruiser lacking horizontal protection. Also, at 12,000 yards the British 381/42 shells would have easily pierced the *Hood*'s maximum vertical protection; of this fact Holland was surely aware.

On this subject, David Mearns and Rob White rightly observe that '[…] the enemy's shells, on a flatter trajectory, would be more likely to strike his side armour rather than his deck armour'.[7] The truth of this statement can be checked by comparing the following values referring to 24 May at 0600:

- The portion of the *Hood*'s hitting space related to the horizontal surfaces of the ship was equal to 5,639 m² (according to a realistic estimation), i.e. the total area of the decks exposed to the so-called plunging fire.[8]
- The portion of the *Hood*'s hitting space related to the vertical surfaces of the ship was about 19,303 m² (according to a realistic estimation), i.e. the surface exposed to shells capable of piercing the *Hood*'s sides, including the parts under the waterline.

Hence, the latter figure is 3.4 times the area of the decks and considering the estimated hit probability of the *Bismarck*'s fifth salvo (SSHP ≈ 12.5%), it is possible to see that the probability of hitting the *Hood*'s vertical surfaces accounts for most of the SSHP, i.e. about 9.7%. Therefore, the likelihood of a 380/47 shell impacting the horizontal surface area of the British battlecruiser (a high-probability event according to many historians) could be lower than a shell possibly striking the sides.

A deeper investigation of the *Bismarck*'s fire terminal effects needs to consider also the varying thickness (e_i)[9] of the armoured belt (305 mm, 178 mm, 127 mm), together with its location above/below the waterline and its aspect angle β with respect to the enemy shells' trajectory, especially those belonging to the salvo fired by the *Bismarck* at 0600. The thickness to perforate (Tp) can be calculated as follows:

$$Tp = e_i / \sin β$$

with β = 63.2°, Tp is roughly equal to 340 mm, 200 mm and 140 mm respectively (Plates 9 and 10). Then according to the perforation capability of the German 380/47 shell (examined in Appendix E), at the distance (15,200 m) and in the geometric firing situation considered all the above armour layers would have been readily pierced. Furthermore, some authors mention the possibility that the fatal shell might have fallen 'short', hitting the hull after completing its trajectory underwater and exploding somewhere near the aft ammunition magazine. Among them, Martin Stephen writes, 'A fashionable and plausible modern view is to suggest the possibility of an underwater penetration.'[10] However, in order to reach the aft 381/42 magazines not only had this shell to pierce the armoured belt under the waterline but also to cross the area where the two big starboard propeller shafts would probably hinder its transit inside the hull, and all that after losing a significant amount of its kinetic energy during its course underwater. It therefore seems unlikely that a possible hit under the waterline might have sent the shell so close to the ammunition magazine that the energy of its explosion was projected inside the latter, also considering the limited explosive charge contained in the 380/47 shell (directrix K, Plate 11).

Some discrepancies emerge in the thickness and distribution of the *Hood*'s horizontal and vertical protection indicated by various reference sources, which imply some difficulties in the investigation of the subject. It has therefore been necessary to assume that in 1941 the deck armour positioned to protect the magazine sections was as in the following table.[11]

Table 15

HMS *Hood* Distribution of deck protection in the area between frames 71-119 (fore magazine) and 259-359 (aft boiler room & aft magazine)					
Deck	Frames				
	71-95	95-119	259-280	280-306	306-359
	thickness mm	thickness mm	thickness mm	thickness mm	thickness mm
Shelter d.	///	///	No armour	No armour	///
Forecastle d.	38	38	38	25	///
Upper d.	19	19	25	51	51
Main d.	76	32	51	38	76
Lower d.	51	51	No armour	51	51

The deck protection was not evenly distributed and was generally weak, although such weakness was altogether relative to the projectile penetration capacity. As the cumulative resistance of more surfaces is not represented by the direct sum of the plates' thickness, the empirical De Marre formula for the equivalent thickness was used (thickness values 'e' refer to parallel armour plates):[12]

$$E_{eq} = (e_1^{1.4} + e_2^{1.4} + \ldots + e_n^{1.4})^{1/1.4}$$

According to the above relation and the values in Table 15, the horizontal overall protection derived from De Marre is equivalent to a plate's thickness of:

Table 16

HMS *Hood* Equivalent deck protection in the area between frames 71-119 (fore magazine) and 259-359 (aft boiler room & aft magazine)					
Deck armour	Frames				
	71-95	95-119	259-280	280-306	306-359
	Equivalent thickness mm	Equivalent thickness mm	Equivalent thickness mm	Equivalent thickness mm	Equivalent thickness mm
	128.9	96.3	84.6	112.6	131

A detailed analysis was performed to estimate the real piercing capacity of the German Psgr 38 cm L/4.4 against side and horizontal armour. For comparison, the deck armour piercing capacity of the Italian 381/50 (15-inch) shell (data from official documents of the Italian Navy)[13] as well as the deck armour piercing capacity of the British 15-inch shell[14] were then referred to the *Bismarck*'s estimated firing range at 0600 (fifth salvo at 15,200 m) and to the *Hood*'s estimated aspect angle (β) at 0600 (63.2°). It was also assumed that:

- the shell penetrated intact (non-shattering penetration);
- the shell impact angle (ω) to the horizontal plane was that pertaining to the firing range (10.6°);
- on impact, the *Hood*'s hull was exactly upright (no ship roll and pitch).

On the basis of the estimation made, the German shell could be expected to penetrate the following armour thickness:

Table 17

Bismarck's future range (m)	15,200
Shell impact velocity (m/sec)	565.4
Shell impact angle on the horizontal plane (ω)	10.6
Hood's aspect angle (β)	63.2
Max. penetrated thickness deck armour (mm)	less than 74 probably 50-55
Max. penetrated thickness side armour (mm)	340-370

Considering the geometry of interception and the maximum thickness that the 380/47 shell was able to penetrate, had the projectile struck the ship's shelter deck or forecastle deck between frames 71-119 and 259-359 it would have been unlikely to directly reach the *Hood*'s main magazines. In particular, the shell might have hit the first deckhouse, between frames 270 and 280, i.e. between directrices A and B (Plates 12 and 13).[15] In this case, it would have been able to reach one of the spaces located just below the upper deck and devoted to the handling of AA 102/45 ammunition.[16] The resulting explosion would in turn have caused the detonation of the projectiles stored in this room, which would have led to the rupturing of the main 102/45 magazine below (located on the lower platform) and that of the adjoining 381/42 propelling charges in a sort of domino effect.[17]

However, a more likely scenario seems that of a 380/47 shell perforating the armourless starboard side under the shelter deck between the above frames (directrix C), passing through the main deck and finally bursting in the proximity of the 102/45 ammunition working spaces. Possible but less likely appears the hypothesis of the German shell striking the main 102/45 magazine or even the adjacent 381/42 'propelling charges' room immediately after perforating the upper part of the armoured belt together with the horizontal plating of the main deck and possibly of the lower deck (directrix D). In fact, however weak the armoured plating of the upper part of the belt, it was able to absorb a substantial amount of the shell's kinetic energy, and thus even to cause it to shatter, also due to the high angle of incidence to the vertical plane (aspect angle β).

For the sake of completeness, another theory should be considered, envisaging the detonation of the 533-mm torpedoes kept near the above-water tubes on the upper-deck amidships. This hypothesis supports what Martin Stephen rightly defines as a 'slightly disturbing explanation', seeing the explosion of torpedoes as a belated consequence of one of the *Prinz Eugen*'s 203/60 hits scored against the British flagship.[18] This hit had started a blazing fire on the battlecruiser's superstructure. Had the fire extended to the torpedoes it would have caused the detonation of the torpedoes' warheads which in turn would have broken the hull and possibly involved the aft ammunition magazine, situated barely 15 m away.

Mearns and White report the findings of the expedition which discovered the wreck of the *Hood* in 2001.[19] The following extracts based on the inspection of the wreck provide an effective reconstruction of the ship's last moments:

> The second shell that hit *Hood* was not clearly seen, but it apparently hit on the boat deck near the mainmast, close to where the first shell had hit and started the fire. It was a shell from *Bismarck*'s fifth salvo, which was seen to straddle Hood with some shells falling short [...]
>
> Our view of the wreckage made it impossible to say whether the damage in this area included the outer bottom plating, but I suspect that it did. Here was all the proof that was needed to confirm that the 15-inch magazines had exploded as was universally believed. The force of the explosion and the extreme heat generated by the burning cordite had broken *Hood*'s back just below the aft turrets, and had blown back the side shell plating on the port side. Had only the 4-inch magazines exploded, such serious damage to the hull wouldn't have extended this far aft [...]
>
> Unfortunately, the precise location of *Bismarck*'s shell penetration will probably never be known. The remains of the 70-metre section where the shell hit is so completely and utterly destroyed that even the task of identifying the wreckage is nearly impossible [...]
>
> Given the extent of the damage we have already documented and the disappointment of not being able to say more about the fatal shell hit on *Hood*, we were grateful to be able to answer one important historical question: had Hood executed the last 20° turn to port? [...] The rudder was undamaged and fixed in the exact position Holland had ordered: on a turn of 20° to port. To be precise, it appears that *Hood* had been still in mid turn when hit [...]
>
> It has been difficult to reconcile the damage *Hood* suffered forward of the superstructure with the various eyewitness testimonies. Ted, himself, recalls seeing the bow intact [...] Ted expected the forward half of the ship to be largely intact – so did I. After all, the main explosion was aft near the mainmast. Could there have been a second explosion in the forward magazines that had ripped the bow apart as dramatically as the stern had been? Certainly the breaks near the forward turrets support this [...] A final piece of wreckage adds fuel to the fire. The conning tower – all 650 tons of it – was found over one kilometre away from the majority of the debris and two kilometres away from the upturned mid-ship section [...] Could the conning tower have been blown free by an explosion of the forward 4-inch and 15-inch magazines and propelled away from the rest of the ship? [...] Even if the flame outside the ship had not ignited the forward magazines, it does suggest that the tower of fire that had vented upwards near the mainmast had also vented horizontally [...] If these flames could vent 300 to 600 feet high could they not also vent 400 feet horizontally to the forward magazines in a ship that was rapidly breaking apart?

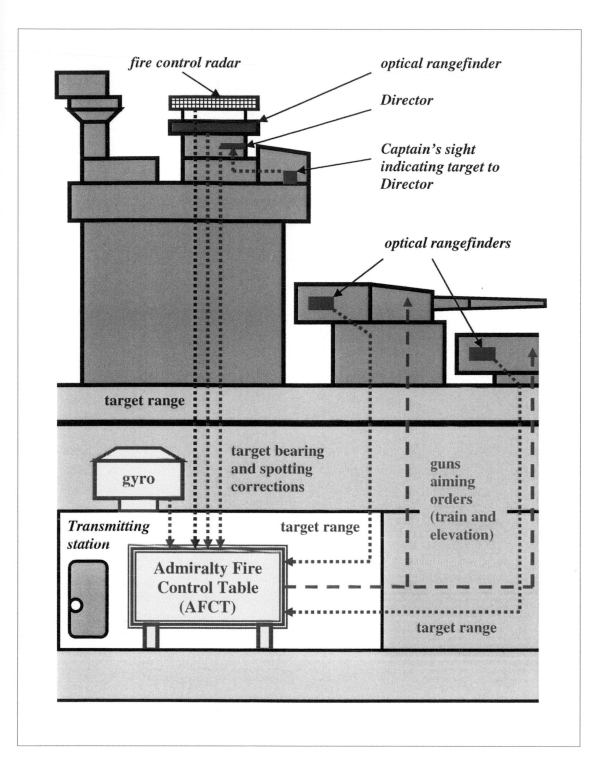

1. British naval fire control system in the Second World War.

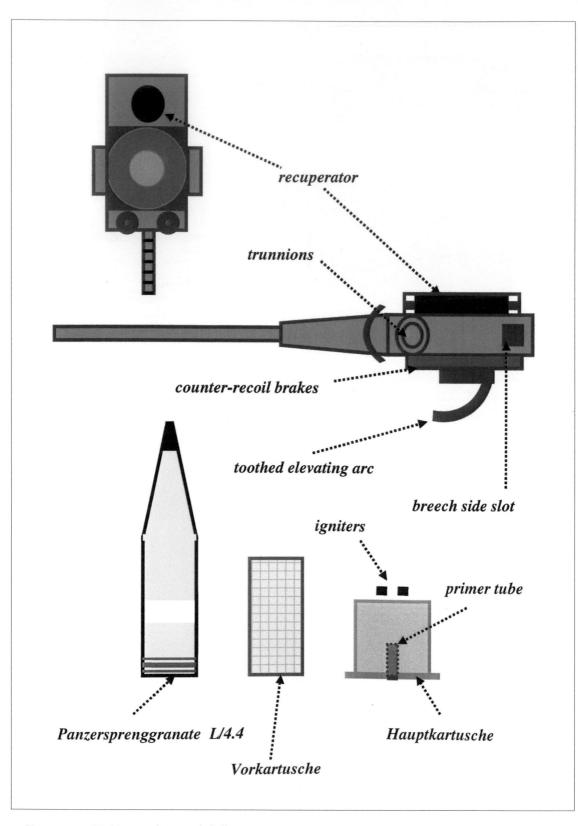

recuperator

trunnions

counter-recoil brakes

toothed elevating arc

breech side slot

igniters

primer tube

Panzersprenggranate L/4.4

Vorkartusche

Hauptkartusche

2. Krupp 38 cm SK C/34 naval gun and shell.

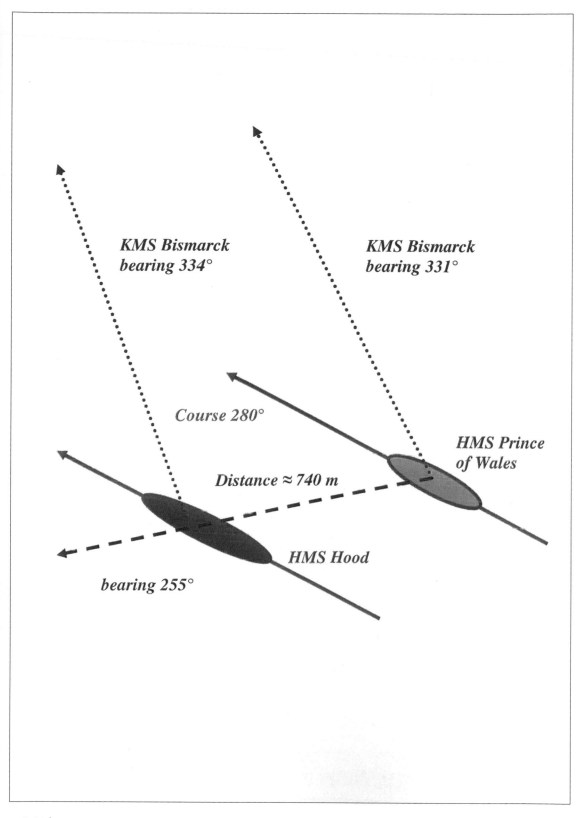

KMS Bismarck
bearing 334°

KMS Bismarck
bearing 331°

Course 280°

HMS Prince
of Wales

Distance ≈ 740 m

HMS Hood

bearing 255°

3. British situation at 0556.

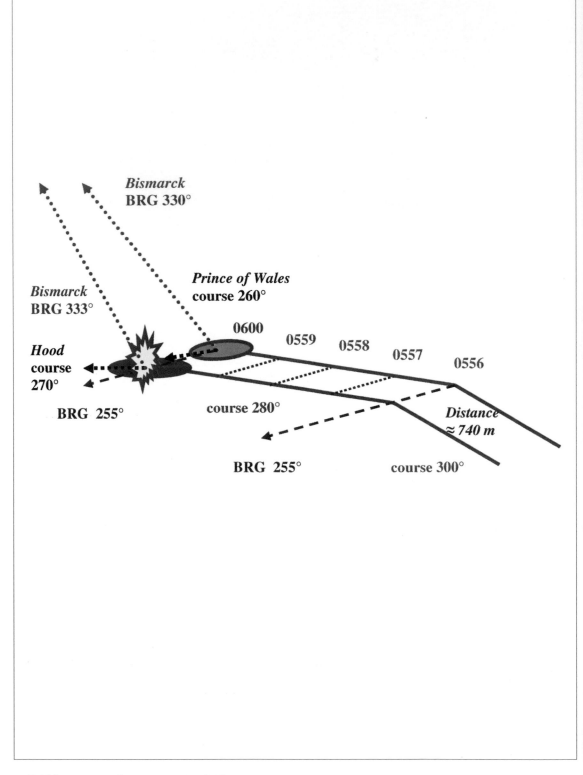

4. British manoeuvre between 0556 and 0600.

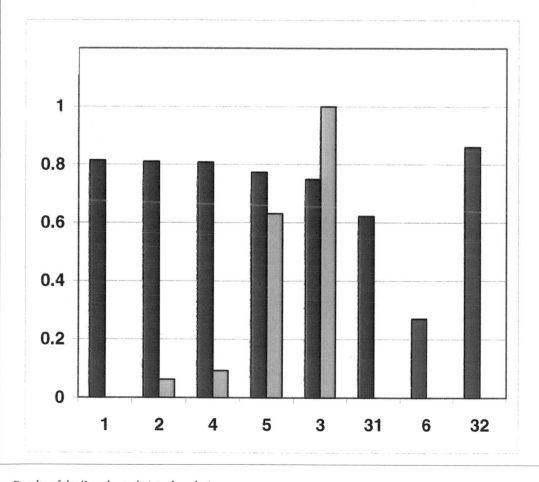

Tactical Situation	Victory	Winner's residual force	Loser's residual force	UK negative events weight
1	UK	0.814	0	0
2	UK	0.81	0	0.061538
4	UK	0.808	0	0.092308
5	UK	0.773	0	0.630769
3	UK	0.749	0	1
31	UK	0.622	0	
6	GE	0.27	0	
32	GE	0.86	0	

4. Results of the 'Lanchester' virtual analysis.

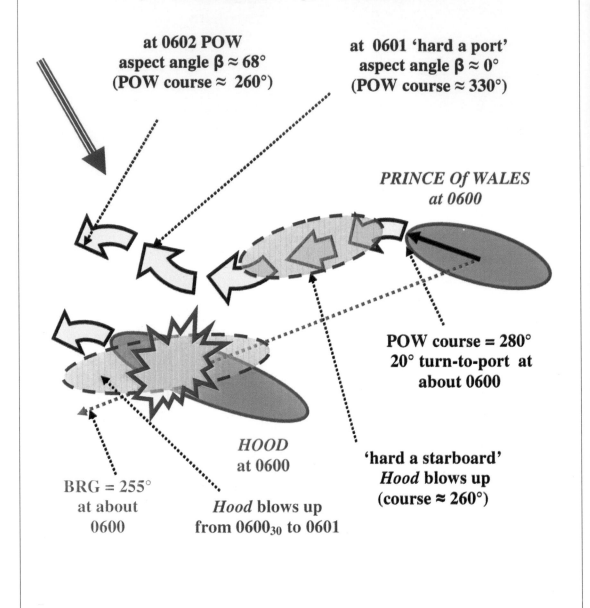

Direction of KMS BISMARCK's fire (from BRG 330°)

at 0602 POW
aspect angle β ≈ 68°
(POW course ≈ 260°)

at 0601 'hard a port'
aspect angle β ≈ 0°
(POW course ≈ 330°)

PRINCE Of WALES
at 0600

POW course = 280°
20° turn-to-port at
about 0600

HOOD
at 0600

'hard a starboard'
***Hood* blows up**
(course ≈ 260°)

BRG = 255°
at about
0600

Hood **blows up**
from 0600₃₀ to 0601

6. The *Prince of Wales'* manoeuvre between 0600 and 0601: as the *Hood* blew up towards 0601, Capt. Leach on the *Prince of Wales*, steaming only 800 yards away from the flagship and still performing the turn to port ordered by Admiral Holland shortly before, had to counter-manoeuvre immediately to avoid the *Hood's* hull sinking rapidly after abruptly coming to a standstill. His orders shortly thereafter were 'hard a-starboard' and 'hard a-port' to keep his ship's port stern away from the sinking battlecruiser dead in the water. It is therefore plausible that at about 0601 the *Prince of Wales'* bow was head on to the *Bismarck*, namely with an aspect angle β approximately equal to 0°.

<u>Theoretical impact point pattern</u> of a gun at a Naval Proving Ground (εp_{xRT} and εp_{yRT} values can be found in the Range Tables)

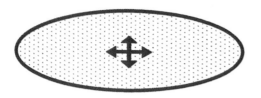

<u>Theoretical impact point pattern</u> of a gun firing under operating conditions at sea (εp_{xsea} and εp_{ysea} values are higher than εp_{xRT} and εp_{yRT}).

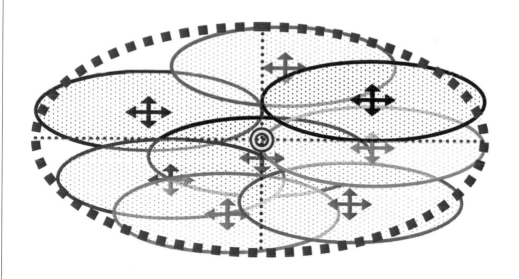

7. Theoretical impact point patterns and the battery beaten zone of an eight-gun battery firing a salvo at the same target under operating conditions. This plane figure is composed of the theoretical impact patterns of the eight guns. The centres of these patterns do not overlap because of errors, namely systematic or slowly time-varying differences of ballistic and geometric quantities between guns, such as initial velocity, parallax and roller-path inclination. In addition, the blast of simultaneous firing increases the dispersion of each individual gun belonging to the same gun turret.

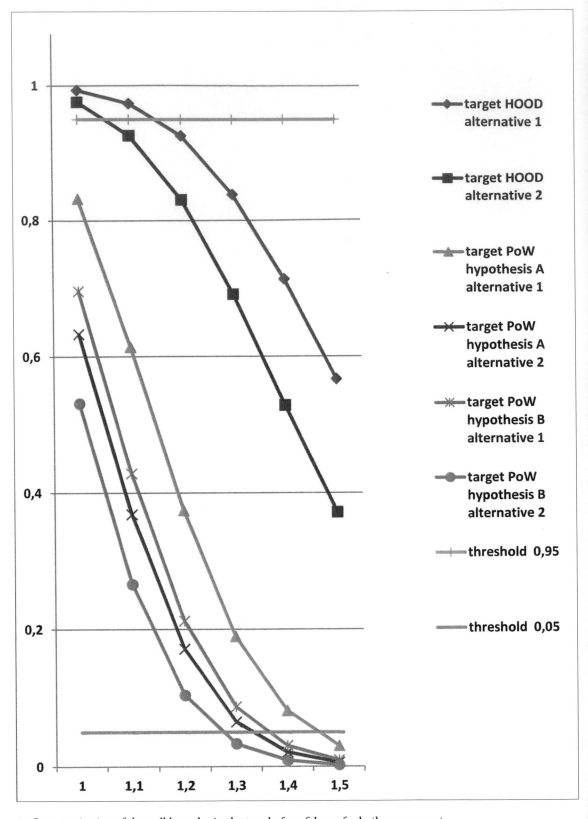

8. Correct rejection of the null hypothesis; the trend of confidence for both engagements.

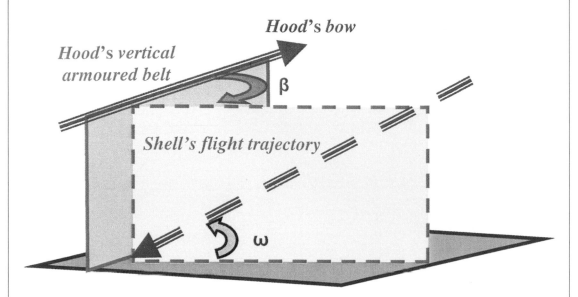

Hood's bow

Hood's vertical
armoured belt

β

Shell's flight trajectory

ω

Hood's horizontal protection

9. Impact geometry.

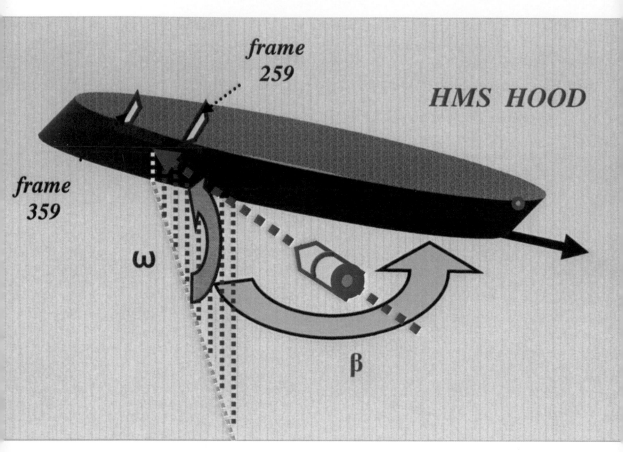

10. The *Bismarck*'s shell trajectory.

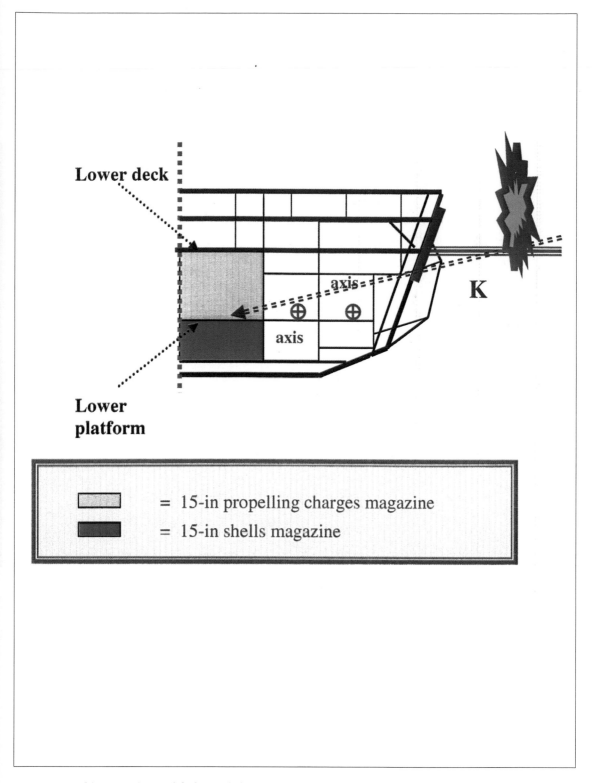

11. HMS *Hood* (May 1941). Simplified unscaled cross-section frame 312.

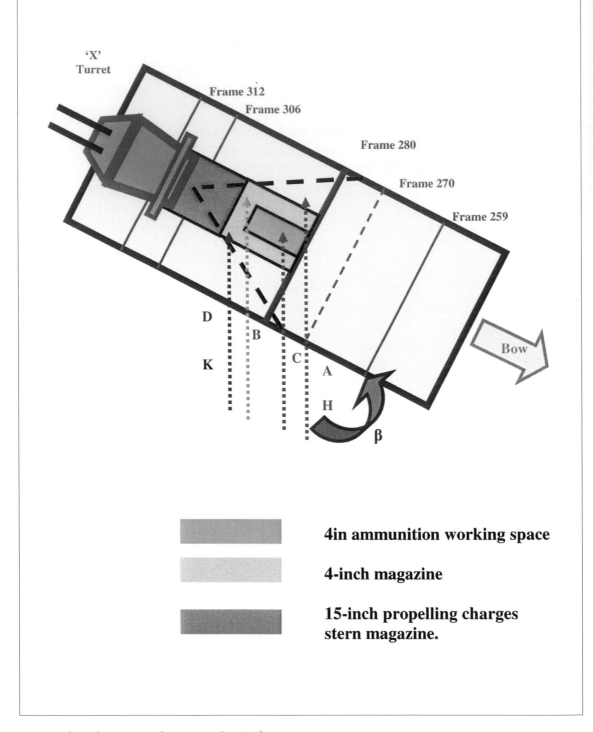

12. Hypothetical geometry of impact on the *Hood*.

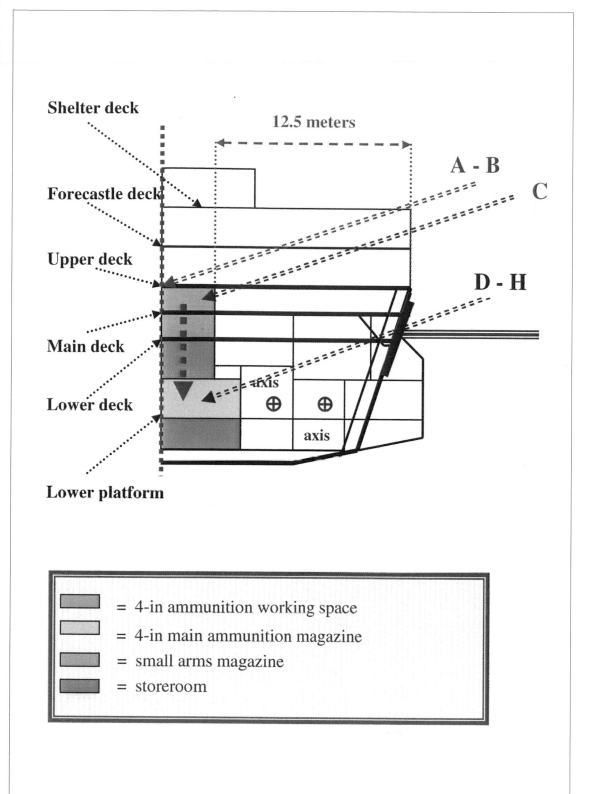

Shelter deck

12.5 meters

A - B

Forecastle deck

C

Upper deck

D - H

Main deck

axis

Lower deck

axis

Lower platform

= 4-in ammunition working space
= 4-in main ammunition magazine
= small arms magazine
= storeroom

13. HMS *Hood* (May 1941). Simplified unscaled cross-section frame 280.

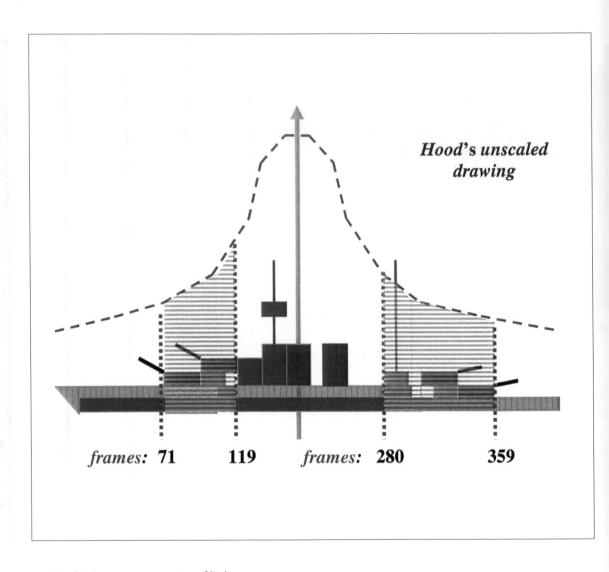

Hood's unscaled drawing

frames: **71** **119** *frames:* **280** **359**

14. Graphic image representation of 'P2'.

15. British 15-inch BL gun and 15-inch shell. (*Author's collection*)

16. British 15-inch BL gun (breech detail) and 15-inch shell. (*Author's collection*)

A final hypothesis considers two concurrent or nearly concurrent hits within the *Bismarck's* fifth salvo: one would have struck the aft magazine and another the forward ones. This could help explain why during the inspection of the wreck the 650-ton heavy conning tower was found so far away from the majority of the debris. Only the explosion of the forward magazines would have been powerful enough to account for this. After all, the considerable distance between the *Hood's* aft and forward magazines (about 100 m) might suggest that with the boiler and turbine rooms in between, the explosion astern was unlikely to involve the fore magazines, even in the event of the boilers bursting due to overpressure.

5.3 The probability of destroying HMS *Hood*: an assessment

History has taught us that the destruction of a large warship by artillery fire alone can take place only if the hits affect ammunition magazines and the ammunition itself. This results either from direct penetration and subsequent explosion or following the detonation in an adjoining and/or communicating area. During the Battle of Jutland the sinking of three British battlecruisers was most probably caused by the explosion of the gun turrets and/or the underlying barbettes spreading to the magazines. Royal Navy designers learnt that lesson and in the interwar period substantially improved the protection of the hull and particularly avoided a direct communication between the barbettes of heavy-calibre turrets and the main ammunition magazines. HMS *Hood* too benefited from such improvements and hence it is possible to discard the hypothesis envisaging the explosion of the ammunition magazines as the result of a shell hitting the *Hood* fair and square on one of the turrets and/or the barbettes.[20] If we exclude the rather unlikely event of an explosion in the torpedo magazine, we are left with two alternative scenarios worthy of further investigation:

- The German shell striking the ammunition magazines immediately and blasting inside them.
- The German shell striking the 102/45 ammunition working space (on the main deck) with the detonation waves propagating into the underlying 102/45 ammunition magazine and the adjoining 381/42 propelling charge magazine.

Whatever the case may be, the fatal 380/47 shell would have got to reach (with a 'P2' probability, Plate 14) the ship's area within the frames encompassing the ammunition magazines, after penetrating the passive defences (with a 'P3' probability). In order to calculate the 'P2' probability, the impact points of the *Bismarck's* hits are assumed to be included in a Gaussian distribution along the *Hood's* keel axis (with its centre in the geometric centre of the ship).[21] Once there, the shell would then have a 'P4' probability of damaging the ship's ammunition magazines. That probability is roughly equal to the ratio between the magazines' volume (slightly increased to include also near misses) and the ship's total volume included in the above frames. After that, the 'P5' probability concerning the correct detonation of the shell needs to be considered, as two out of the total hits scored by the German battleship (both on the *Prince of Wales*) did not detonate.[22] All these events are summarised in the following table:

Table 18

Event	
2	The shell hits the ship's area between the frames in question, including the ammunition magazines
3	The armour between the frames in question is pierced by the hitting shell
4	The shell arrives inside the volume where the shell explosion is surely able to induce the magazine deflagration
5	The shell detonates correctly

All the events included in the above table are *compatible* with each other (i.e. they are not mutually exclusive), and *independent* (i.e. they are not mutually affected). Hence the probability of them occurring all together and bringing about the explosion of the ammunition magazines (Pe) is equal to the product of each event's probability of happening (Theorem of Compound Probability):

$$Pe = P2 * P3 * P4 * P5$$

However, the event explosion is conditioned by, or *dependent on*, the actual impact on the British unit of 380/47 shells fired by the German battleship: event '1' (compatible with 'e') with probability of occurrence P1. Hence we can express with P (e/1) the conditional probability of the explosion (e) given the hit/s (1). When two events are compatible and dependent, the joint probability of 'e' and '1' occurring [P(e ∩ 1)] is, in the situation under investigation, equal to:

$$P (e \cap 1) = P1 * P (e/1)$$

As the hypothesis assumed here is that the explosion was neither the result of an incident from within the *Hood*[23] nor of a hit scored by the *Prinz Eugen*[24] then:

$$P (e/1) = Pe$$

Hence the joint probability of 'e' and '1' is:

$$P (e \cap 1) = P1 * Pe$$

On the other hand, event '1' can be subdivided into two *incompatible* (i.e. mutually exclusive) alternatives which cover all the possible events included in a *Hood*-hit scenario:

1a The *Hood* is struck by *only one* shell (exactly one) out of the four effective salvoes fired (32 shells altogether without the *hit in the fifth salvo only* constraint, i.e. 32/2nd-3rd-4th-5th);

1b The *Hood* is struck by *at least two* shells (two or more) out of the four effective salvoes fired (32 shells altogether without the *hit in the fifth salvo only* constraint).

Alternative 1a

Had this been the case, the two outcomes, namely forward *and* aft ammunition magazine struck, are necessarily *incompatible*. By the Law of Total Probability, the probability of occurrence of an outcome against the other is given by the sum of the probabilities attributed to each of them:

$$Pk1a = P1a * (P2_{bow} * P3_{bow} * P4_{bow} * P5) + P1a * (P2_{stern} * P3_{stern} * P4_{stern} * P5) =$$

$$= P1a * (P2_{bow} * P3_{bow} * P4_{bow} * P5 + P2_{stern} * P3_{stern} * P4_{stern} * P5) =$$

$$= P1a * (P_{eBOW} + P_{eSTERN})$$

where:

- P1a: probability of occurrence of event 1a;
- P_{eBOW} $= (P2_{bow} * P3_{bow} * P4_{bow} * P5)$;
- P_{eSTERN} $= (P2_{stern} * P3_{stern} * P4_{stern} * P5)$

Alternative 1b

In this case the two events are *compatible* with each other, thus the probability of occurrence of either the first outcome or the second is expressed by the following relation:

$$Pk1b = P1b * (P_{eBOW} + P_{eSTERN} - P_{eBOW} * P_{eSTERN})$$

where P1b is the probability of occurrence of event 1b.

As alternatives 1a and 1b are incompatible, by once again applying the Law of Total Probability, the expected probability of occurrence of the event '*Hood* hit in the magazines by at least one shell' is given by the sum of the probabilities attributed to each of them. Hence the probability that the *Hood's* sinking was the consequence of the blowing up of the ammunition magazines after being hit by exactly one or at least two 380/47 shells out of an 8-shot effective salvo fired by the German battleship is the following:

$$Pk = Pk1a + Pk1b =$$

$$= P1a * (P_{eBOW} + P_{eSTERN}) + P1b * (P_{eBOW} + P_{eSTERN} - P_{eBOW} * P_{eSTERN})$$

then the estimated probabilities are:

- $P2_{bow} \approx P2_{stern} \approx 0.082$ (8.2%)
- $P3_{bow}{}^{25} \approx P3_{stern} \approx 0.78$ (78%)
- $P4_{bow} \approx 0.45$ (45%)
- $P4_{stern} \approx 0.66$ (66%)
- $P5 = 0.7$ (70%)
- $P_{eBOW} \approx 0.02$ (2%)
- $P_{eSTERN} \approx 0.03$ (3%)

The following table indicates the highest SSHP probability per each salvo fired by the *Bismarck* on the *Hood* (according to the hypothesis of perfectly-on-target firing):

Table 19

Salvo	2nd	3rd	4th	5th
Shells (n)	8 (2 + 4 + 2)	8	8	8
Time	0557	0558	0559	0600
SSHP (kkk = 1)	≈ 0.075	≈ 0.109	≈ 0.116	≈ 0.125

hence:

$$P1a \approx 0.1045$$
$$P1b \approx 0.87$$
$$Pk1a \approx 0.005$$
$$Pk1b \approx 0.043$$
$$Pk\text{-}32/2nd\text{-}3rd\text{-}4th\text{-}5th \approx 0.048 \ (4.8\%)$$

The above Pk refers to the four effective salvoes fired, a total of 32 shells without the *hit in the fifth salvo only* constraint. Conversely, assuming that the hit/s was/were from the fifth salvo only, i.e. 32/5th (perfectly-on-target fire):

$$P1a \approx 0.031$$
$$P1b \approx 0.021$$
$$Pk1a \approx 0.0016$$
$$Pk1b \approx 0.00104$$
$$Pk\text{-}32/5th \approx 0.0026 \ (\approx 0.3\%)$$

Finally, if only the fifth salvo is considered, only 8 shells (8/5th) with perfectly-on-target fire:

$$P1a \approx 0.393$$
$$P1b \approx 0.265$$
$$Pk1a \approx 0.02$$
$$Pk1b \approx 0.013$$
$$Pk\text{-}8/5th \approx 0.033 \ (3.3\%)$$

An attempt to quantify roughly the effect of the above Pk values on the number of effective full salvoes (NS) fired necessary for a cumulative Pk (CPk), i.e. the probability to hit with at least one shell, of 95% would give:

$$CPk = 0.95 = 1 - (1 - Pk)^{NS}$$

$$(1 - Pk)^{NS} = 0.05$$

$$NS = \frac{\text{Log } 0.05}{(1 - Pk)}$$

Hence, considering Pk-8/5th, the result is:

$$= \frac{\text{Log } 0.05}{(1 - 0.033)} \approx 90 \text{ salvoes} = 720 \text{ effective shots fired}$$

On the other hand, even considering:

- $P2_{bow} = P2_{stern} = 10\%$
- $P3_{bow} = P3_{stern} = 100\%$ (the German shells definitely pierce the armour)
- $P5 = 100\%$ (the German shells definitely detonate)

the Pk is:

$$Pk\text{-}32/2nd\text{-}3rd\text{-}4th\text{-}5th \approx 0.106 \ (10.6\%)$$

$$Pk\text{-}8/5th \approx 0.073 \ (7.3\%)$$

In the latter case for a CPk of 95% the number of shells to fire would be:

$$= \frac{\text{Log } 0.05}{(1 - 0.073)} \approx 40 \text{ salvoes} = 320 \text{ effective shots fired}$$

Hence to achieve a 95% probability of sinking the *Hood*, the *Bismarck* should have fired as many as 40 full salvoes under the same kinematic and geometric conditions of the 5th salvo. But reality was not like that. The *Hood* blew up after just *four effective 380/47 salvoes* fired with a total of only 32 shots (5 salvoes with 40 shots altogether). The explosion of one or both 15-inch ammunition magazines inside the *Hood* is therefore to be regarded as a highly improbable event. Furthermore, had a systematic error actually affected German firing, then the Pk would have been definitely lower, causing a proportional decrease in the likelihood of the event and hence a contextual increase in the number of salvoes needed to achieve that result.

It is, however, possible that the hypothetical systematic error was gradually reduced thanks to the corrections ordered by the *Bismarck's* first gunnery officer. In this scenario the fifth salvo may have been perfectly on target or perhaps affected by a moderate error, which would have also increased the chances of two or more shells of the fifth salvo – instead of just one – hitting the *Hood* at the same time. This would, among other things, provide a better explanation of the fact that the ship's conning tower lies at the bottom of the ocean about 2 km away from the midsection: one shell might have struck the aft magazine and another one of the same salvo the forward magazine. The ensuing explosions would have been powerful enough to throw the 650-ton heavy tower that far away. Besides, the alternative explanation of this fact appears even less realistic; namely that the deflagration wave of the aft magazine propagated through the 100 m length of the engine and boiler rooms, finally causing the corresponding deflagration of the forward 15-inch propelling charges.

Oddly enough, only two days later fate dictated that an equally low-probability event occurred – this time luck was with the British as if to restore the balance of power. On 26 May, a Swordfish torpedo bomber operating from HMS *Ark Royal* succeeded in scoring an incredible hit. It struck the starboard side of the German battleship's stern with a 450-mm torpedo, heavily damaging both rudders – the only part of the *Bismarck* vulnerable to this kind of weapon. The rudder was only 5.5 m long *v.* the ship's total length of 250 m. A very rough probability estimation of this event, namely of a torpedo hitting the rudder, indicates a scant 2.2% (assuming that the torpedo hits the ship in the first place!)

The damaged rudders prevented the *Bismarck* from escaping back to France and ultimately caused her sinking. Incapable of manoeuvring their ship, the crew could neither shake off their pursuers (the albeit slower *Rodney* and the *King George V* in particular) nor make effective use of their 380/47 guns when it came to ballistic contact. This finally happened on 27 May 1941, between 0847 and 1036, the time of the *Bismarck*'s sinking. The final battle (fought on the anniversary of the Battle of Tsu-Shima between Russia and Japan in 1905) was not really a battle as such but more of an execution. At 0902, the *Bismarck* artillery control posts had already been destroyed and the few working guns left were fired in local control with low precision. Out of 2,876 shots of any calibre fired by the British battleships a few hundred hit the target, rapidly turning the ship into a huge pyre.[26]

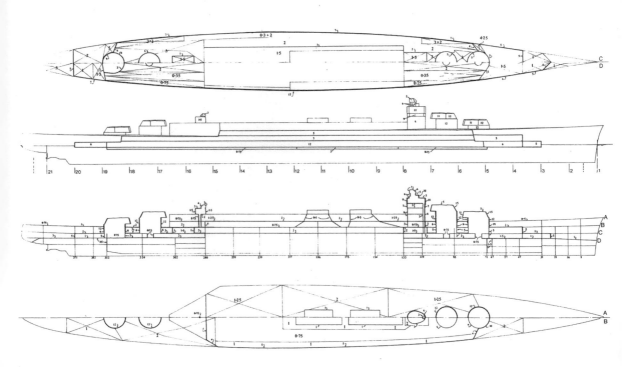

Fig 22: The *Hood*'s armour layout, courtesy of J. Roberts, *The Battlecruiser Hood*.

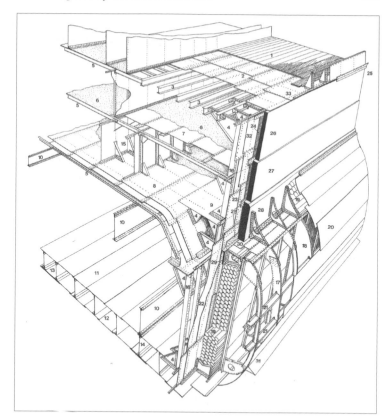

Right: Fig 23: The *Hood*'s midships structure (at forward engine room), courtesy of J. Roberts, *The Battlecruiser Hood.*

Below: Fig 24: Penetrative power of 38 cm Psgr L/4.4 800 kg shell (face-hardened armour); adaptation of an original Krupp graph.

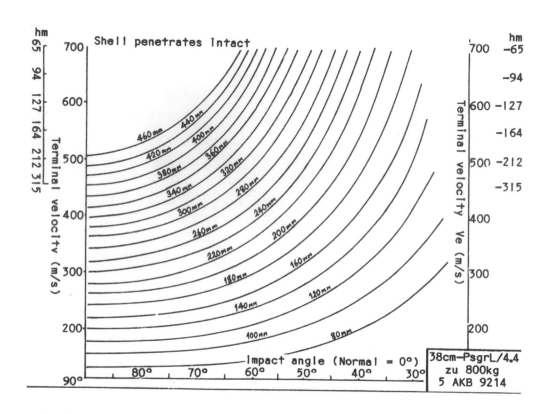

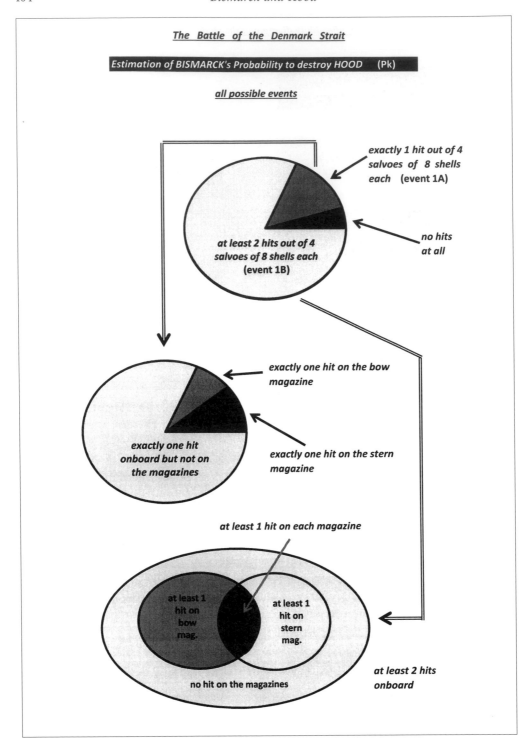

Figure 25.

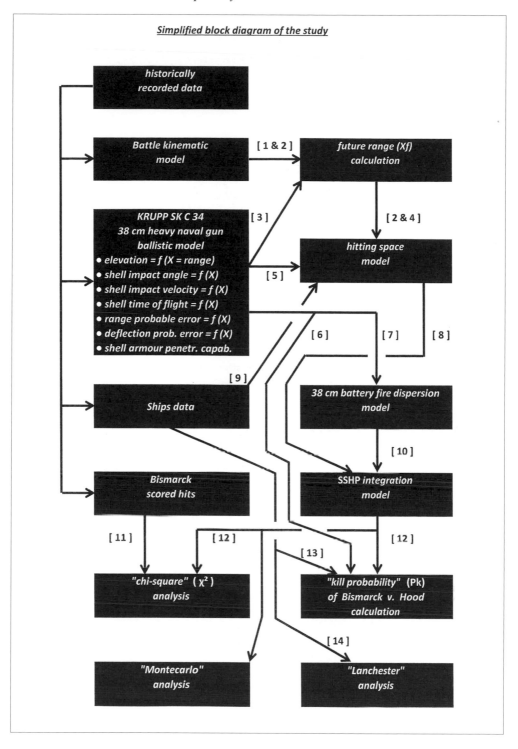

Figure 26.

6

A New Perspective

The results provided by the technical statistical analysis debunk a few popular 'myths' and suggest a new perspective on the Battle of the Denmark Strait. In particular:

- The likelihood of a systematic error affecting the German battleship's firing at the *Hood* is higher than the alternative hypothesis, i.e. the *Bismarck*'s firing perfectly on target. Consequently, the claims of extreme accuracy of the *Bismarck*'s firing in the first stage of the battle should accordingly be revised. Of course, if it could be proven beyond all doubt that the *Bismarck* scored more than one hit in the 3rd or 4th salvo, that would substantially affect the results and hence the conclusions of the analysis. On the other hand, the *Bismarck*'s first gunnery officer demonstrated outstanding ability supported by the excellent performance and efficiency of the German ordnance.[1] In fact, KK Schneider's successful action resulted from the most effective assessment of the evolving tactical situation. Given the theoretical force ratio, promptness in responding to fire with 'full salvoes rapid' was more important and urgent than checking accuracy.[2] He took a risk ... calculated in a matter of seconds: it was of paramount importance to seize that fleeting instant when the large British ships were fighting but unable to train all their guns on the targets because of the unfavourable approach course. The German officer followed his intuition and seized the propitious moment. Trying to fire perfectly on target would have taken him precious minutes. In fact, the ladder procedure prescribed the firing of more dispersed salvoes and the careful evaluation of the scores for a longer time. Instead, he focused on rapidly exploiting the favourable circumstances while continuing to make the necessary corrections with just a few minutes before a dramatic change of situation. As soon as the British naval group was able to bring all its guns to bear, the Germans would have most definitely have suffered the effects of ballistic inferiority and the *Hood* would have also redirected her fire on the *Bismarck*. Of course, Schneider could not realistically have expected an immediate and decisive success – which he nonetheless achieved – but he had to do his utmost to erode the great superiority of the enemy and try to cause maximum damage. Schneider was outstanding because he recognised the pre-eminent tactical necessity without letting himself be wrongly seduced by the search for sterile – and, in that situation, counterproductive – specialist perfection. He therefore proved to be well aware of the naval operational requirements that must always prevail over the arid technicalities of 'pure' gunnery.

- Given the rather 'flat' trajectories of the German shells at the fighting distance of the confrontation between the *Bismarck* and the *Hood*, the frequent mention by historians of plunging shells with a steep angle of descent is utterly inappropriate. I sincerely hope my study helps to prevent the perpetuation of this common scholarly error. Furthermore, although it is possible that the fatal shell hit one of the *Hood*'s after decks, it is more likely that the shell struck the ship's side, penetrating into the interior and exploding. Reconstructions indicate that the explosion took place in the vicinity of the 381/42 aft magazines. Actually, bursting in the AA 102/45 ammunition working spaces located below the upper deck by the X 381/42 turret seems much more realistic. The detonation of the AA medium-calibre projectiles would then propagate in the propelling charges magazine.

- Analysis of the engagement between the *Bismarck* and the *Hood* clearly indicates the totally casual nature of the explosion of the unfortunate battlecruiser. Certainly, the armoured protection of the latter was insufficient. All the same, an enemy shell causing the main 15-inch magazine to blow up was a low-probability event – all the more so considering that such a result was achieved with only 32 shells fired for effect.[3] The inconceivability of the explosion of the 'Mighty Hood' struck the collective imagination so strongly that the effectiveness of the *Bismarck*'s guns achieved legendary status. Historians themselves were not spared from this belief; in their writings the fighting potential of the famous battleship often appears to be over-exaggerated.

- By contrast, the expected *Bismarck* hit probability in the engagement between her and the *Prince of Wales* fully matching the observed hits indicates that German firing this time was probably on target or affected by a very limited systematic error.

- As for the *Prince of Wales*' 356/45 firing, it is clear that she fired most effectively between 0553 and 0600 scoring – even under unfavourable conditions – as many as three hits against the *Bismarck*. The restricted dispersion of the British guns, the excellent alignment of the heavy-calibre battery and, above all, the outstanding ability of the first gunnery officer, Lt Cdr McMullen (who until recently had been the first gunnery officer of the *Hood*) account for this very good performance, whose excellence can be inferred from the table at the end of this chapter comparing times, rounds fired and hits. We should not allow ourselves to be misled by the lack of hits after 0600, as mechanical breakdowns and violent rudder movements to evade enemy fire substantially hindered any efforts to strike again. Conjecturing whether things might have been different had McMullen remained on the *Hood* is futile. By contrast, we should wonder why the excellent firing performance of the *Prince of Wales* – surely not inferior to that of the *Bismarck* – has never been adequately recognised, both shortly after the battle and in the following 60 years. Given the lack of official and unofficial documents on this issue, we can only guess, but it is plausible that considering Churchill and Pound's disapproval of Capt. Leach's difficult but totally right decision to break off the engagement, any expression of praise of the *Prince of Wales*' effective firing could have proven counterproductive. Strangely enough, historians of later times have always described and commented

Battleship *Prince of Wales*, 28 October 1941. (*Imperial War Museum, London*)

on the battle along the lines of the reports of the British boards of inquiry. They have hardly mentioned high accuracy and effectiveness of the battleship's ordnance, while they have always underlined the mechanical defects of the large-calibre guns as if wishing to justify the controversial (yet necessary) decision to disengage from combat. Incidentally, Wake-Walker, who replaced Holland at the head of the British group, did not oppose Leach's orders. Ultimately, Leach was awarded the Distinguished Service Order for his part in the battle, but the *Prince of Wales* began to be surrounded by a negative aura often perceived by the superstitious crews. In fact, it was rumoured in the Royal Navy that the new battleship was a 'Jonah' – an ill-omened ship.[4]

- Losers usually get all the blame and Vice Admiral Holland is no exception to this rule. He is commonly remembered as the ambitious officer who was defeated despite his superior forces. Holland's most significant mistakes include:
  ※ his order to turn north, issued at about 0010 on 24 May. This order lost him bearing on the enemy (at the beginning of the battle the after turrets of the two British ships were unable to bear), but it was a reaction to Wake-Walker's loss of contact. Perhaps given the adverse weather conditions and the real

radar performance, Wake-Walker's units should have tried to close the distance to continue shadowing effectively;

❇ having not more directly involved Wake-Walker's heavy cruisers in the battle;

❇ having kept the *Hood* in the lead of the British formation and handled his squadron rather inflexibly, which significantly limited the freedom of the *Prince of Wales* to manoeuvre and fire; and

❇ having not engaged the *Bismarck* in the first crucial minutes of the battle, as the enemy ships had been mistakenly identified.

In spite of Holland's multiple tactical mistakes before and during the battle, the insistence on the merely defensive rationale behind his closing manoeuvre, i.e. his sole purpose being to avoid the enemy plunging fire, cannot but appear ungenerous and hardly credible. Instead, it is likely that the British Admiral was prompted by the urgent need to increase the hit probability of his group, thus preventing the enemy from breaking into the central Atlantic. He could not let the opportunity to stop his opponents pass him by; he had to try to inflict decisive damage because that was the only way left to accomplish his mission.

Finally, no one has ever discussed Admiral Tovey's 'mistake'; namely his taking at face value Leach's optimistic declaration that the *Prince of Wales* was fully operational and ready to take her place in the Fleet. The brand-new battleship was actually still struggling with mechanical problems when she was ordered to join the *Hood* in the action against the *Bismarck*, and Tovey's decision was not without effects on the outcome of the battle. In fact, apart from the *Hood* blowing up, the loss of efficiency of the *Prince of Wales'* heavy guns was probably the worst event that occurred to the British side.

Table 20

Firing ship	Bismarck	Prince of Wales
Target	Hood	Bismarck
First hit after (min)	5	3
First hit after salvoes (n)	5	6
Shots fired under central control (n)	40	55
Total salvoes fired (n)	5	18
Salvoes per min (n)	1	2
Total hits observed (n)	1	3
Average rounds fired per hit (n)	40	18
Average rounds per salvo (n)	8	3

Conclusion

No one will ever be able to say with certainty what exactly happened on that fateful day; namely to describe in detail the circumstances determining the evolution and the outcome of the Battle of the Denmark Strait. The event lasted only a total of 16 minutes. However, over the last 60 years, legions of historians and *aficionados* have consumed plenty of ink on this subject which, conversely, has neither brought all the facts surrounding that spectacular and tragic battle into focus nor dissipated the vapours of the 'fog of war', thus leaving doubts and blind spots.

There were few survivors of the great battleships sunk between 24 May and 27 May 1941, and those who survived have by now joined the men who then lost their lives. Only a careful investigation of the elements available can help to shed light on some otherwise mysterious aspects. However, since certainty in knowledge is unattainable, my purpose has been to search for a key to a more credible interpretation of the event. In my study I have tried to highlight the fact that this well-known story – compiled shortly after the end of the battleship *Bismarck* and often reported somewhat uncritically in countless subsequent writings – does not always accord with a more realistic interpretation of that memorable event.

The technical statistical analysis has produced results that warrant some reflection and possibly a deeper investigation. In any case, they prove that it is sometimes necessary – in respect of even the most established interpretations – to maintain an ever-vigilant critical spirit.

To claim a monopoly of correctness […] is not in my intention. I have, however, endeavoured to explode a few legends, and to refute prejudices with facts.

Cajus Bekker

Appendix A

Kinematic model of the courses followed by the opposing naval groups from 0537 to 0609 on 24 May 1941

The information available from different German and British sources concerning the kinematics of the battle is generally consistent on the courses taken by the two opponents, but it often differs on times and on single manoeuvres.[1] As a result, accurately determining the relative positions of the groups at any one instant becomes altogether difficult. It is true that there are a few geometric data (listed below) subjecting the description of the manoeuvres to some constraints. However, a degree of uncertainty about the kinematics continues to exist. The elements contained in many works are not always consistent and reliable. And, in addition, the loss of the *Bismarck*'s War Diary has deprived us of particularly important pieces of the data puzzle. At any rate, the data derived from the records taken on the *Prinz Eugen* are highly reliable, despite the cruiser's freedom of manoeuvring during the battle resulting in her not strictly following the course of her flagship.

The schematic reconstruction (kinematic model) proposed below is deemed adequate, as it is capable of mediating – with a good approximation – among all the available elements. This reconstruction covers the kinematic situation under way in the time interval between 0556 and 0609, subdividing the ballistic phase into one-minute intervals. Times are referred to in whole minutes and rely on German sources. The adopted model is subject to the following constraints:

1. both naval groups sailing at an equal speed of 28 knots, as reported by all available sources;

2. the present range resulting from the reconstruction made for the *Bismarck*'s fifth salvo (fired at 0600 and hitting the *Hood*) was of about 15,500 m. This figure is in accordance with German reports and is essentially consistent with the *Prince of Wales*' firing data. Considering the *Bismarck–Hood* relative motion and the shell flight time, this distance was correlated with a predicted or future range of 15,200 m. When the *Bismarck* scores the fatal hit, the *Hood*'s aspect angle (her course inclination angle) is calculated to be 63.2°;

3. the *Bismarck*'s bearing taken by the *Prince of Wales* at 0600 was approximately equal

to 330°, resulting from the chart of the salvoes' fall of shots that is based on the data registered onboard during the battle (ref. 65, p. 40);

4. as reported by Chesneau (ref. 29, p. 159), shortly before 0600 Holland ordered a second 20° turn to port. For this reason the *Prince of Wales* – initially sailing on course 280° and at a distance of just 741 m (810 yards) from the flagship – risked ramming the *Hood*'s sinking wreck. In that situation, between 0600 and 0603, the *Prince of Wales* performed swift manoeuvres to avoid that risk. The 380/47 shell that hit the *Prince of Wales* just before 0602 struck the side plating of the compass platform (roughly in the middle) and exited the room in the proximity of the back port corner without exploding. Thus the aspect angle of the British battleship was then equal to about 70° (assumed value: 67.9°). Leach, still recovering from the shock of the hit, ordered an emergency turn to port (ref. 15, p. 5);

5. the training of the *Bismarck*'s guns at 0602, i.e. at the beginning of the engagement with the *Prince of Wales*, was roughly equal to 310°, as reported by von Müllenheim-Rechberg: '[…] and her guns now point at a bearing of about 310 degrees' (ref. 34, p. 175);

6. the *Bismarck*'s assumed present range from the *Prince of Wales* at 0602 was 14,000 m, as reported by von Müllenheim-Rechberg: 'Because our courses were converging, the range soon closed to 14,000 m and the Prince of Wales was taking shells from both the German ships' (ref. 34, p. 89). This distance is correlated with a predicted (future) range of 13,700 m;

7. the 380/47 shot that hit the *Prince of Wales* between 0604 and 0605 struck the hull, after travelling about 80 feet underwater, with an angle of entry between 40° and 50° (ref. 22, p. 62). Applying these data to the ship's bow, the aspect angle is assumed to be 135°;

Battle of the Denmark Strait: the *Bismarck* fires a full salvo on the *Prince of Wales* at a bearing of about 310°, 24 May 1941. (*Wilhelmshavener Zeitung*)

8. the course followed by the *Prince of Wales* that is considered in this study is generally consistent with the chart of the salvoes fired by this unit (ref. 61, p. 40);

9. the *Bismarck*'s cease-firing distance is substantially compatible with the range relative to a time close to that of the (partial) 0609 salvo. It is then plausible that Lütjens gave the command to cease firing towards 0609, at a range of 22,000 m, according to German sources (ref. 35, p. 90).

A great effort has been made to provide the most accurate reconstruction of the battle. Nonetheless, errors may still exist, especially in connection with distance. However, they should be moderate; namely not over a few hundred metres (with specific reference to the ballistic phases with an average value of ± 1% of the range). Considering the firing dispersion of the *Bismarck*'s Krupp SK C/34 guns as a function of distance, this value does not appear to significantly affect the final results of the analysis.

Bismarck's Krupp SK C/34 38 cm heavy naval gun breech and recuperator. (*Podzun Pallas Verlag*)

Table 21

					Bismarck kinematic situation			
Time hhmm	Salvo (n)	Course (°)	Speed (kt)	Train (°)	True bearing from *Hood* (°)	*Hood* present range* (m)	*Hood* predicted range** (m)
0556	1	220	28	294.4	334.4	18,900	18,500
0557	2	220	28	294.1	334.1	18,000	17,600
0558	3	220	28	293.9	333.9	17,100	16,700
0559	4	220	28	293.6	333.6	16,300	16,000
0600	5	220	28	293.2	333.2	15,500	15,200
0601?	6	220	28	293.1	333.1	14,900	14,800

Table 22

	Hood kinematic situation		
Time hhmm	Course (°)	Speed (kt)	Train (β) (°)
0556	280	28	54.4
0557	280	28	54.1
0558	280	28	53.9
0559	280	28	53.6
0600	270	28	63.2
0601	265**	28**	68.1**

Table 23

					Bismarck kinematic situation			
Time hhmm	Salvo (n)	Course (°)	Speed (kt)	Train (°)	True bearing from *Prince of Wales* (°)	*Prince of Wales* present range* (m)	*Prince of Wales* predicted range* (m)
0601?	6	220	28	290.9	330.9	14,900	14,500
0602	7	195	28	312.9	327.9	14,000	13,700
0603	8	200	28	308.5	328.5	14,300	14,400
0604	9	255	28	250.9	325.9	15,200	15,600
0605	10	265	28	240.1	325.1	16,300	16,700
0606	11	270	28	234.6	324.6	17,600	18,300
0607	12	270	28	232.1	322.1	19,000	19,700
0608	13	270	28	230	320	20,400	21,200
0609	14	270	28	228.1	318.1	21,900	22,800

Table 24

Prince of Wales kinematic situation			
Time hhmm	Course (°)	Speed (kt)	Train (β) (°)
0601	330.9	28	0.9
0602	260	28	67.9
0603	150	28	178.5
0604	190	28	135.9
0605	190	28	135.1
0606	140	28	184.6
0607	140	28	182.1
0608	140	28	180
0609	140	28	178.1

* *rounded to the nearest hundredth*
** *computed by the* Bismarck's *C38 K*

It is worth noting that the *Bismarck*'s predicted range has been calculated using an iterative algorithm based on the relevant kinematic data (the ships' speed and course; the shell's time of flight) and assuming that speed and course remain unchanged for the time of flight of the shell. This algorithm proves effective as it is able to achieve convergence of the calculated range with the real future range in only five successive iterations:

present ship-to-ship range (range 1)
▼
shell's time of flight 1
▼
ships' relative movement over the time of flight 1
▼
range 2 [$\Delta 1 = |(\text{range 1}) - (\text{range 2})|$]
▼
shell's time of flight 2

•
•

range 'n' [$\Delta_{n-1} = |(\text{range 'n–1'}) - (\text{range 'n'})| = 0$]
▼
range 'n' = predicted range

Of course, this calculation procedure can be performed only by digital computers. Mechanical analogue fire-control computers installed aboard the warships of the Second World War solved the problem differently – the movement of their inner gears reproduced all the relevant kinematic data in an analogue way.

Appendix B

HMS *Hood* and HMS *Prince of Wales*: size of the hitting space (HS) and SSHP calculation procedure

1. Introduction

For the purpose of a probability study concerning artillery fire, the geometric shape of the intended target has to be rendered less complex than it really is. Certainly, investigating the real shape produces more accurate results virtually. However, that would make it altogether difficult to define the hitting space (HS) on which we have to integrate the probability density function – to calculate the SSHP – expressing the fire dispersion, i.e. the distribution of the shots' impact points in the horizontal plane.[1]

The width and height of the ship varying with its length justifies the need to assume a target characterised by a simplified shape and dimensions and yet whose projection on the water plane is as faithful as possible with the real target. The assumed target is therefore defined as follows:

- the horizontal surface area (S_t) is equal to the projection upon the horizontal plane of the target's real decks, i.e. the target area exposed to the shells striking the decks;
- the bulwarks are considered perpendicular to the total surface area;
- the internal volume above the waterline (V_{TOT}) is equal to the real volume of the ship's top side;
- the mean height from the waterline is considered equal to the ratio:

$$hm = V_{TOT} / S_t$$

This target is significantly simplified when compared with the real target but is, at the same time, on an average equivalent with the actual target. However, the curved profile of the waterways poses an additional problem requiring some further simplifications:

- the assumed target's shape is a parallelepiped of rectangular base;
- the target length (L) is equal to the real target's maximum length;
- the target mean beam (A) is equal to the ratio:

$$A = S_t / L$$

The HS (see Figs 27 and 28 at the end of this appendix) is principally defined by:

- A dimension on the x axis deriving from the three geometric elements listed below:
  - ✳ the projection of the target onto the plane of the line of fire inclined at the β angle;
  - ✳ the projection of the target's mean height (hm) above the waterline upon the horizontal plane determined by the shell's impact angle (ω) – ω is the inclination of the shot's trajectory on impact with respect to the horizontal plane:

$$Bx = hm / \tan \omega$$

  - ✳ a distance (Cx) in front of the target, at which a shot falling short of the ship is however capable of hitting and causing damage after travelling a short but not marginal distance, which can be covered underwater (Cxu) or in the air if the shell bounces off the water (ricochet hits, Cxr).

- A dimension (Dy) on the y axis which is equal to the projections of the target's length (L) and mean beam (A) upon the normal plane of the line of fire inclined at the β angle expressing the bearing of the target itself:

$$Dy = L * |\sin \beta| + A * |\cos \beta|$$

The results of the trials carried out by both the US Navy in 1912 and the Imperial Japanese Navy in 1924 are considered in order to calculate Cxu. At that time, it emerged that shells falling short and impacting the water with an angle (ω) between 10° and 30° were still capable of striking the target's hull after covering a moderate distance underwater provided they possessed enough kinetic energy to:
  - ✳ overcome water resistance from the falling point up to the immersed part of the target's hull;
  - ✳ and after that, still had enough energy to produce an appreciable impact on the keel.[2]

Determining Cxr is very difficult as many factors influence the shell's trajectory after water impact, among which are the impact angle width, the shell's kinetic energy at impact, the shell's rotational motion (for gyro flight stabilisation) and the sea state (amplitude of the waves). The assumed maximum value of Cxr is 30 m. The target course inclination angle (aspect angle) β is also important for the Cx value. In fact, if the β angle is less than 10°, the probability of an underwater hit or of a ricochet hit is considered zero.

The elements discussed so far are meant to define the dimensions of the hitting space. This plane figure includes all and only the intersection points between the striking trajectories (above and below water) and the sea surface. In order to calculate the SSHP, the hitting space dimensions have to be further simplified to make the integration procedure easier (see Fig. 29):
  - lateral dimension: Dy

- longitudinal dimension:

$$Dx = (S_t + S1 + S2) / Dy$$

where:

S_t is as defined above;
S1   is the locus of points in the horizontal plane including the shells striking the above-water target's vertical surface (the above-water parts of the broadsides and the sides of the superstructures):

$$S1 = Bx * Dy$$

S2   is the locus of points in the horizontal plane including the shells striking the underwater target's vertical surface area:

$$S2 = Cx * Dy$$

2. Relevant dimensions of HMS *Hood* and HMS *Prince of Wales*

HMS Hood
- L   262.2 m
- maximum width at waterline and at bulges   29.7 m – 31.7 m
- hm   8.9 m
- S_t 5,639 m²

HMS Prince of Wales
- L   227 m
- maximum width   31.5 m
- hm   10.4 m
- S_t 5,406 m²

The estimation of the mean height above waterline and of the deck surface area of the ships under investigation is based on scale drawings.

3. Underwater route (Cxu) of striking, *short* shells

In this investigation, the Cxu value is the length of the underwater distance covered by a shell falling in the water *slightly short* with an angle of incidence (ω) between 10° (with tighter angles, the shell ricochets) and 30° (with wider angles, the shell sinks almost immediately) and with a certain impact velocity upon entry into the water (Vω)

depending on the range. Therefore, the following elements have to be considered:

    a.   the kinetic energy of the shell on water impact (KEω);

    b.   the shell's coefficient of hydrodynamic resistance (Ch);

    c.   the keel resistance.

Underwater hits (scored by the *Bismarck*) are considered only when the shot, having covered the remaining distance under water, still possesses enough kinetic energy to overcome the resistance of the target's keel and obtain at least the complete penetration of the plating (KEcpp). It is further assumed that the underwater impact on the side of the hull always took place with a vertical angle ω of 0°. In a *complete penetration of the plating* situation, the shell gets through the total thickness of the plating but the process saps the remaining kinetic energy; hence the projectile comes to a halt after piercing the plates. It is therefore necessary to calculate the resistance of the keel for each British ship and, in turn, the energy required for the complete penetration of the plating. John Roberts reports that the *Hood's* plating thickness at the anti-torpedo bulge totalled 1.5 inches (38 mm).[3] However, for the *Prince of Wales* Alan Raven and John Roberts indicate a bulge total thickness equal to 1.75 inches (44.5 mm).[4]

    If we consider:

- the empirical De Marre formula to calculate the velocity of complete penetration of the plating (Vcpp) of a surface of known thickness T for a projectile with calibre C and weight W with angles of impact β and ω (ψ is the so-called De Marre constant):

$$Vcpp = (T^{0.7} * \psi * C^{0.75}) / (\sin \beta * \sin \omega * W^{0.5})$$

- the mean velocity, Vm, is calculated by taking the velocity of the projectile both upon entry into the water and at target impact:

$$Vm = (V\omega + Vcpp) / 2$$

- Newton's Law (as in Prandtl's formula) concerning resistance to objects (with cross-section S and mean velocity Vm) moving in a fluid with density 'ρ' is:
$$R = 0.5 * \rho * Ch * S * Vm^2$$

- the distance value (however approximately known) Cxu$_{known}$ (about 80 feet): the distance covered under water by the shell striking the *Prince of Wales* under the waterline at a known water impact velocity (Vω) and with an inclination angle (β) of about 135° between 0604 and 0605

then we can calculate the shell underwater resistance factor, Ch:

$$KEcpp = 0.5 * (W / g) * Vcpp^2$$
(the kinetic energy needed for the complete penetration of the hull plates)
$$KE\omega = 0.5 * (W / g) * V\omega_{known}^2$$
(the kinetic energy at water impact)

$$\Delta KE = KE\omega - Kecpp$$

$$R * Cxu_{known} = \Delta KE$$

$$R = \Delta KE \, / \, Cxu_{known}$$

$$Ch = R \, / \, (0.5 * \rho * S * Vm^2)$$

Once we know Ch, we can calculate R for every Vm, i.e. for every Vω related to the proper predicted range, and hence the maximum Cxu (measured from the ship's side) at which a projectile fired from any distance and having fallen in the water slightly short can still strike:

$$Cxu = \Delta KE \, / \, R$$

4. SSHP calculation procedure

In this study, the expression 'single shot hit probability' (SSHP) indicates the probability of a successful hit out of the infinite number of shots a battery of the same calibre guns with the same ballistic properties could theoretically fire. Here the investigated gun battery is that of the battleship *Bismarck*. Calculating the SSHP under the general geometric and ballistic conditions affecting each battery salvo involves integrating the specific function that describes the battery fire dispersion and is extended to the target simplified HS domain. That implies the need to consider the standard deviation σ_B of the distribution of the falling points of the shots fired by the entire battery, where σ_B is bigger than the standard deviation σ_G of a single gun of the battery. Integration is performed by partitioning the target simplified hitting space (HS) domain into a set of rectangles of equal dimensions (20 rectangles are considered). The accuracy of the results thus obtained clearly depends on the size of the rectangles whose dimensions are (see section 1):

$dx = Dx$ (longitudinal width of each rectangle)
$dy = Dy \, / \, 20$ (transversal width of each rectangle)

The compromise adopted between the maximum obtainable precision and the complexity of the calculation appears sufficiently adequate for the purpose of this investigation. The algorithm used here to integrate the battery fire dispersion on the simplified HS domain starts from the rectangle centred on the target. The hit probability value thus obtained is the elementary probability associated with the considered rectangle only, which is part of the whole simplified HS. Then, the calculation is applied in sequence to the remaining rectangles in order to extend the integration of the falling points distribution function to the overall simplified HS domain (see Fig. 4 at the end of this appendix). The result of the integration is the required SSHP. Owing to the evolution of the kinematic and geometric conditions during the battle, the above procedure has to be repeated for each one of the *Bismarck*'s salvoes.

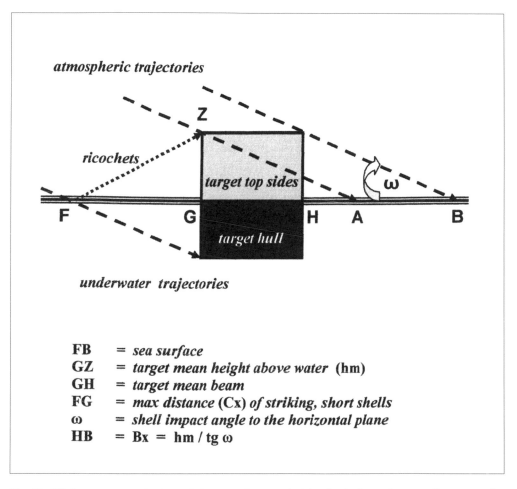

FB = *sea surface*
GZ = *target mean height above water* **(hm)**
GH = *target mean beam*
FG = *max distance* **(Cx)** *of striking, short shells*
ω = *shell impact angle to the horizontal plane*
HB = **Bx** = **hm / tg ω**

Fig 27: Hitting space, projection of the target's mean height (hm) above the waterline upon the horizontal plane determined by the shell's impact angle ω.

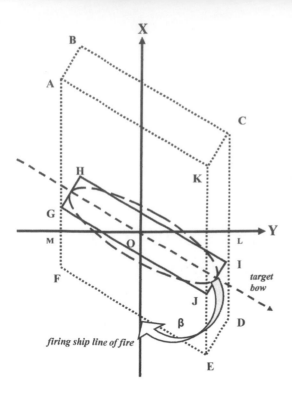

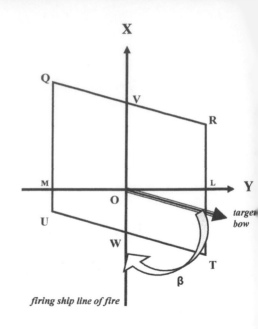

ABCDEF = *hitting space* (HS)
O = *target center*
β = *target course inclination angle (or aspect angle)*
ML = *Dy*
GH = *A*

QRTU = *parallelogram equivalent to the hitting space area*
       and with the same ML dimension
O = *target geometric center*
ML = *Dy*
UQ = *Dx*

Above left: Fig 28: Hitting space, projection of the target onto the plane of the line of fire inclined at the β angle.

Above right: Fig 29: Simplified hitting space.

Left: Fig 30: Simplified hitting space domain (only 3 out of the 20 rectangles considered are displayed here).

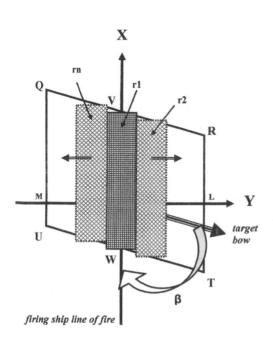

r1, r2, rn = *20 integration rectangles*
ML = *Dy*
UQ = *Dx*

Appendix C

Fire dispersion of the *Bismarck*'s 380/47 gun battery and SSHP calculation

In this appendix, reference is sometimes made to Italian technical regulations and customs, given the author's experience and career as an Italian Navy officer. However, for clarity, similarities and differences with the regulations of other navies (the Royal Navy, and the Kriegsmarine) are briefly outlined.

The Theory of Errors,[1] an important branch of statistics, will be examined in this appendix only in relation to artillery fire against targets lying in the horizontal plane. Our purpose is to measure the quantities affecting the dispersion of the impact points of the shells fired by the *Bismarck*'s battery of heavy-calibre guns. Knowing the magnitude of dispersion is essential to the calculation of the hit probability of a single shot (SSHP) fired by the German battleship's battery. This calculation also requires the knowledge of target distance, orientation and size, which have already been examined in Appendices A and B.

1. Gun fire errors

The *systematic errors* of a single gun equally affect each shot, as they depend on several unchanging causes pertaining to the weapon's functioning and sights. Vector composition of causes produces the global systematic error resulting in a translation of the impact points whose entity may or may not depend on the time of flight of a projectile.[2] Dispersion is instead due to fortuitous fluctuations, *variable errors*, affecting the velocity vector of every projectile fired by that gun, namely the vector's orientation and intensity.[3] Some of these fluctuations intervene only at firing, while others can occur at any point in the trajectory. These fluctuations are due to several factors pertaining to both ballistic features (barrel, gun mount, launch charge, projectile) and weather conditions (wind and air density). Any fluctuation involving one of the ballistic or meteorological features results in a specific accidental error, i.e. a basic alteration of the shot's trajectory. The mix of accidental errors causes a change in trajectory, which is the result of the vector composition of all the basic alterations. Systematic errors can be largely corrected by employing specific technical procedures, whereas accidental errors are unavoidable as they are mostly peculiar to a specific gun-ammunition combination. Vector addition of systematic errors to accidental errors further affects the point of fall of the projectile.

According to the Theory of Errors, the distribution of impact points follows the normal or Gaussian distribution; hence for a hypothetical infinite number of shots there are as many impact points creating a characteristic point pattern, two-dimensional and infinitely extended in every direction, representing the above distribution. This distribution presents a heavy concentration around a particular mean point – the centre of the distribution. From this centre outwards (whatever the direction) the distribution thins out progressively: in any direction the density has a Gaussian distribution.

Italian technical regulations consider the ellipse whose axes coincide with the projection on the horizontal plane of the line of fire (x axis) and with its perpendicular (y axis) meeting at the centre of the distribution of the impact points. The length of each semi axis is, by definition, four times the probable error 'εp' (or 2.7 times the standard deviation 'σ') of the distribution.[4] Hence, in each direction the diameter of the ellipse contains about 99.3% of the infinite impact points.[5] This ellipse is called the theoretical horizontal impact point pattern, as the impact points lie in the horizontal plane.[6]

2. Fire dispersion at a naval proving ground and range tables

For operational purposes the performance of each gun-ammunition combination is extensively reported in the range tables. This document is filled in on the basis of tests and trials carried out in a proving ground and gives details concerning the projectile's possible trajectories as well as the measure of dispersion as a function of the firing range. Dispersion is expressed in different forms according to the technical procedures adopted by different navies. For instance, the Italian *Regia Marina* considered the so-called *Striscie al 50%* (50% zones),[7] while the range tables for the guns mounted on the ships of the Royal Navy or the *Kriegsmarine* referred to the probable error. However, all these quantities assumed a theoretical population of an infinite number of projectiles fired.

The raw data behind the figures contained in the range tables are obtained through firing tests under accurately controlled conditions involving the following:
- The use of a single gun mounted on land firing at fixed distances. The gun's aiming equipment is accurately checked before each firing.
- For each distance 's' shots are fired. The projectile's weight and external profile are carefully controlled before firing and must comply with technical specifications. Similar preventive checks are carried out on storage temperature and on the weight of the launch charges. In addition, the latter must belong to the same production batch to keep variations in ballistic properties of the propellant to a minimum.
- Weather conditions along the trajectory are monitored and recorded during each firing. Weather parameters such as wind, temperature and humidity must not exceed pre-set limits.
- The point of fall of each projectile is measured by appropriate instruments (theodolites). When all the rounds have been fired, the raw data concerning the actual measurement of the trajectory are processed with specific reference to the standard atmospheric

conditions assumed for range table values. The data thus obtained are used to calculate all the characteristic elements of the various trajectories[8] by means of a specific set of integration algorithms and, currently, of a computer.[9] The range tables used by navies also indicate the dispersion according to the firing range.

In the British, German and Italian range tables these quantities refer to a *population* of infinite impact points, although, as previously mentioned, the tests carried out at a naval proving ground employ only a limited number of shots for each firing range; hence statistical inference is applied to achieve the desired data. In spite of controls, dispersion still occurs and is mainly due to:

- a. fluctuations in the initial velocity for the imperfectly uniform ballistic properties of the launch charges even if from the same production batch;
- b. horizontal and vertical vibrations of the gun barrel on firing;
- c. interference from gas propellants on the shell initial trajectory up to a few calibres off the muzzle.[10]

It is therefore possible to write the following theoretical equations expressing the dispersion (due to accidental errors) in range and deflection (x and y axes respectively) for a gun firing at a naval proving ground:[11]

$$\varepsilon p_{xRT} = \sqrt{(\varepsilon p^2_a + \varepsilon p^2_b + \varepsilon p^2_c)}$$

$$\varepsilon p_{yRT} = \sqrt{(\varepsilon p^2_b + \varepsilon p^2_c)}$$

For the rest of this analysis, standard deviation 'σ' rather than probable error 'εp' will be used to express the dispersion of the *Bismarck*'s gunfire, because the former can be used easily to calculate the single shot hit probability (SSHP).[12] Thus:

$$\sigma_{xRT} = \sqrt{(\sigma^2_a + \sigma^2_b + \sigma^2_c)}$$

$$\sigma_{yRT} = \sqrt{(\sigma^2_b + \sigma^2_c)}$$

3. Fire dispersion of an individual gun under standard operating conditions

Fire dispersion of a single gun as reported in the range tables is actually lower than is actually observed under operational circumstances where the laboratory-like conditions of a proving ground can hardly be reproduced. Actual operating conditions thus contribute to new accidental variations (independent of each other as well as of the causes of dispersion in the proving ground), adding further fluctuations to the velocity of each shot. Thus, if we indicate with σ_{xG} and σ_{yG} the standard deviation of the impact points on the x and y axes due to the new causes of variations, and use the following symbols to indicate the new causes of variations shot by shot:

- d. change of initial velocity for variations in the launch charges (usually not sorted by batch);
- e. change of velocity for the use of projectiles of slightly different weight;
- f. change of the ballistic coefficient for the use of projectiles of slightly different weight;
- g. error in the correction for motion of the firing ship;
- h. change of velocity along the trajectory for wind exceeding the range table standard;
- i. change of velocity for random variations of air density along the trajectory exceeding the range table standard;
- j. change of gun train and elevation for oscillation of the signal transmitted from the fire-control station;
- k. change of gun train and elevation for slackening of the transmission chains;
- l. change of gun train and elevation for mistakes made by the operators in charge of the gun laying[13]

it is possible to write for one gun:

$$\sigma_{xG} = \sqrt{(\sigma^2_d + \sigma^2_e + \sigma^2_f + \sigma^2_g + \sigma^2_h + \sigma^2_i + \sigma^2_j + \sigma^2_k + \sigma^2_l)}$$

$$\sigma_{yG} = \sqrt{(\sigma^2_g + \sigma^2_h + \sigma^2_j + \sigma^2_k + \sigma^2_l)}$$

As the new causes of variations are independent of those present at a naval proving ground, we can write for an individual gun firing under actual operating sea conditions:

$$\sigma_{x\,sea\,G} = \sqrt{(\sigma^2_{xRT} + \sigma^2_{xG})}$$

$$\sigma_{y\,sea\,G} = \sqrt{(\sigma^2_{yRT} + \sigma^2_{yG})}$$

According to Italian technical regulations, the value of dispersion at sea of an efficient gun must not exceed 1.5 times the range table value. For the sake of simplicity, the limit of 1.5 times the range table standard will be assumed for the following computations, also assuming that the *Bismarck* being brand-new (and, unlike the *Prince of Wales*, having undergone months of tests and trials at sea), the efficiency of her weapon systems was unquestionable:

$$\sigma_{x\,sea\,G} = 1.5 * \sigma_{xRT} \qquad\qquad \sigma_{y\,sea\,G} = 1.5 * \sigma_{yRT}$$

4. Fire dispersion of a battery under standard operating conditions

A battery is a set of guns of the same calibre. The battery fires a salvo when all the guns fire against the same target simultaneously. In that situation, systematic errors affecting the firing of each individual gun, with respect to the mean gun of the battery, imply that the various centres of dispersion, i.e. the centres of the guns' theoretical impact patterns, do not overlap. This in turn results in an increase of the battery beaten zone.[14] Under operating conditions, the battery beaten zone is, as already mentioned in Chapter 4, the plane figure made up by the arrangement of the theoretical impact point patterns of the salvo firing guns (Plate 7).

In particular, systematic errors include:
- m. discrepancy between the true initial velocity of each gun and the mean value applied to the fire-control system to compute the predicted gun range;
- n. error in the parallax correction for each gun made by the fire-control system;
- o. resetting error of the receivers providing the range computed by the fire-control system;
- p. error for roller-path inclination diversely affecting each gun;
- q. discrepancy between the real firing range for each gun and the range computed by the fire-control system, due to the distance between the guns and the director (on the *Bismarck* the mean distance ΔL between the fore top director and the fore and aft turrets was 62.5 m, thus: q = ΔL * cos train);
- r. error due to different height above water of the turrets (on the *Bismarck* the difference Δh between low and high turrets was 4 m, thus: r = Δh / tan impact angle ω);
- s. error for transient (dynamic) distortion of ship structure (due to sea waves) diversely affecting each gun;
- t. error due to the effects on the shot trajectory because of interference from muzzle blasts produced by the simultaneous firing of the guns in the same turret.[15]

In an n-gun battery for each systematic error type there usually exists:
- a mean value of the error producing the shift of the battery beaten zone centre; this effect is usually eliminated (or reduced to a minimum) by the corrections applied by the first gunnery officer before issuing the order of 'rapid fire';
- n-quantities (generally differing from each other) equal to the difference between the quantity of the systematic error of each gun and the previous average value. These quantities are responsible for the non-overlapping of the theoretical mean points of impact referring to the firing of each gun, thus increasing dispersion. Each quantity usually has a component on the x and y axes, and it is possible to estimate the standard deviation for every one of them:

$$\sigma_{x\,syst} = \sqrt{(\sigma^2_{x\,syst\,'m'} + \dots + \sigma^2_{x\,syst\,'t'})}$$
$$\sigma_{y\,syst} = \sqrt{(\sigma^2_{y\,syst\,'n'} + \dots + \sigma^2_{y\,syst\,'t'})}$$

In order to quantify the total dispersion of the battery caused by the two components, systematic and accidental errors, it is possible to combine them in the following mathematical equations that, even if not rigorous, provide a reasonable estimate of this quantity:[16]

$$\sigma_{x\,sea\,battery} = \sqrt{(\sigma^2_{x\,sea\,G} + \sigma^2_{x\,syst})}$$

$$\sigma_{y\,sea\,battery} = \sqrt{(\sigma^2_{y\,sea\,G} + \sigma^2_{y\,syst})}$$

5. Estimated dispersion of the *Bismarck*'s 380/47 battery

On the basis of the aforesaid, we can now estimate the standard deviation with reference to the theoretical distribution of the impact points of the projectiles fired by the *Bismarck*'s battery.[17] To this purpose, for each range value derived from the kinematics of the engagement against the British units the estimation involves the following steps:

(A)   referring to the range tables for the Krupp 380 L/47 SK C/34 gun, consider the probable errors, εp_{xRT} and $\varepsilon p_{yRT,}$ (section 2);

(B)   convert the probable errors to the corresponding standard deviation values σ_{xRT} and σ_{yRT};

(C)   increase the above standard deviation values by 50% to allow for actual single gun operating conditions (section 3);

(D)   attribute a realistic standard deviation value to each systematic error (section 4);

(E)   deduce the change of range and deflection for variations in the ballistic quantities affected by the systematic errors ($\sigma_{x\,syst}$ and $\sigma_{y\,syst}$);[18]

(F)   apply the relations as in section 4 and calculate the standard deviation values, $\sigma_{x\,sea\,battery}$ and $\sigma_{y\,sea\,battery}$, defining the total dispersion of the *Bismarck*'s battery.

Because of the uncertainty inherent in the arbitrary attribution of a value to systematic errors (step D), the results thus obtained cannot be considered totally reliable. It follows that a suitable range of variation needs to be computed, i.e. one in which the actual battery standard deviation values are definitely contained. As the values initially attributed to systematic errors were deliberately low,[19] our results are at the lowest limit of the range for possible variation, and at the upper limit the values obtained by multiplying the difference between the estimated dispersion and the range table dispersion (i.e. between the estimated standard deviation and the range table standard deviation) by a 'kkk' factor increasing from 1 to 1.5:

$$1 \leq kkk \leq 1.5$$

hence:

$$incremented\,\sigma_{x\,sea\,battery} = \sigma_{xRT} + kkk * (estimated\,\sigma_{x\,sea\,battery} - \sigma_{xRT})$$

$$incremented\,\sigma_{y\,sea\,battery} = \sigma_{yRT} + kkk * (estimated\,\sigma_{y\,sea\,battery} - \sigma_{yRT})$$

The single shot hit probability (SSHP) for each salvo fired by the *Bismarck*'s battery is then determined by calculating the integral of the function expressing the battleship's firing dispersion extended to the target's hitting space.

6. Estimated standard deviation of the *Bismarck*'s 380/47 single gun firing dispersion under standard operating conditions at sea

The following table illustrates steps A, B and C of the previous section to determine the standard deviation values:

Table 25

Engagement with HMS *Hood*							
Time	Salvo (n)	Probable error (m) (range tables)		Standard deviation (m) (range tables)		Estimated standard deviation (m) (one gun at sea)	
		range	deflection	range	deflection	range	deflection
		εp_{xRT}	εp_{yRT}	σ_{xRT}	σ_{yRT}	$\sigma_{x\,sea\,G}$	$\sigma_{y\,sea\,G}$
0557	2 L	101.9	4.4	151.1	6.5	226.7	9.8
	2 C	101.4	4.3	150.3	6.4	225.5	9.6
	2 S	101	4.2	149.7	6.2	224.6	9.3
0558	3	100.4	4	148.9	5.9	223.4	8.9
0559	4	99.8	3.8	148	5.6	222	8.4
0600	5	99.1	3.6	146.9	5.3	220.4	8

Table 26

Engagement with HMS *Prince of Wales*							
Time	Salvo (n)	Probable error (m) (range tables)		Standard deviation (m) (range tables)		Estimated standard deviation(m) (one gun at sea)	
		range	deflection	range	deflection	range	deflection
		εp_{xRT}	εp_{yRT}	σ_{xRT}	σ_{yRT}	$\sigma_{x\,sea\,G}$	$\sigma_{y\,sea\,G}$
0601?	6	98.7	3.3	146.3	4.9	219.5	7.4
0602	7	98.2	3.1	145.6	4.6	218.4	6.9
0603	8	98.6	3.3	146.2	4.9	219.3	7.4
0604	9	99.4	3.7	147.4	5.5	221.1	8.3
0605	10	100.4	4	148.9	5.9	223.4	8.9
0606	11	102.3	4.5	151.7	6.7	227.6	10.1

The salvoes fired by the *Bismarck* at 0607, 0608 and 0609 were not considered, as they were partial salvoes with only 5 shells fired altogether.

7. Estimated systematic errors and calculation of the battery firing dispersion

According to steps D and E, to determine the standard deviation of the *Bismarck*'s battery we first have to estimate the quantities from 'm' to 't' listed in section 4, representing a realistic error basket. The values indicated in Table 27 appear realistic to quantify (to 1σ) the systematic errors of a battery composed of 8 heavy-calibre guns mounted in 4 turrets. The same values were considered for the *Bismarck*'s engagements with both the *Hood* and the *Prince of Wales*.[20] Tables 28 to 31 indicate the values calculated for the above systematic errors ($\sigma_{x\,syst}$ and $\sigma_{y\,syst}$):

Table 27

Estimated values attributed to quantities 'm'–'t' (at 1σ) affecting range							
m	n	o	p	q	r	s	t
(m/sec)	(1°/60)	(1°/60)	(1°/60)	(m)	(m)	(1°/60)	(m/sec)
3.5	0	3.5	3.5	ΔL * cos train	Δh / tan ω	3.5	3.5

Estimated values attributed to quantities 'm'–'t' (at 1σ) affecting deflection							
m	n	o	p	q	r	s	t
(m/sec)	(1°/60)	(1°/60)	(1°/60)	(m)	(m)	(1°/60)	(m/sec)
0	3.5	3.5	3.5	0	0	3.5	1.75

Table 28

Engagement with HMS *Hood*						
Time	0557	0557	0557	0558	0559	0600
Salvo	2 L	2 C	2 S	3	4	5
Future range	18,000	17,600	17,200	16,700	16,000	15,200
Train	294.1	294.1	294.1	293.9	293.6	293.2
Shell's impact angle ω	13.8	13.3	12.9	12.3	11.5	10.6
Variation in range due to variation of +10 m/sec in muzzle velocity*	364.4	357.4	350.3	341.5	329	314.6
Variation in range due to variation of 1°/60 in gun elevation**	20.4	20.8	21.2	21.7	22.4	23.2
Variation in range due to variation of 1% in air density*	40.8	39.1	37.3	35.2	32.4	29.3
Variation in range at 1σ due to 'm'	127.5	125.1	122.6	119.5	115.2	110.1
Variation in range at 1σ due to 'o'	71.4	72.8	74.2	76	78.4	81.2

Variation in range at 1σ due to 'p'	71.4	72.8	74.2	76	78.4	81.2
Variation in range at 1σ due to 'q'	25.5	25.5	25.5	25.3	25	24.6
Variation in range at 1σ due to 'r'	8.1	8.5	8.7	9.2	9.8	10.7
Variation in range at 1σ due to 's'	71.4	72.8	74.2	76	78.4	81.2
Variation in range at 1σ due to 't'	127.5	125.1	122.6	119.5	115.2	110.1
σx syst	220.3	218.9	217.5	215.9	213.8	211.5
σx 1 gun at sea	226.7	225.5	224.6	223.4	222	220.4
σx battery at sea	316.1	314.3	312.7	310.7	308.2	305.5

Table 29

Engagement with HMS *Hood*						
Time	0557	0557	0557	0558	0559	0600
Salvo	2 L	2 C	2 S	3	4	5
Future range	18,000	17,600	17,200	16,700	16,000	15,200
Train	294.1	294.1	294.1	293.9	293.6	293.2
Variation in deflection at 1σ due to 'n'	18.3	17.9	17.5	17	16.3	15.5
Variation in deflection at 1σ due to 'o'	18.3	17.9	17.5	17	16.3	15.5
Variation in deflection at 1σ due to 'p'	18.3	17.9	17.5	17	16.3	15.5
Variation in deflection at 1σ due to 's'	18.3	17.9	17.5	17	16.3	15.5
Variation in deflection at 1σ due to 't'	63.8	62.6	61.3	59.8	57.6	55.1
σy syst	73.6	72.1	70.6	68.8	66.2	63.2
σy 1 gun at sea	9.8	9.6	9.3	8.9	8.4	8
σy battery at sea	74.2	72.7	71.2	69.4	66.7	63.7

Table 30

Engagement with HMS *Prince of Wales*						
Time	0601?	0602	0603	0604	0605	0606
Salvo	6	7	8	9	10	11
Future range	14,500	13,700	14,400	15,600	16,700	18,300
Train	290.9	312.9	308.5	250.9	240.1	234.6
Shell's impact angle ω	9.9	9.1	9.8	11	12.3	14.2
Variation in range due to variation of +10 m/sec in muzzle velocity*	301.9	287.2	300.1	321.8	341.5	369.7

Variation in range due to variation of 1°/60 in gun elevation**	23.9	24.8	24	22.8	21.7	20.1
Variation in range due to variation of 1% in air density*	26.6	23.7	26.2	30.8	35.2	42.1
Variation in range at 1σ due to 'm'	105.7	100.5	105	112.6	119.5	129.4
Variation in range at 1σ due to 'o'	83.7	86.8	84	79.8	76	70.4
Variation in range at 1σ due to 'p'	83.7	86.8	84	79.8	76	70.4
Variation in range at 1σ due to 'q'	22.3	42.5	38.9	20.5	31.2	36.2
Variation in range at 1σ due to 'r'	11.5	12.5	11.6	10.3	9.2	7.9
Variation in range at 1σ due to 's'	83.7	86.8	84	79.8	76	70.4
Variation in range at 1σ due to 't'	105.7	100.5	105	112.6	119.5	129.4
σx syst	209.7	211.6	211.8	212.1	216.7	223
σx 1 gun at sea	219.5	218.4	219.3	221.1	223.4	227.6
σx battery at sea	303.6	304.1	304.9	306.4	311.2	318.6

* from the range tables of the Ansaldo 381/50 naval gun
** from the range tables of the Krupp 380/47 naval gun

Table 31

Engagement with HMS *Prince of Wales*						
Time	0601?	0602	0603	0604	0605	0606
Salvo	6	7	8	9	10	11
Future range	14,500	13,700	14,400	15,600	16,700	18,300
Train	290.9	312.9	308.5	250.9	240.1	234.6
Variation in deflection at 1σ due to 'n'	14.8	13.9	14.7	15.9	17	18.6
Variation in deflection at 1σ due to 'o'	14.8	13.9	14.7	15.9	17	18.6
Variation in deflection at 1σ due to 'p'	14.8	13.9	14.7	15.9	17	18.6
Variation in deflection at 1σ due to 's'	14.8	13.9	14.7	15.9	17	18.6
Variation in deflection at 1σ due to 't'	52.9	50.3	52.5	56.3	59.8	64.7
σy syst	60.6	57.5	60.2	64.7	68.8	74.6
σy 1 gun at sea	7.4	6.9	7.4	8.3	8.9	10.1
σy battery at sea	61.1	57.9	60.7	65.2	69.4	75.3

8. SSHP of each of the *Bismarck*'s 380/47 salvoes

The following tables present the results of the battery fire dispersion integration on the target hitting space, carried out to calculate the SSHP for each salvo fired by the *Bismarck* during the battle. As mentioned in section 5, the uncertainty surrounding the estimate of the 380/47 battery dispersion makes it necessary to consider a range of variations large enough to definitely contain the actual value of standard deviation referring to the distribution of the impact points throughout the engagement. This margin is determined by a varying kkk factor multiplying each estimated standard deviation, thus increasing the value of the latter compared to the initial estimate. For each salvo we will then have as many SSHPs as the kkk coefficients. However, the criterion discussed in Appendix D limits – on the basis of realistic constraints – kkk range of variation and consequently reduces the uncertainty surrounding the *Bismarck*'s battery dispersion and the SSHPs.

The SSHP values will be used to perform the chi-square statistical analysis described in Appendix D. As mentioned before, the last partial salvoes fired by the German battleship, namely the 12th at 0607, the 13th at 0608 and the 14th at 0609 (only 5 shots altogether), were not considered in the calculations. In this last phase of the engagement, the *Bismarck*'s firing at *Prince of Wales* was hindered by the smoke screen laid down by the British battleship, and hence probably no longer on target. Besides, the 0601 salvo might still have been aimed at the sinking *Hood*. In fact, the *Bismarck*'s fifth salvo was fired against the *Hood* at about 0600. The explosion probably took place around 0601, at about the time of the *Bismarck*'s sixth salvo; hence there was probably no time for the astonished artillery crew to shift target and fire on the *Prince of Wales* straight away. However, even had the crew reacted promptly, the *Prince of Wales*' manoeuvres to avoid the sinking wreck of the *Hood* were such that at 0601 she was heading towards the *Bismarck* with a very tight aspect angle. In this situation the German SSHP was very low, with little chance of hitting the target.

At any rate, the first 380/47 shell to hit the *Prince of Wales* struck shortly after 0602.

Table 32

Engagement with HMS *Hood*								
Time (hhmm)	Future range (m)	Salvo	kkk factor	σx sea battery (m)	σy sea battery (m)	Target 'hitting space' dimensions		SSHP (%)
						ML (m)	UQ (m)	
0557	18,000	2 s-sL	1	316.1	74.2	225	91.6	4.6
		2 shells	1.1	332.6	81	225	91.6	4.52
			1.2	349.1	87.7	225	91.6	4.4
			1.3	365.6	94.5	225	91.6	4.25
			1.4	382.1	101.3	225	91.6	4.09
			1.5	398.6	108.1	225	91.6	3.92
	17,600	2 s oC	1	314.3	72.7	225	93.1	10.25

		4 shells	1.1	330.7	79.3	225	93.1	9.37
			1.2	347.1	86	225	93.1	8.57
			1.3	363.5	92.6	225	93.1	7.85
			1.4	379.9	99.2	225	93.1	7.2
			1.5	396.3	105.9	225	93.1	6.61
	17,200	2 s-sS	1	312.7	71.2	225	94.5	4.67
		2 shells	1.1	329	77.7	225	94.5	4.62
			1.2	345.3	84.2	225	94.5	4.52
			1.3	361.6	90.7	225	94.5	4.39
			1.4	377.9	97.2	225	94.5	4.24
			1.5	394.2	103.7	225	94.5	4.08
0558	16,700	3	1	310.7	69.4	224.5	96.5	10.95
		8 shells	1.1	326.9	75.8	224.5	96.5	10.03
			1.2	343.1	82.1	224.5	96.5	9.2
			1.3	359.2	88.5	224.5	96.5	8.44
			1.4	375.4	94.8	224.5	96.5	7.76
			1.5	391.6	101.2	224.5	96.5	7.15
0559	16,000	4	1	308.2	66.7	223.8	99.6	11.54
		8 shells	1.1	324.2	72.8	223.8	99.6	10.61
			1.2	340.2	78.9	223.8	99.6	9.75
			1.3	356.3	85	223.8	99.6	8.96
			1.4	372.3	91.1	223.8	99.6	8.25
			1.5	388.3	97.3	223.8	99.6	7.6
0600	15,200	5	1	305.5	63.7	243.7	102.4	12.52
		8 shells	1.1	321.4	69.5	243.7	102.4	11.6
			1.2	337.2	75.4	243.7	102.4	10.75
			1.3	353.1	81.2	243.7	102.4	9.96
			1.4	368.9	87.1	243.7	102.4	9.22.
			1.5	384.8	92.9	243.7	102.4	8.55

Table 33

Engagement with HMS *Prince of Wales*								
Time (hhmm)	Future range (m)	Salvo	kkk factor	σx sea battery (m)	σy sea battery (m)	Target 'hitting space' dimensions		SSHP (%)
						ML (m)	UQ (m)	
0601?	14,500	6	1	303.6	61.1	27.4	257.2	5.74
		8 shells	1.1	320	66.7	27.4	257.2	5.03
			1.2	335.1	72.3	27.4	257.2	4.44
			1.3	350.8	78	27.4	257.2	3.95
			1.4	366.5	83.6	27.4	257.2	3.54
			1.5	382.3	89.2	27.4	257.2	3.19

0602	13,700	7	1	304.1	57.9	219.3	119.6	14.62
		8 shells	1.1	320.3	63.2	219.3	119.6	13.54
			1.2	335.8	68.6	219.3	119.6	12.53
			1.3	351.7	73.9	219.3	119.6	11.6
			1.4	367.5	79.2	219.3	119.6	10.74
			1.5	383.4	84.6	219.3	119.6	9.95
0603	14,400	8	1	304.9	60.7	29.7	242	5.88
		8 shells	1.1	320.8	66.3	29.7	242	5.14
			1.2	336.6	71.9	29.7	242	4.54
			1.3	352.5	77.4	29.7	242	4.04
			1.4	368.4	83	29.7	242	3.62
			1.5	384.3	88.6	29.7	242	3.26
0604	15,600	9	1	306.4	65.2	175.1	105.5	11.09
		8 shells	1.1	322.3	71.2	175.1	105.5	10.04
			1.2	338.2	77.1	175.1	105.5	9.12
			1.3	354.1	83.1	175.1	105.5	8.3
			1.4	370	89.1	175.1	105.5	7.57
			1.5	385.9	95.1	175.1	105.5	6.93
0605	16,700	10	1	311.2	69.4	177.1	99.4	10.01
		8 shells	1.1	327.4	75.8	177.1	99.4	9.04
			1.2	343.7	82.1	177.1	99.4	8.18
			1.3	359.9	88.5	177.1	99.4	7.43
			1.4	376.1	94.8	177.1	99.4	6.77
			1.5	392.4	101.2	177.1	99.4	6.18
0606	18,300	11	1	318.6	75.3	41.9	170	4.53
		8 shells	1.1	335.3	82.2	41.9	170	3.96
			1.2	352	89	41.9	170	3.5
			1.3	368.7	95.9	41.9	170	3.11
			1.4	385.4	102.7	41.9	170	2.79
			1.5	402.1	109.6	41.9	170	2.51

Technical sources

Access to the data reported in the range tables for the Krupp SK C/34 38 cm L/47 gun was absolutely essential to this analysis. The *Historisches Archiv Krupp*[21] kindly provided the longitudinal and lateral probable error for the *Panzersprenggranate* L/4.4. The longitudinal dispersion value for the same shell was also indicated in graphical form by:

- Whitley, together with the main ballistic functions of the gun and the penetration capacity of the shell. In particular, this text contains an English translation of the Krupp graph 5AkB 1861a;[22]
- Skwiot, together with the main ballistic functions of the gun and the original Krupp graph 5AkB 1861a.[23]

Ballistic functions such as elevation, impact angle, time of flight and impact velocity are also reported by Campbell in numerical form for a few selected ranges.[24]

Appendix D

Statistical analysis of the *Bismarck*'s firing accuracy

1. The statistical analysis

Obtaining a representative sample is crucial in any statistical analysis. For values of *n* (sample size) equal to or greater than 30 (large samples) the distribution approximates to the normal. The approximation to the normal distribution improves as *n* increases. Hence for smaller samples (*n* < 30) the sampling distribution is not normal, with increasingly negative variations as *n* decreases. The statistical analysis of small samples must therefore resort to the Small Sample Theory of William Sealy Gosset (1908), an approach that also provides reliable results for values of *n* >30.

Considering that there were just over 30 effective shots fired on the *Hood* before she blew up (32 including 8 of the 2nd adjustment salvo described as 'straddling' by the *Bismarck*'s first gunnery officer) and that not many more were fired on the *Prince of Wales*, the above theory can be applied to the analysis of the samples made up of the 380/47 shells fired by the German battleship.

For the purpose of this analysis the chi-square (χ^2) test has been performed. This test is a hypothesis test proposed by the academic Karl Pearson[1] and later refined by R. A. Fisher.[2] This procedure is recognised as particularly appropriate when comparing the theoretical (expected) probability of an event (Fe) with its real (observed) frequency of occurrence (Fo), in order to test if the null hypothesis (H_0) is true; namely to ascertain whether the sample (by which Fo is determined) is representative of the population (to which Fe refers). When a divergence is observed of the real from the expected outcome, this method allows us to understand if the divergence is due to accidental errors or to systematic errors. Basically, Pearson proposed a requirement for rejecting (with a certain degree of confidence) the assumed hypothesis, i.e. the null hypothesis, if the level of confidence provided by the test results is equal or superior to the associated threshold value. This usually happens when the observed statistic markedly differs from theoretical expectations based on the null hypothesis, which leads to the conclusion that such a discrepancy cannot reasonably be related to random fluctuations. The threshold (called *level of significance* and expressed by the correlation coefficient *r*) sets the risk level;

namely the risk of wrongly rejecting the null hypothesis. Usually 'practical certainty' is achieved when *r* is between 95% and 99% (excessively strong and consequently dubious with higher percentages correlation). However, it is altogether possible to consider other levels of significance associated with lower confidence and higher risk margins. Whenever that is the case, practical certainty cannot be achieved, but the null hypothesis can be considered *less likely* or *more likely*. In short, the χ^2 basic computational equation is:

$$\chi^2 = \sum_{i=1}^{k} \frac{(Fo_i - Fe_i)^2}{Fe_i} \qquad (1)$$

where:
- k is the number of classes into which the possible events 'i' are divided;
- Fo_i is the number of observations for each class;
- Fe_i is the expected theoretical frequency for each class (asserted by the null hypothesis) which equals the total sample size multiplied by the expected probability of each class of events.

Consultation of the chi-square distribution for one or more degrees of freedom (df) of the investigated hypothesis then shows the probability of observing the null hypothesis. The degrees of freedom (an integer greater than zero) is essentially equal to:

$$df = k - 1 - p \qquad (2)$$

where 'p' is the reduction in degrees of freedom necessary to estimate some population parameters in order to calculate the theoretical (expected) frequencies. The null hypothesis can be rejected when the chi-square statistic is larger than the threshold value associated with the accepted level of confidence and the number of df.

2. Applying Pearson's chi-square test to the outcome of the *Bismarck*'s gunfire

In this study the chi-square test is employed for an outcome analysis of the *Bismarck*'s gunfire; hence the following has to be considered:

Theoretical probability (P_T) to hit (object of the analysis)

Expected frequency of hits per sample of size *n*: $Fe = n * P_T$

Number of hits observed = Hit frequency of occurrence: $Fo = M$

(3)

Other prerequisites include:
    a.   obtaining a sample as large as possible ($n > 30$);
    b.   an expected frequency per single event equal to at least 5; lower values negatively affect the test reliability.

The test will therefore investigate the following null hypothesis:

$H_0 =$ the *Bismarck's* gunfire was perfectly on target for both ships engaged during the battle, the *Hood* and the *Prince of Wales* (no systematic firing error throughout the engagement).

This hypothesis implies that the hit probability of a single 380/47 shot (SSHP) is to be based on the assumption that throughout the battle the centre of the infinite shots falling point pattern coincided with the target's centre – an event apparently taken for granted by most historical reconstructions. This is therefore the assumption behind the computation of the SSHP values associated with each of the *Bismarck's* salvoes.

It is worth noting that the hits observed are necessarily a sample drawn from a population of *infinite* shots theoretically fireable by the *Bismarck's* heavy-calibre battery. Therefore the distribution of the (observed) sample will certainly have the same standard deviation as the (expected) population. When the two distributions diverge, this can only be attributable to a systematic error, which in turn can only take place if the centre of the sampling distribution does not share the same centre as the target's (as assumed by the null hypothesis). In order to meet the test requirement for the adequate sample size (in our analysis n is made up of the shots fired for effect) the calculation included all the effective salvoes fired by the *Bismarck* in each one of the two engagements against the *Hood* and the *Prince of Wales* respectively. Otherwise, the number of shots fired for each salvo ($n = 8$) would have been largely insufficient.[3] This approach is allowed by the additive property of the chi-square test in so far as the following is considered:
  • the sum ($\Sigma\chi^2$) of the partial χ^2 results obtained after calculating the above equation (1) for each salvo;
  • the sum (Σdf) of the degrees of freedom attributed to each salvo;
  • the level of probability of correctly rejecting the null hypothesis on the basis of $\Sigma\chi^2$ and Σdf.

Furthermore:
  • whenever the test additive property is used, Yates' continuity correction factor must not be applied, as results would become overcorrected;[4]
  • whenever artillery weapons are employed, there are two possible outcomes: *hit* or *missed*. If the salvo includes a number of shots greater than one then the outcome is defined as: *target hit by exactly 'i' shots out of 'n'* (where $0 \leq i \leq n$). Hence, in the event considered, the number of classes 'k' is 9 for each salvo;
  • the value given to 'p' in equation (2) above must be calculated taking into account the following elements:
      ❋   two population parameters need estimating to calculate the SSHP and then the P_T, i.e. the two standard deviations, σx longitudinal and σy lateral to the line of

fire, determining the Gaussian distribution of the 380/47 shots' falling points;

❋ as the expected frequencies of the two possible outcomes (*target hit* or *target missed*) must be equal or above the threshold level of 5, two close salvoes are considered together in order to increase the number of shells from 8 to 16 (this approach is allowed by the additive property of the chi-square test). This implies the need to adopt the mean P_T value of the two salvoes – a mathematical calculation that makes sense because the firing battery was the same and the salvoes in question were fired at short time intervals on the same target.

The reduction in degrees of freedom 'p' can now be performed, estimating two population parameters for each salvo (the two standard deviations) and one population parameter for each couple of close salvoes (the mean P_T value).

Hence, for each couple of close salvoes of 8 shells fired by the *Bismarck* we have:

$$df = k - 1 - p = (9 - 1 - 2) + (9 - 1 - 2) - 1 = 11$$

On the aforesaid basis, we can assert that the computations performed meet all the chi-square test reliability requirements.

3. Statistical analysis of the *Bismarck*'s gunfire: results and discussion

The following tables sum up the results of the statistical analysis considering a variation of the 'kkk' factor of:

$$1 \leq kkk \leq 1.5$$

Table 34

Bismarck v. Hood						
Alternative	Confidence of H_0 (null hypothesis) correct rejection					
	kkk=1	kkk=1.1	kkk=1.2	kkk=1.3	kkk=1.4	kkk=1.5
1 = 1 hit out of 32 shells fired	0.993	0.973	0.924	0.835	0.709	0.562
2 = 2 hits out of 32 shells fired	0.975	0.924	0.828	0.687	0.524	0.367

Table 35

Bismarck v. Prince of Wales							
Hyp.	Altern.	Confidence of H_0 (null hypothesis) correct rejection					
		kkk=1	kkk=1.1	kkk=1.2	kkk=1.3	kkk=1.4	kkk=1.5
A*	1 = 3 hits	0.835	0.618	0.378	0.192	0.083	0.031
A*	2 = 4 hits	0.635	0.37	0.172	0.066	0.021	0.006
B**	1 = 3 hits	0.691	0.424	0.209	0.086	0.03	0.009
B**	2 = 4 hits	0.525	0.261	0.102	0.032	0.009	0.002

* *hypothesis A = 40 shells fired*
** *hypothesis B = 48 shells fired*

The graph of Plate 8 represents the trend of confidence for both engagements, namely the probability of correctly rejecting the null hypothesis, as a function of a kkk variation. A comparison of the data implies that the same kkk value is applied to calculate dispersion in both encounters.

It is then possible to observe that:

- the usual level of confidence for rejecting or accepting with certainty the null hypothesis is respectively from 99% to 95% and from 1% to 5%. In our scenario, the distribution is discrete; hence it appears reasonable to assume 95% and 5% as upper and lower limits. In this way, situations of too strong or too weak correlation are excluded as unlikely (values higher than 95% in favour of rejection or lower than 5% in favour of acceptance). Thus, the (mean) confidence levels for kkk values lower or equal to 1.1 (for the engagement with the *Hood*) and greater or equal to ≈ 1.36 (for the encounter with the *Prince of Wales*) cannot be considered valid. The true standard deviation (σx and σy) of the distribution of the shots fired by the *Bismarck*'s battery was then probably between the following values (the lower and upper limits of the intervals are excluded):

Table 36

Bismarck v. Hood					
Time	Salvo	Battery standard deviation in range (σx sea battery) (m)		Battery standard deviation in deflection (σy sea battery) (m)	
		limit		limit	
		lower kkk = 1.1	upper kkk = 1.36	lower kkk = 1.1	upper kkk = 1.36
0557	2	330.8	373.4	79.3	96.6
0558	3	326.9	368.9	75.8	92.3
0559	4	324.2	365.9	72.8	88.7
0600	5	321.4	362.6	69.5	84.7

Table 37

Bismarck v. Prince of Wales					
Time	Salvo	Battery standard deviation in range (σx sea battery) (m)		Battery standard deviation in deflection (σy sea battery) (m)	
		limit		limit	
		lower kkk = 1.1	upper kkk = 1.36	lower kkk = 1.1	upper kkk = 1.36
0601?	6	319.3	360.2	66.7	81.3
0602	7	320	361.2	63.2	77.1
0603	8	320.8	362	66.3	80.8
0604	9	322.3	363.6	71.2	86.7
0605	10	327.4	369.6	75.8	92.3
0606	11	335.3	378.7	82.2	100

- on the basis of the aforesaid reasons it seems fair to assume that the acceptable kkk coefficient of variation lies around 1.22. In this case, the mean confidence of correctly rejecting the null hypothesis for the engagement with the *Hood* is about 85% – i.e. there is about an 85% probability that the *Bismarck's* firing at the *Hood* was affected by a substantial systematic error. This result refers to the salvoes fired at the *Hood* as a whole. Obviously, this does not exclude the possibility that the last effective salvo fired (the fifth at 0600) – and only that one – might have been unaffected by significant systematic errors, having benefited from the continuous corrections applied by the first gunnery officer;
- considering the SSHP data (see Appendix C), a higher number of hits could have been reasonably expected (at least two out of four 8-shot salvoes) in the event of perfectly centred firing at the *Hood*. However, even the possible simultaneous occurrence of two hits scored with the fifth salvo would not have altered the conclusion that a quite likely systematic error, at least, affected the first three effective salvoes fired, while the probability of three or more hits in the same salvo is rather low;
- by contrast, around the same kkk value, the null hypothesis concerning the encounter with the *Prince of Wales* is accepted – i.e. it is possible to maintain that during the second engagement the *Bismarck's* firing was not affected by a significant systematic error. In fact, with kkk = 1.22 the overall confidence level of correctly rejecting the null hypothesis for the engagement with the *Prince of Wales* is around 17% only. The failure to reach the optimal threshold of 5% may be due to a residual systematic error, as eliminating systematic errors, if theoretically possible, remains wishful thinking in the real world. In fact, they are 'physiologic' if for no other reason than the limit of accuracy of optical rangefinders (even if stereoscopic like the *Bismarck's*) and optical sights of the time. It is worth mentioning that, when properly functioning, they still produced an error in range of about 1% (equal to 152 m for 15,200 m range). Besides, manual aiming at a target steaming several miles away realistically

involved an error of at least 2 mils (equal to 30.4 m for 15,200 m range), as it was very difficult to precisely aim at the geometrical centre of the target;

- if two hits within the fifth salvo appear likely, then the same can be said for the seventh salvo. Actually, for all kkk values the SSHPs to score exactly two hits are always higher in the seventh salvo than in the fifth.

Table 38

Time hhmm	Salvo (n)	kkk	SSHP (%)	Probability of scoring	
				exactly 1 hit out of 8 fired shells (%)	exactly 2 hits out of 8 fired shells (%)
0600	5	1	12.52	39.3	19.7
		1.1	11.6	39.1	18.0
		1.2	10.75	38.8	16.4
		1.3	9.96	38.2	14.8
		1.4	9.22	37.5	13.3
		1.5	8.55	36.6	12.0
0602	7	1	14.62	38.7	23.2
		1.1	13.54	39.1	21.4
		1.2	12.53	39.3	19.7
		1.3	11.6	39.1	18
		1.4	10.74	38.8	16.3
		1.5	9.95	38.2	14.8

In addition, there is no strong evidence against a possible double hit by the *Bismarck* within the seventh salvo fired at the *Prince of Wales*. Hence, it appears reasonable to consider the confidence level of the null hypothesis correct rejection in a coordinate way, namely comparing – for the two engagements – the results for the same alternative.

Table 39A

Alternative 1	kkk = 1.18
Bismarck v. Hood	H_0 correct rejection 85.1%
Bismarck v. Prince of Wales	H_0 correct rejection 16.5%

Table 39B

Alternative 2	kkk = 1.28
Bismarck v. Hood	H_0 correct rejection 85.6%
Bismarck v. Prince of Wales	H_0 correct rejection 16.4%

For the engagement between the *Bismarck* and the *Hood* the confidence level for the H_0 correct rejection is approximately equal to 85%, which supports the idea of substantial systematic error/s affecting the *Bismarck*'s firing against the *Hood*, whereas for the engagement with the *Prince of Wales* the level of confidence is about 17% thus supporting the hypothesis of a perfectly centred firing.

4. The 'Monte Carlo' method

To better investigate the results obtained with the chi-square test a 'Monte Carlo' simulation was also performed, on the basis of the SSHPs of the *Bismarck*'s salvoes. The simulation included 10,000 computer evaluations of the model. The results are indicated in the following table:

Table 40

kkk	Mean expected hits on *Hood*			Mean expected hits on *Prince of Wales*
	2nd 3rd 4th salvo	5th salvo	total	total
1	2.3	1	3.3	4
1.1	2.2	0.9	3.1	3.6
1.2	2	0.8	2.8	3.3
1.3	1.9	0.8	2.7	3
1.4	1.7	0.7	2.4	2.8
1.5	1.6	0.7	2.3	2.5

The intrinsic 'noise' involved in this approach suggests that a ± 0.1 range of variation for the above results has to be considered (decimals are statistically significant in spite of the discrete nature of shell hits). The Monte Carlo results obtained with kkk = 1.22 (the most probable kkk value according to the chi-square test) indicate that the *Bismarck* would have scored two hits on the *Hood* between 0557 and 0559, and one hit at 0600, had her firing been perfectly on target. As no definite hits were actually scored by the *Bismarck* within that time frame, the hypothesis that her second, third and fourth salvoes were not perfectly on target is validated.

By contrast, the results concerning the hits on the *Prince of Wales* support both the hypothesis of a well-centred firing by the *Bismarck* and, specifically, alternative 1 (three hits).

Appendix E

Specifications of Krupp large-calibre guns on board the German units participating in the battle

Table 41

Bismarck's 380/47 gun data		Notes
Calibre	380 mm (a)	14.96 inch
Weight including breech	110.7 tons	
Breech block weight	2.8 tons	horizontal sliding block breech
Weapon length overall	19,630 mm (b)	(b) = (c) + (f)
Bore length	18,405 mm (c)	length = (e) + (g) + (h)
Exact bore length in calibres	48.43 (d)	(d) = (c) / (a)
Official bore length in calibres	47	
Rifling length	15,982 mm (e)	42.06 calibres
Block length	1,225 mm (f)	
Chamber length	2,230 mm (g)	
Chamber and rifled bore connecting section length	193 mm (h)	
Chamber diameter	445.7 mm	
Chamber volume	319 litres	
Grooves	90	right-handed
Depth of grooves	4.5 mm	
Width of grooves	7.76 mm	other sources 7.5 mm
Width of lands	5.5 mm	other sources 5.7 mm
Twist	from 1 in 36 cal. to 1 in 30 cal.	increasing
Inclination of grooves	from 5° 0' 19" to 5° 58' 42"	increasing
Shell weight	800 kg	
Propelling charge total weight	212 kg	
Working pressure	3,200 kg/cm²	
Bore time	35.7 ms	

Recoil	1,050 mm	normal
Muzzle velocity (new bore)	820 m/sec	
Max. range (naval installation)	35,550 m	max. elevation 30° shell Psgr L/4.4
Supply of shells per gun	105 (125 max.)	
Standard bore life	250 ESR	Equivalent Service Rounds (at full charge)

Table 42

Ammunition & components	**Total weight (kg)**	**Explos. weight (kg)**	**Length (mm)**	**Notes**
Panzer-sprenggranate L/4.4	800	18.8	1,672	APCBC[1] shell[2] fitted with base fuse only:[3] *shells used during the battle* (Psgr L/4.4–m Hb)
Sprenggranate L/4.5	800	32.6	1,710	HE shell fitted with nose and base fuse (Spgr L/4.5–m Hb)
Sprenggranate L/4.6	800	64.2	1,748	HE shell fitted with nose fuse only (Spgr L/4.6 – m Hb)
Ballistic cap			665	Made of light alloy and screwed to the shell nose
Copper bands				3 near the base
Shell max. diameter			397 379.8	including copper bands body only
Bodenzünder (BdZ C/38)				Type C/38 base fuse
Kopfzünder (KZ 27)				Type KZ 27 nose fuse
Hauptkartusche	182.5	112.5	818 (case)	Main propelling charge in brass case (diameter 420 mm). Powder type: RPC/38[4]
Primer tube		1.25		Type C/12 nA St. screwed to the main charge case base; the primer contained the black powder igniter
Vorkartusche	100	99.5		Fore charge in silk bag; powder type: RPC/38 with *Bleiring* (a thin sheet of lead clearing the bore of copper particles)
Coarse-grained black powder igniters		2.25		500 g at the base and 750 g at the top of the main propelling charge; 1000 g at the base of the fore charge

Bismarck's 380/47 shell data

Table 43

Bismarck's gun mounting data	Notes
Total revolving weight: 1,640 tons	Weight includes turret armour and ready rounds stowed in the turret.

Bismarck fitting out at the Blohm & Voss shipyard, turrets *Anton* and *Bruno*, Hamburg, 1939. (*Blohm & Voss*)

Rangefinder weight: 8 tons	
Distance apart of gun axes: 375 mm	
Elevation limits: from −5.5° to +30°	Max. range for 800 kg shells at 30° elev. was 35,550 m. At 45° elevation (possible only for coast defence guns, *Siegfried*) the max. range could reach 42,100 m, and at 45° elevation for a 495 kg HE shell (muzzle velocity = 1050 m/sec) max. range was 54,900 m
Max. elevating speed: 6° / sec	
Loading angle: +2.5°	Loading at fixed elevation angle: after each salvo the gun was brought to the loading elevation angle and after loading it was brought to bear at the angle of elevation calculated for the following salvo.
Training limits: 215° ÷ 145° (referring to the bow:) 35° ÷ 325°	For turrets *Anton* and *Bruno* For turrets *Cäsar* and *Dora*
Max. training speed: 5.4° / sec	
Firing cycle at 4° elevation: 26 sec	(2.3 rounds / min)[5]
Cradle	see note [6]
Servo systems	see note [7]

Armour penetration of the *Bismarck*'s 380/47 *Panzersprenggranate* L/4.4 under specific ballistic impact conditions

The Krupp 5AkB 9214 table presents the penetration data derived from tests carried out at a naval proving ground and refers to a 38 cm 800 kg *Panzersprenggranate* L/4.4 against a KC face-hardened (vertical) armour (normally KC steel was not used for deck protection). Official penetration data of horizontal protection plates are not available.

The tests assumed impact at a right angle on vertical surfaces[8] (the real value of the vertical impact angle varying with the range was not considered) and non-shattering penetration.[9] The Krupp table provides the penetration data *v.* the shell striking velocity (the relative velocity between the firing ship and the target is not considered) and *v.* the plate aspect angle (β) at impact.[10]

At 0600, the future range of the *Bismarck*'s fifth salvo was 15,200 m; hence the shell striking velocity was 565.4 m/sec. On impact, the *Hood*'s aspect angle β was 63.2°. In this situation the Krupp table indicates that the 38 cm *Panzersprenggranate* was expected to pierce about 370 mm.

Ballistic penetration is a very complex phenomenon for which a well-defined scientific theory does not yet exist. Different sources often give different penetration figures for the same shell, as some data are derived from empirical formulae while others are gathered from tests carried out at proving grounds.

For penetration tests at a naval proving ground a reduced charge is used to obtain the same impact velocity as at the investigated distance. In addition, by orienting the steel plates it is possible to reproduce the angles of impact resulting from the terminal angle of falling (ω) at a given distance as indicated in the range tables. As these tests are performed under real-life conditions, the results are only influenced by the actual performance of the projectile; namely by its possible fracture during penetration. In that event the energy absorbed by fracturing substantially reduces the level of penetration. The breakage of the projectile usually occurs when the armour thickness is nearly the same as the calibre and when the ω and/or β angles are not close to 90°. The main objective of penetration tests was to evaluate the ability of the projectile to penetrate the side armour of enemy ships. Therefore tests envisaging very low angles of obliquity (ω) with plates simulating deck protection were infrequent.

The penetration data indicated in the Krupp 5AkB 9214 table are reported below. For comparative purposes the table includes the penetration data for the British 381/42 shell (879 kg; 732 m/sec muzzle velocity) as well as for the 381/50 shell (885 kg; 870 m/sec muzzle velocity) fired by the Ansaldo-OTO 381/50 gun (Model 1934). See ref. 3 and ref. 15 for the British ordnance, and ref. 76 for the Ansaldo-OTO gun data. The Royal Navy and the Italian Navy data were gathered from proving ground tests:

Table 44

Calibre	Range (m)	Impact velocity Vω (m/sec)	Impact angle (ω)	Impact angle (β)	KC side armour penetration (mm)	Deck protection penetration (mm)
380/47	15,000	568	0	90	530	NA
	19,000	521	0	90	480	NA
	20,000	511	0	90	470	NA
	24,000	473	0	90	420	NA
	26,000	469	0	90	410	NA
381/42	16,500	≈ 490	≈ 16	90	≈ 340	51
	20,100	≈ 460	≈ 22	90	≈ 310	76
	23,800	≈ 440	≈ 28	90	≈ 265	102
381/50	19,000	591	11.6	90	416	67
	20,000	569	13.7	90	402	74
	24,000	528	18.5	90	348	105
	26,000	513	21.2	90	325	126

Other sources report the following penetration data:

Table 45

Calibre	Range (m)	Impact velocity Vω (m/sec)	Impact angle (ω)	Impact angle (β)	KC side armour penetration (mm)	Deck protection penetration (mm)
380/47	10,000	641	5.8	90	510	NA
	15,000	568	10.4	90	474	NA
	20,000	511	16.4	90	364	NA
	25,000	473	23.8	90	308	100
	30,000	457	31.9	90	NA	120

In any event, the penetration capacity of the *Panzersprenggranate* L/4.4 exceeded the strength of the *Hood*'s side armour at 15,200 m range (in the battle situation 340-370 mm perforated thickness), while at the same range the deck armour penetrated thickness was from 50 to 55 mm.

Table 46

Prinz Eugen's 203/60 gun data		Notes
Calibre	203 mm (a)	8 inch
Weight including breech	20.7 tons	
Breech block weight	0.45 tons	horizontal sliding block breech
Weapon length overall	12,150 mm (b)	(b) = (c) + (f)
Bore length	11,518 mm (c)	(c) = (e) + (g) + (h)
Exact bore length in calibres	56.7 (d)	(d) = (c) / (a)
Official bore length in calibres	60	
Rifling length	9,527 mm (e)	46.9 calibres
Block length	632 mm (f)	
Chamber length	1,873 mm (g)	
Chamber and rifled bore connecting section length	118 mm (h)	
Chamber diameter	218.1 mm	
Chamber volume	70 litres	
Grooves	64	right-handed
Depth of grooves	2.4 mm	
Width of grooves	5.76 mm	
Twist	from 1 in 40 cal. to 1 in 35 cal.	increasing
Inclination of grooves	from 4° to 5°	increasing
Shell weight	122 kg	
Propelling charge total weight	50.8 kg	
Working pressure	3,200 kg/cm²	
Recoil	625 mm	normal
Muzzle velocity (new bore)	925 m/sec	
Max. range (naval installation)	33,540 m	max. elevation 37°
Supply of shells per gun	160 (189 max.)	
Standard bore life	510 ESR	Equivalent Service Rounds (at full charge)

Table 47

Prinz Eugen's 203/60 shell data				
Ammunition & components	Total weight (kg)	Explos. weight (kg)	Length (mm)	Notes

Panzer-sprenggranate L/4.4	122	2.9	895	APCBC shell fitted with base fuse only
Sprenggranate L/4.7	122	5	956	HE
Sprenggranate L/4.7	122	9.8	953	HE
Ballistic cap				Made of light alloy and screwed to the shell nose
Copper bands	NA	NA	NA	
Shell max. diameter	NA	NA	NA	
Bodenzünder (BdZ C/38)				Type C/38 base fuse
Kopfzünder (KZ 27)				Type KZ 27 nose fuse
Hauptkartusche	47.9	29.7	875 (case)	Main propelling charge in brass case. Powder type: RPC/32[11]
Primer tube		1.25		Type C/12 nA St. screwed to the main charge case base, the primer contained the black powder igniter
Vorkartusche		21.1	900	Fore charge in silk bag; powder type: RPC/32 with *Bleiring* (a thin sheet of lead clearing the bore of copper particles)
Coarse-grained black powder igniters		0.54		160 g at the base and 180 g at the top of the main propelling charge; 200 g at the base of the fore charge

Table 48

Prinz Eugen's gun mounting data	Notes
Total revolving weight: 249 tons 262 tons	The upper value is for turrets *Anton* and *Dora*. Weight includes turret armour and ready rounds stowed in the turret.
Rangefinder weight: NA	
Distance apart of gun axes: 216 mm	
Elevation limits: from –10° to +37°	Turret *Anton* had a lower limit of –9°
Max. elevating speed: 8° / sec	
Loading angle: +3°	Loading at fixed elevation angle: after each salvo the gun was brought to the loading elevation angle and after loading it was brought to bear at the angle of elevation calculated for the following salvo.
Training limits: 215° ÷ 145° (referring to the bow): 35° ÷ 325°	For turrets *Anton* and *Bruno* For turrets *Cäsar* and *Dora*
Max. training speed: 8° / sec	
Firing cycle at 4° elevation: 21 sec	(2.9 rounds / min)[5]
Cradle	see note 6
Servo systems	see note 7

Appendix F

Applying Lanchester's Laws of Concentration to the battle

A 'what if' approach to the Battle of the Denmark Strait allows an investigation into the influence of each negative event that occurred to the British side more thoroughly. As mentioned in Chapter 3, there were five significant negative events. The different events can be evaluated only by means of a quantitative analysis. However, the intrinsic limitations of this empirical method require that the results obtained are to be considered purely indicative and worthy of interest not in absolute but in relative terms for a comparative evaluation.

A simple step-by-step procedure described in notable books on naval warfare has been followed in order to avoid the difficulties connected with the solution of the differential equations expressing Lanchester's Laws.[1] The following formula was used to quantify the initial 'staying power' (STP) of each warship participating in the battle:

$$STP = ship\ speed\ *\ \sqrt{(full\ load\ displacement\ *\ amour\ weight)}$$

The physical dimension of this quantity is:

$$metric\ tonnes\ *\ metres\ /\ second$$

Thus the staying power is expressed as power.

The power erosion (ER) performed by the ship-borne artillery was then quantified/determined according to the following formula:

$$ER = shell\ W\ *\ shell\ MV\ *\ shell\ penetration\ capacity\ *$$

$$n\ guns\ onboard\ *\ \%\ of\ efficient\ guns\ *\ \%\ of\ guns\ able\ to\ bear\ *$$

$$\%\ of\ the\ ship\ residual\ STP$$

where:

shell W	=	shell weight in metric tonnes;
shell MV	=	shell muzzle velocity in metres / second;
shell penetration capacity	=	related to that of the Krupp 38 cm SK C/34 gun. In this way the related quantity is expressed by a pure number;
n guns onboard	=	total number of heavy guns on the ship.

The physical dimension of this quantity is:

$$\text{metric tonnes * metres / second}$$

i.e. also the erosion performed by the artillery is expressed as power.

It is worth noting that the percentage of the ship residual STP allows the evaluation of the progressive degradation of the gun efficiency resulting from the erosion caused by enemy artillery.

Although the five negative events – and their alternatives – are the drivers of this analysis, many additional conditions (54 altogether) were taken into account to determine if the erosion could be attributed, when a target shift could take place, and which ship became the new target. Furthermore, had the British battlecruiser not blown up, a maximum delay of 10 minutes from the beginning of the battle (0553) was assumed for the *Hood*'s target shift from the *Prinz Eugen* to the *Bismarck*.

Notes

Introduction and Chapter 1

1. The huge IJN *Yamato* became operational in December 1941.
2. Not only was the new vessel 3 knots faster than the fastest armoured ship ever built but she also boasted a number of large-calibre guns 2.5 times the 'standard' of the so-called 'pre-Dreadnought'.
3. In 1902, General Vittorio Cuniberti of the Engineer Corps of the *Regia Marina* published a very important article reported by *Jane's Fighting Ships* in the same year with the title 'An ideal battleship for the British fleet'. As a result of the latest technologies, Cuniberti predicted the advent of battleships characterised by:
    - an increase in displacement up to 21,000 tons compared to the 17,000 tons of the heaviest contemporary ships;
    - a greater number of heavy guns with the same calibre: twelve 305-mm guns *v.* the usual number of four;
    - an armoured belt with a maximum thickness of 305 mm;
    - a propulsion plant providing a top speed of 24 knots *v.* 18 knots of the fastest battleship of that time.
4. Steam turbines for naval use were developed in Britain by Charles Parsons from 1880 to 1887. During a naval parade at Spithead in 1887, he successfully demonstrated the high speed provided by the new propulsion system on the *Turbinia* (a small vessel he had built). The first torpedo boats derived directly from that vessel – they were slim, very fast and fitted with torpedoes. Not until 1900 were propulsion plants developed with power and technical features suitable for installation aboard heavy ships.
5. These units were not in service at the time of the Russo-Japanese War from 1904 to 1905. The building of HMS *Dreadnought* was approved on 13 January 1905. The ship was launched on 10 February 1906 and commissioned on 11 December 1906.
6. The German Navy adopted the same concept with a few significant differences: German units were fitted with high-quality but lower-calibre guns and were better armoured than their British counterparts.
7. Battlecruisers were usually longer than battleships. German vessels generally differed from their British counterparts in protection from +3 to 5%, armament –5%, propulsion from –3 to –5%.
8. During the Battle of the Falkland Islands on 8 December 1914, the battlecruisers HMS *Invincible* (later Hood's flagship at the Battle of Jutland) and HMS *Inflexible* of Admiral Sturdee defeated the German squadron of Admiral Von Spee.
9. The risk for Britain was to win a Pyrrhic victory over the German fleet and at the same time lose world supremacy because of the substantial damage it would inevitably cause to the Royal Navy.
10. See J. Steinberg, *Yesterday's Deterrent* (London, 1965).
11. These battlecruisers had temporarily joined the Grand Fleet. They were commanded by Admiral Hood aboard his flagship HMS *Invincible*. At 1830 British time (1930 German time) battlecruisers *Derfflinger* and *Lützow* fired three salvoes which hit the flagship from a distance of 8,200 m. The *Invincible* blew up, killing nearly all her crew including Admiral Hood.

12. Admiral Evan-Thomas's state-of-the-art battleships – the first in the world to mount 381-mm guns – had been temporarily assigned to Beatty's fleet as a replacement of Hood's squadron.

13. At the Battle of Jutland the British forces totalled 149 units (1,250,000 tons displacement and 60,000 men) whereas the German forces amounted to 99 units (660,000 tons displacement and 45,000 men).

14. Battlecruisers were initially conceived by Adml Sir John Fisher as the 'exploring force of the fleet', able to easily outmanoeuvre (thanks to their high speed) and destroy (with their overwhelming firepower) enemy armoured cruisers.

15. After the explosion of the *Queen Mary* he famously remarked, 'There seems to be something wrong with our bloody ships today!'

16. For the sake of comparison, at the time some battle units in the Royal Navy had a displacement of over 30,000 tons and 381 mm guns.

17. The Principles of War have been studied and thoroughly discussed since the birth of General Staff for the armed forces and war 'schools'. Their aim is to explain the rationale behind the chaos of war and to provide military leaders at all levels, facing the difficult task of decision-making in the fog of war, with a specific frame of reference as well as criteria for guide and support. The Principles of War are the typical product of a rationalist school of thought from the late Enlightenment, especially those contained in Baron de Jomini's writings (a Swiss general who served under Napoleon) and much later in those of Admiral Mahan (the father of the concept of Sea Power). In 1806, de Jomini wrote that only a few fundamental principles guide the conduct of war, the foremost being the Force Concentration Principle. This school of thought is still largely the basis of Anglo-Saxon military *modus operandi* and thus of NATO (the British officially adopted the first set of Principles of War in 1920), for surface, naval and (since the first decade of the twentieth century) air operations. The Principles of War – in the light of Kant's philosophy with Clausewitz as main representative in the military field – have surely softened their initial prescriptive quality. Clausewitz never regarded the principles as prescriptive. It is true he listed a few and investigated their importance. Even so, on more than one occasion he pointed out that there are neither fixed rules nor foregone conclusions. However, they play a significant role in planning and conducting military operations at all levels: strategic, operational (or theatre-wide tactical), tactical and even technical (both for weapon systems and for projectiles). As we progress from one level to the next, we experience a restriction of space-time within the event horizon. The binding quality of the principles tends to increase up to the rigidly prescriptive of the technical level, which justifies the adoption of controlled-by-doctrine fire systems, i.e. operated automatically according to pre-established criteria and logic blocks.

18. The most significant results were independently achieved:
    - In 1902 by Lt (later RAdml) Jehu Valentine Chase US Navy (see *The Navy as a Fighting Machine* [Appendix C] by RAdml Bradley Fiske US Navy, published in 1916 and reprinted by the Naval Institute Press of Annapolis in 1988). Chase's study was classified secret up to 1972.
    - In 1915 by M. Osipov in Russia and by Ambroise Baudry, a French naval officer.
    - In 1916 by RAdml Bradley Fiske US Navy, and the British air engineer Frederick Lanchester.

19. This fact is so true and meaningful as to be mentioned even in St Matthew's Gospel in the well-known Parable of the Talents, in which the increase in resources of those who already possess them and the contemporaneous decrease of those who lack them are clearly evident: 'For unto every one that hath shall be given, and he shall have abundance: but from him that hath not, even that which he hath shall be taken away.'

20. Planning is discussed in Chapter 3 of Sun Tzu's book, sections 8 and 9.

21. This necessity is also expressed in St Luke's Gospel (14:31): 'What king, going to encounter another king in war, will not sit down first and take counsel whether he is able with ten thousand to meet him who comes against him with twenty thousand?' – R = 0.5.

22. In Chapter 3, Sun Tzu wrote, 'If our forces are five to [the enemy's] one, attack him [...] if equally matched, we can offer battle; if slightly inferior in numbers, we can avoid the enemy.' However, both Napoleon and Nelson proved that there is a reasonable chance of success also for a quantitative inferiority margin if the action is carried out with the right timing, great determination and a certain amount of aggression, a clear grasp of the situation and great mastery of manoeuvring.

At Austerlitz (2 December 1805), Napoleon won with 74,000 men *v.* 86,000 ($R_{FR} \approx 0.86\ v.\ 1$). At Trafalgar (21 October 1805), Nelson attacked and won with 27 vessels against 33 ($R_{UK} \approx 0.82\ v.\ 1$).

23. The initial version of Plan Z, submitted to Hitler around mid-1938, envisaged ending construction by 1948.

24. The planned H-44-class battleships had a displacement of 144,000 tons and an armament including eight 508-mm guns mounted on four twin turrets and firing two-ton projectiles.

25. The first of the five H-39-class armoured ships armed with 40 cm Krupp SK C/34 guns (406/47 firing 1,030 kg shells) which were to follow the F class (i.e. Bismarck class) was laid down at the Blohm &Voss dockyard in Hamburg immediately after Hitler's approval on 18 January 1939. However, construction was interrupted in September of the same year and definitively stopped on 25 November 1941. The hull was scrapped for reuse of the steel for other units. The seven large-calibre guns made by Krupp for these ships became part of coastal batteries.

26. The strategy of sea denial, as its name suggests, aims to prevent an enemy from using the sea. It therefore means suppressing the enemy's maritime commerce as well as hindering the deployment of naval forces from the sea in general, and amphibious operations in particular.

27. This force ratio refers solely to major units deployed in the Atlantic or elsewhere. The French fleet is not included.

28. In 1939, five King George V-class units were still under construction.

29. In 1939, the two Bismarck-class units were not ready yet. Moreover, three Deutschland-class units were modern battlecruisers rather than battleships, as first classified. In 1943, they were reclassified as heavy cruisers.

30. Another five were under construction.

31. W. Wegener, *Die Seestrategie des Weltkrieges* (Berlin, 1929).

32. Commerce raiders also joined in these operations but cannot be included in the heavy units class.

33. These operations were continued by merchant cruisers, and increasingly by U-boats.

34. The destruction of the PQ17, an Allied convoy to Russia, by the *Luftwaffe* and U-boats was made possible by the threat posed by the *Tirpitz* in the area. However, this threat derived its deterrent potential not from the *Tirpitz*'s offensive actions but from the *Bismarck*'s successful deeds, as is well explained in the book by P. Lund & H. Ludlam: *I Was There: On PQ17 The Convoy to Hell* (Slough, 1968).

35. In particular, the new plants produced much higher working pressure and higher steam temperature, i.e. from around 17.5 kg/cm² ($\approx$ 250 psi) and 150 °C ($\approx$ 320 °F) respectively of the *Dreadnought* to around 58 kg/cm² and 450 °C of the *Bismarck*. These improvements were obtained through the adoption of better techniques for steam plants (especially the introduction of the superheater) as well as the use of diesel oil instead of coal with the necessary adaptation of boiler burners. The latter was declared necessary by the British Admiralty as early as 1903 and was carried out with Adml Fisher as First Sea Lord starting with the Queen Elizabeth-class battleships from 1914.

36. An increase in speed of 1 knot corresponds to an exponential increase in power determined by the thinness of the hull and by drag.

37. The *Deutschland* was the first capital ship in the world with the innovation concerning the hull and propulsion: eight MAN diesels for a total power of 56,000 hp and a maximum speed of about 28 knots, a displacement of 12,100 tons standard and 16,000 tons full load (10,000 tons officially declared). Her protection, effective against 203-mm shells, consisted of Krupp cemented armour with a maximum belt thickness equal to 60 mm (increased to 100 mm in the succeeding *Admiral Graf Spee*).

38. The shell weighed 560 kg; the nominal rate of fire was 3 rounds per minute.

39. Because of her totally different design and general features, the IJN *Yamato* is not considered here.

40. RN *Vittorio Veneto* is generally considered the first fast battleship ever built, as armament, protection and speed fulfilled the requirements for this kind of vessel later expressed and followed by the major navies.

Chapter 2

1. The employment of heavy ships for the invasion of Norway (Operation *Weserübung*) instead had the aim of supporting from the sea an attack of terrestrial forces, defending them from enemy counterattack and contributing to the landing of German troops.

2. Admiral Günther Lütjens was born in Wiesbaden in 1889 and entered the Naval School in Kiel in 1907. He graduated twentieth out of 160 midshipmen in his class and in 1935 he was Captain of the light cruiser *Karlsrühe*. As an Admiral he served as Chief of Personnel and later as Chief of Torpedo Boats. During the invasion of Norway in 1940, he replaced Adml Marschall on board the *Gneisenau* as Fleet Commander. He was decorated with the Knight's Cross.

3. Other sources indicate values ranging from 113,690 to 122,000 gross register tons.

4. 'Distant' because it was not implemented close to German ports or, more generally, near the coast of German-occupied Europe.

5. Only the *Renown* underwent a major refit in the late '30s, including a redesign of the bridge structure. The refit work was completed in September 1939.

6. The ships had recently returned to Brest from Operation Berlin. The *Scharnhorst* needed an urgent overhaul of her propulsion, while the *Gneisenau* was bombed (4 April 1941) and then torpedoed (6 April 1941), suffering heavy damage.

7. Chief of Staff of the German Admiral was KzS Netzbandt, former commanding officer of the *Scharnhorst*.

8. First gunnery officer was KK Adalbert Schneider.

9. First gunnery officer was KK Jasper; second gunnery officer was KK Schmalenbach.

10. First gunnery officer was Lt Cdr Moultrie.

11. First gunnery officer was Lt Cdr McMullen.

12. Part of the forces could be deployed in the protection of important locations and high-value resources or in preparation for an attack.

13. These ships could carry nearly 9,000 tons of fuel and 400 tons of lubricating oil, together with ammunition of different calibres, spare parts, provisions and water. They were equipped with repair shops and a sick bay. They reached a speed of about 22 knots and an endurance of 12,500 nautical miles at 15 knots.

14. The *Bismarck* cost about 196 million *Reichsmarks* and had a crew of some 2,000 men. Moreover, in 1941 it was the one and only truly fast battleship of the *Kriegsmarine*.

15. The *Bismarck* left Gotenhafen at 0200 on 19 May, after a period of trials and battle practice in the Baltic Sea. The two German ships reached Bergen around 0900 on 21 May. It was perhaps the urgent need to steam on and beat the enemy to the draw that made Lütjens decide against refuelling the *Bismarck* in Bergen. This decision was to prove crucial a few days later, in the light of subsequent events.

16. A most innovative vessel for her time, with 5,000 ton full load displacement, six 152/55 guns and six seaplanes. It was launched in 1933 and stricken in 1960.

17. The option of passing north of the USSR and then breaking out into the Pacific was available but not considered. This was probably due to the excessive distance, to the difficulty of refuelling and resupplying and, last but not least, to the dangerous presence of massive floating ice. However, this route had already been followed successfully by the German former merchant cruiser *Komet* (merchant raider *Schiff 45*) and might have been passable again in May 1941, given that the relationship between Nazi Germany and the Soviet Union was then still good. (Operation Barbarossa started on 22 June 1941 with no forewarning.)

18. However, it is well known that during Operation Cerberus from 11 to 12 February 1942, the battleships *Scharnhorst* and *Gneisenau*, together with the heavy cruiser *Prinz Eugen*, followed this route to return to Germany from France.

19. The *Bismarck* left Bergen at 1930 on 21 May.

20. The *Bismarck* too had a radar set installed aboard, but on 23 May the jolts caused by the firing against Wake-Walker's ships put the forward radar out of action beyond repair.

21. This force included the battleship *King George V*, the battlecruiser *Repulse* and the aircraft carrier *Victorious*, as well as light cruisers and torpedo boats.

22. Old *Hood's* maximum speed was 28 knots because of some problems requiring a propulsion overhaul. The *Prince of Wales*, although brand-new, was unable to steam faster than 28 knots in those loading conditions.

23. The ship had been commissioned on 19 January 1941, nearly three months before completion on 31 March 1941.

24. It is worth noting that the armour of the *Prince of Wales* was generally thicker than that of the *Bismarck*.

25. The *Prince of Wales* joined up with the cruisers *Suffolk* and *Norfolk*.

26. The hull was not armoured in that area.

27. On 25 May, the forward boiler room was no longer serviceable because of flooding through the damaged bulkheads.

28. The message he sent to the *Seekriegsleitung* at 0801 indicates that by then his decision had already been taken.

29. About 4 minutes elapsed from 0556, when the German battleship opened fire, to 0600, when the *Hood* was mortally hit.

30. This is a clear example of 'surpassing the culminating point' of success (on Germany's part), a situation mentioned by Clausewitz and well described by Professor E. Luttwak in his book, *Strategy: The Logic of War and Peace* (Cambridge MA, 2001).

Chapter 3

1. It is worth noting that since 1900, the increase in the effective range of naval guns had reversed the favourable geometry of this manoeuvre. In fact, at Trafalgar, Nelson and Collingwood approached in double line ahead at a right angle to Villeneuve's Franco-Spanish line offering the port side, because until the middle of the nineteenth century the range of the side guns was so limited that it prevented effective firing against the enemy sailing on a perpendicular course when the opponent was conveniently located for bearing. However, when the distance was short enough the enemy could not be engaged by most of the available guns as it was by then in the no-firing bearing (about $\perp 20°$ abeam). Later, with increased range and guns fitted in rotating turrets, it was most favourable to offer the side to the enemy sailing in line ahead. In this situation all the main ordnance could engage, whereas the opponent could employ the forward guns only. Therefore the development of new technologies for naval guns reversed the concepts of favourable and unfavourable positions in the famous 'crossing the T' manoeuvre. The new version was performed for the first time at the Battle of Tsushima (27 May 1905) when Admiral Togo, the Commander of the Japanese fleet, outmanoeuvred the Russian ships of Admiral Rojestvensky, crossing the T twice. During the Second World War, on a few celebrated occasions, the manoeuvre was performed in its new version by RAdml Merrill, US Navy, at the Battle of Empress Augusta Bay (2 November 1943), and VAdml Oldendorf, US Navy, at the Battle of Surigao Strait (25 October 1944), a part of the larger Battle of Leyte Gulf.

2. To allow for the adjustment of gun pointing and subsequently fire at a distance ensuring adequate hit probability.

3. This is what happened in the abovementioned Battle of Empress Augusta Bay when RAdml Merrill ordered numerous turning manoeuvres.

4. To win back the bearing, the British group should have steamed at a speed higher than the *Bismarck*, i.e. greater than 28 knots. However, this was impossible because the *Hood's* condensers had vacuum problems, and 28 knots was the maximum speed that the *Prince of Wales* could sustain under her load conditions.

5. See ref. 16, p. 402.

6. See ref. 29, p. 156.

7. This ship, as well as the others, exploded under the fire of German battlecruisers, among which was SMS *Derfflinger* commanded by KzS Hartog (who replaced Admiral Hipper as commander of the German battlecruisers at the battle for a few hours). The first gunnery officer was the famous KK Georg von Hase. In the interwar period he wrote a well-known book of memoirs of the Battle of Jutland entitled *Die zwei weissen Völker!*

8. Never again would the Royal Navy give one of its units either the name *Hood* or the motto *Ventis Secundis* ('with favourable winds') assigned to Holland's unlucky ship.

9. This procedure involved the simultaneous firing of three groups of shells within the same salvo of adjustment: the central group on the basis of the future target distance calculated by the firing table (the German C38 K), another group considering a 400 m shorter distance, and the last group for a 400 m longer distance. In this way, a sort of double-bracket in flight was created. By observing the projectile fall patterns relative to the target, it was easily possible to work out the right distance.

10. The Lanchester Laws analytically expressing the advantages secured by the principle of force concentration indicate, among other things, a quadratic dependence of attainable results (dependent variable) on the initial force superiority over the opponent (independent variable); hence even an initial limited favourable margin can yield significant results.

11. The most famous of earlier episodes is that involving the French vessel *Orient* going down after the explosion of the ammunition magazine under gunfire from HMS *Bellerophon* at the Battle of the Nile (Abukir Bay) on 1 August 1798.

12. Both groups had radar. German stereoscopic rangefinders had been known in Britain since the First World War. However, the Royal Navy still preferred coincidence rangefinders (first developed by Barr & Stroud around 1889) as they were very simple to operate. Electro-mechanical fire-control tables were fitted onboard all units participating in the battle: C38 K on German ships, AFCT on the *Prince of Wales* and Dreyer Table Mk V on the *Hood*. The latter's obsolete design may have failed to give the best support to the firing against the *Prinz Eugen* considering the fast range changes occurring until 0600. However, that is not known for sure.

13. During the Second World War many navies made the same mistake. One example worth mentioning is that of the Japanese Kongo-class battlecruiser. The first of this class was built in Britain and was the first in the world to mount 356/45 guns. Together with her sister ships she underwent reconstruction in the '30s and subsequently operated as a fast battleship, in spite of lacking protection. *Kirishima* (the fourth of the Kongo class) sank near Savo Island after being hit heavily by USS *Washington* at the Battle of Guadalcanal (15 November 1942).

14. When the *Hood* exploded, the heavy cruiser *Norfolk* was about 30,000 yards away (see ref. 29, p. 163). Her torpedoes could cover a maximum distance of about 11,000 yards. This fact, added to a possible speed nearly 4 knots faster than the German vessels proceeding at 28 knots, could have made it possible to launch her torpedoes against the *Bismarck* just before 0600, the crucial phase of the battle, if at 0247 on 24 May, i.e. when Wake-Walker regained contact with the enemy, he had been given the order to close distance and attack.

15. It was the skilful use of numerical superiority (together with a favourable speed margin) that was the key to Harwood's success at the Battle of the River Plate on 13 December 1939, when with one heavy cruiser *(Exeter)* and two light cruisers *(Ajax* and *Achilles)* he attacked the far more powerful KMS *Admiral Graf Spee*.

16. The high-level features of the German ships lower the initial force ratio to a more realistic 1.5 to 1 for the British group.

17. With a 2 to 1 force ratio Sun-Tzu suggests dividing one's own forces. This strategy allows an attack on the enemy from two different directions.

18. On that occasion, Wake-Walker did not seem to share the spirit of initiative shown by Nelson at the Battle of Cape St Vincent (14 February 1797).

19. See ref. 29, p. 173.

20. When the *Hood* blew up, her hull split in two and the *Prince of Wales* risked colliding with the wreckage still floating. Capt. Leach had to perform an emergency evasive manoeuvre because, in accordance with Holland's order just before 0600 to turn 20° to port ('2 blue'), the *Prince of Wales* was heading at 14 m/s straight into the broken hull of HMS *Hood* only a few hundred metres away.

21. Radio transmission of tactical signals did not require a short distance between the units involved; the reverse was true for flag signals.

22. Actually, the *Bismarck* was longer and wider than the *Prinz Eugen* of 38.5 m and 14.5 m respectively.

23. At 0535, British lookouts aboard the *Prince of Wales* sighted the German ships and, at 0545, the Germans saw their pursuers. At 0537, the *Hood* was given the 'enemy in sight' communication.

24. The *Hood* was recognised shortly after being sighted.

25. Which did not happen at the previously mentioned Battle of the River Plate when the *Admiral Graf Spee* divided the fire of her main armament between HMS *Exeter* and the two light cruisers HMS *Ajax* and HMNZS *Achilles*.

26. If the *Bismarck* had divided fire between the *Hood* and the *Prince of Wales*, each salvo would have included a lower number of projectiles. Hence fewer data would have been available to determine the centre of each salvo.

27. It is unknown if the order was given shortly before or after the first out of the total three 356/45 projectiles hit the *Bismarck*. More realistically, these events were unconnected; namely the decision to redirect the *Prinz Eugen's* fire was not taken in an attempt to divert the fire of the British battleship but for the reason illustrated later. In fact, thanks to the heavy armour of the *Prince of Wales* the 203/60 shells of the *Prinz Eugen* could produce only marginal damage, as in fact happened.

28. The formation and falling time of the water pillars raised by the different projectiles were: for the 380 shell, a height range from 0 to about 60 m in about 5 seconds; for the 203 shell, maximum pillars of about 45 m in about 3 seconds.

29. This hypothesis is quite improbable in view both of the famous power of the 'Mighty Hood' and of the realistic effectiveness of a 203/60 shell.

30. This data refers to the average rate of fire actually sustained during the battle.

31. The initial salvoes (usually the first three or four) were for adjustment and the British procedure prescribed a reduced number of shots. From 0553 to 0602, only a total of 55 shots were fired with the 18 salvoes, leaving out another three salvoes (for a total of four shots only) fired between 0603 and 0604:30 in local control by the Y turret (quadruple after 356/45 turret). Therefore the average was a little over three shots per each of the 18 salvoes above.

32. During the battle the *Prinz Eugen* fired a total of 179 203/60 shells. It is not certain whether the *Bismarck's* sixth salvo (at 0601) was fired against the *Prince of Wales* or, more likely, for hysteresis against the sinking *Hood*. In that case, 48 380/47 shots were fired against the British battlecruiser, the first eight off target as well as the last eight, the *Hood* having abruptly altered her position under the effect of the explosion. Therefore the total of 32 effective shots against the battlecruiser would remain unchanged, whereas only 45 would have been fired at the *Prince of Wales* (only 40 effective, excluding the last five erratic shots fired by the *Bismarck*).

33. See ref. 22, pp. 61-62.

34. A few sources, among which are Roskill (ref. 16, p. 406 and ref. 17, p. 132), Schofield (ref. 38, p. 36), Kennedy (ref. 31, p. 96) and von Müllenheim-Rechberg (ref. 34, p. 91) indicate a 380/47 calibre instead of 203/60, while Stephen (ref. 21, p. 81) and Raven (ref. 15, p. 5) consider the possibility of a 203 shell. Conversely, Tarrant (ref. 22, pp. 56 and 62) is definite on the 203 calibre. A detailed analysis concerning 380/47 hit probability will be provided later.

35. The *Prince of Wales* went down, together with the *Repulse*, during the Battle of Kuantan (east of Malaya) at 1320 local time on 10 December 1941. The whole Force Z commanded by Admiral Tom Phillips was destroyed by repeated Japanese air attacks (Japanese aircraft took off from Vietnamese airfields).

36. See ref. 22, p. 44.

37. There is no certainty about the number of 380/47 shells hitting the *Hood*. Probably it was just one, as discussed later.

38. Incidentally, the British were unaware of the hits scored then. It took the testimonies of the (few) survivors from the *Bismarck*, who were (rather hastily) rescued by Royal Navy units in the area.

39. See ref. 33, p. 99; ref. 40, p. 220; ref. 61; ref. 72; and P. Colombier 'HMS Hood: le héros déchu de la Royal Navy' in *LOS!* magazine No. 7, March/April 2013.

40. See ref. 40, p. 220, note 60.

41. B. A. Fiske, *The Navy as a Fighting Machine* (Annapolis, 1988).

42. See ref. 46, p. 109.

43. *On first approximation*, it is possible to assume events A, B, C and D as marked by an equal probability of occurrence/non occurrence [$P(i0) = P(i1) = 0.5$], i.e. *uncertain occurrence*. In fact:

- if in the night before the battle Holland had not ordered a change of course (after losing visual/radar contact with the enemy), event A would probably not have occurred. With two possible alternatives (changing the course heading north or keeping on the initial interception course) the probability associated with each one of them is assumed equal to 50%;
- if the *Prince of Wales* had completed the tune-up of her large-calibre guns before the battle, event B would probably not have occurred. On the other hand, the technical expertise gained from the completion of the *King George V* (the first of her class) should have made the tune-up of the second unit 356/45 battery easier, even with less time available. Moreover, the support given by Vickers technicians aboard the *Prince of Wales* during the battle would have been important. As a consequence, it was not certain whether the 356/45 battery could be effectively employed in the battle or not; hence, on first approximation, it can be justly assumed an estimated 50% for P(B0);
- if the ship engaged by the *Hood* had not been the *Prinz Eugen*, event C would not have occurred. With two possible alternatives (engagement of the *Prinz Eugen* or engagement of the *Bismarck*), the probability associated with each one of them is assumed equal to 50%;
- if Wake-Walker's ships had played a more active role in the battle, event D would not have occurred. With two possible alternatives (participation or non-participation in the battle), the probability associated with each one of them is assumed equal to 50%.

44. According to the Law of Total Probability, the probability of occurrence of one of the incompatible events is given by the total of the Po estimated for each event.

45. However, the occurrence of the other negative events (A+B+C+D: inappropriate interception manoeuvre, engagement of the wrong ship, mechanical breakdowns of the *Prince of Wales*, and missed employment of Wake-Walker's cruisers) would have resulted in serious damage being inflicted to the British group, again a Pyrrhic victory. Situation 31 can therefore be considered the mirror image of situation 6.

46. D. Irving, *Hitler's War* (London, 2001).

Chapter 4

1. The target's sturdiness is its ability to harmlessly reflect the incident energy and/or absorb it unscathed. As the energy transfer by ammunition to the target occurs by an exponential law that is a function of the target distance, then, among other factors, the target size is evidently important to sturdiness.

2. Systematic errors of a salvo are registered between the salvo centre (i.e. the salvo falling points centre) and the target geometrical centre.

3. Accidental errors provoke the dispersion of impact points around the salvo centre.

4. See ref. 34, p. 89.

5. See ref. 38, p. 32.

6. See ref. 31, p. 88.

7. Von Müllenheim-Rechberg in his celebrated book remembers: 'Suddenly' a petty officer (machinist) wrote of our first hit from the Prince of Wales, 'we sensed a different jolt, a different tremor through the body of our ship: a hit, the first hit!' (See ref. 34, p. 93.) It is worth noting that the kinetic energy liberated by 356/45 shells on impact was lower than that of 380/47s covering the same distance. This testimony supports the idea that a separate hit could by no means be ignored.

8. Adjustment is a procedure preliminary to effective firing. Through the observation of the salvo falling points the gunnery officer tries to make the centre of the battery beaten zone coincide with the target centre. The battery beaten zone is made up by the sum of each elliptical area whose axes contain 99.3% of the infinite shots theoretically fired by every single gun of the battery (infinite impact point pattern).

9. See ref. 34, p. 87.

10. With this procedure the salvo was subdivided into three-round groups. In the Italian *Regia Marina* the groups were typically two, four and two for an eight-gun battery (this is the subdivision considered for this study):

- The first was called 'Short group'. It was fired with a shorter range than that determined on elevation and deflection values supplied by the firing table, and aimed at achieving an 85% likelihood of obtaining 'real' laddering between groups. The standard procedure indicated 400 m as the range difference between groups in the ladder.
- The second was called 'Base group'. It was fired according to elevation and deflection values supplied by the firing table. These values were calculated on the basis of the average distance (the average of the ranges determined by rangefinders trained on the target) and bearing acquired through directors.
- The third was called 'Long group'. The range used for settings was 400 m longer. In this way, the adjustment salvo probability of kill was greatly reduced. However, the probability of straddling was maximised: the shells of two groups landed on either side of the target or the shells of a single group landed on target straight away. In any case, as the range difference between groups was known, it was quite easy to determine the corrections necessary to fire effectively; namely when the centre of impact points was on target, hence maximising the probability of kill.

11. See ref. 34, p. 89.
12. A Gaussian function or bell curve.
13. 'The hitting space (in range) for a target is the distance behind the target, measured parallel to the line of fire, that a shot striking the top of the target will strike the horizontal plane through the base of the target. It includes the projection of the target's vertical height upon the plane of the water and the target's horizontal dimension in the line of fire (or depth). It may also include a distance in front of the target within which impacts are likely to produce underwater or ricochet hits on the target. The hitting space in deflection is the width of the target.' (Naval Ordnance & Gunnery, Volume 2: Fire Control. US Navy NAVPERS 10798, p. 66).
14. A copy of the original data of dispersion for the Krupp SK C/34 gun with its L/4.4 *Panzersprenggranate* used by the *Bismarck* during the battle was kindly provided in graph form by the *Historisches Archiv Krupp*, HA Krupp, WA 52-429-0, WA 52-429-1, WA 52-429-2, WA 52-429-3.
15. F_E was obtained by multiplying the number of the fired rounds by the value of the theoretical hit probability inferred from the calculated SSHP.
16. See ref. 34, p. 87.
17. With the *hit in the fifth salvo only* constraint the probability of exactly one hit decreases to 3% (5% with at least one hit in the fifth salvo).
18. In this regard, both Admiralty boards of inquiry, after hearing from all eyewitnesses (the survivors of both parts included), reached the conclusion that the *Hood* had been sunk by one or more shells belonging to the fifth salvo fired by the *Bismarck*.
19. This document is kept at the National Archives in London and is part of the collection ADM 234/444. The sinking of the *Hood* is discussed on page 10, while the damage suffered by the *Prince of Wales* is described on page 11.
20. See ref. 14, pp. 56 and 62, and ref. 22, p. 62.
21. The slightly higher value calculated for alternative 2 (of both hypotheses) attributing the hit to the *Bismarck* is not sufficient to tip the scales in favour of the higher calibre.

Chapter 5

1. Obviously, the British did not definitely know the characteristics of German 380/47 guns.
2. The model target was a ship-portion with the same architecture and armour thickness as the *Hood*.
3. The British 15-inch gun had more curved trajectories because of the lower muzzle velocity (732 m/sec *v.* 820 m/sec) and because of the heavier shells.
4. From the operational and strategic point of view instead, the attempt of the Royal Navy task force to interdict the German group was thoroughly defensive and was in reaction to the German attempt to break the British *distant blockade*.
5. In his article, 'The loss of HMS Hood – A Re-Examination' (Warship International Naval Research

Organization, 1987-2007) William J. Jurens undertook a very accurate analysis of these aspects.

6. See ref. 16.
7. See ref. 33, p. 96.
8. See Chapter 4, note 13.
9. e' or 'E' (later in the text) is for the French word *épaisseur* meaning 'thickness'.
10. See ref. 21, p. 80.
11. For these data see ref. 35, p. 61 and ref. 29, p. 145. When in doubt, a smaller thickness was considered.
12. Jacob de Marre was a famous French scholar of terminal ballistics whose lifetime spanned the end of the nineteenth century and the beginning of the twentieth.
13. The horizontal armour penetration capacity of the Italian 381/50 shell (74 mm at 20,000 m range) was considered because no data concerning the German shells were available. In any event, it must be noted that:
    - the Italian shell was heavier than the German (885 kg *v.* 800 kg);
    - the horizontal penetration of the Italian shell referred to a slightly higher impact velocity (569 m/sec *v.* 565.4 m/sec);
    - the impact angle to the horizontal plane of the Italian shell was wider than that considered for the German shell (13.7° *v.* 10.6°). Hence the deck penetration capacity of the Italian 381/50 shell (74 mm) at 20,000 m was surely higher than that of the German Psgr 38 cm L/4.4 at 15,200 m.
14. Table 68 in ref. 15, p. 278 indicates for a 15-inch shell (879 kg) a deck penetration capacity of 2 inches (51 mm) at a range of 18,000 yards (≈ 16,500 m), with an impact velocity of ≈ 490 m/sec and an impact angle (ω) of 16°.
15. This is the area from which the huge fire pillar was seen erupting at 0601.
16. The average inclination of the trajectory necessary to reach the 102/45 ammunition working space is quite compatible with the shell's angle of entry (considering the predictable deflection downwards of the shell's trajectory following the loss of velocity on perforating decks and bulkheads). This was possibly the sequence of events, but only if the impact on the main deck took place close to the starboard waterway, otherwise the projectile would have probably passed above the ammunition working spaces and storerooms and travelled deep into the port side of the ship causing minor damage.
17. The latter was located above the same-calibre shell magazine probably for stability reasons, although this architectural option was most risky given the high vulnerability of launch charges, which in the Royal Navy were kept in simple silk bags. Later, in the battleships designed and built by all navies, the large-calibre shell magazines were to be located above the propelling charge ones.
18. See ref. 21, p. 80.
19. See ref. 33, pp. 199-207.
20. Incidentally, she was due to have more armour added to protect the decks as part of a major refit which was cancelled on the outbreak of hostilities.
21. A Gaussian distribution of hitting shells' impact points appears realistic because unguided artillery ammunition fall and spread on the surface as a function of firing dispersion.
22. In ref. 22, p. 58 Tarrant writes in this regard: *'The defective bursting qualities of the German shells – four out of the seven had failed to explode and one only partially exploded – obviously saved Prince of Wales from serious damage.'*
23. This hypothesis appears to be realistic and hence acceptable. It is nonetheless worth mentioning that quite a few military units sank because of an explosion *from within*, i.e. not in a naval battle, among which are the following:
    - The US battleship *Maine* went down while in port in Havana due to the explosion of the fore ammunition magazine on 15 February1898. Some Spanish agents were blamed – perhaps unjustly so – for the event which started the Spanish-American War in the same year.
    - The French battleship *Liberté* sank in port in Toulon after the accidental explosion of her ammunition magazine on 25 September 1911.
    - The Italian battleship *Brin* sank in port in Brindisi after her ammunition magazines exploded as a result of an act of sabotage by Austrian agents on 27 September 1915.

- The Italian battleship *Leonardo da Vinci* sank in port in Taranto after the explosion of her aft ammunition magazine caused by an act of sabotage by Austrian agents on 2 August 1916;
- The Japanese battleship *Mutsu* sank while moored at a buoy in Hiroshima Bay (Kure) as a result of the accidental blowing up of her aft ammunition magazine on 8 June 1943.

24. This assumption is equally realistic and acceptable, although a few authors, among whom are Martin Stephen (see ref. 21, p. 80) and Mark Simmons (*Warships International Fleet Review* London: Seymour, August 2008, p. 56), do not exclude the possibility that the fatal shell may have been fired by the *Prinz Eugen* shortly before Lütjens ordered the heavy cruiser to take the *Prince of Wales*.

25. The horizontal surface was considered not completely penetrable, with the exception of the area above the 102/45 ammunition working space at stern.

26. HMS *Rodney* fired 380 406/45 rounds and 716 152/50 rounds; HMS *King George V* fired 339 356/45 rounds and 660 133/50 rounds; HMS *Norfolk* and HMS *Dorsetshire* fired 527 and 254 203/50 shells respectively.

Chapter 6

1. The only reservation about German artillery materiel used in the battle concerns ammunition reliability.

2. The excellent Krupp SK C/34 gun had a very high rate of fire: theoretically, it could fire every 26 seconds.

3. I do not share the opinion of Admiral Lord Chatfield, who declared at the time that the lethal hit could not have been a stroke of good luck for the Germans.

4. See ref. 10.

Appendix A

1. Not all clocks onboard the fighting ships read the same time. Likewise, gyrocompasses were not aligned equally. Also, the measure of distance calculated through the rangefinder could not boast the same precision as obtained through today's radar. In fact, British coincidence rangefinders were less efficient than German stereoscopic ones, whose range of error would not exceed 1-2% of the distance measured by experienced operators under normal operative conditions. Finally, British rangefinders (unlike the German instruments) had great difficulty in measuring the distance when the object, e.g. a pillar of smoke, had blurred contours.

Appendix B

1. This is a function of two independent Gaussian variables; namely the distribution along the x axis for the distance and the y axis transverse to it – in other words, a bell-shaped tri-dimensional curve.

2. If the impact angle (ω) is less than 10°, the shells tend to bounce flat and significantly deviate to the right (by the rotation impressed on them at firing). If the impact angle is more than 30°, the shells sink rapidly at a rather short distance from the falling point.

3. See ref. 35, p. 56.

4. See ref. 15, p. 284.

Appendix C

1. See J. R. Taylor, *An Introduction to Error Analysis, The Study of Uncertainties in Physical Measurements* (Mill Valley CA, 1982).

2. A possible resetting error of a range measuring sensor (a rangefinder or a radar) produces a constant range error of the shot's impact points. By contrast, a possible error concerning the projectile's initial velocity (constant velocity error) results in an error increasing with the flight time. On the other hand, a possible angular error affecting the director or the radar and the reference direction of the ordnance causes an error increasing with the range and hence with the flight time.

3. It is possible to distinguish between short-term fluctuations (shot by shot) and longer-term fluctuations with slow variations that are hardly appreciable shot by shot and produce sensible effects only when the gun barrel has fired many projectiles. The gradual decrease in initial velocity caused by the progressive erosion of the barrel is a typical example. In this analysis, long-term errors are included in systematic errors for the sake of simplicity.

4. The probable error is the quantity (between the expected and the observed point of fall) including 50% of the population of hypothetically infinite shots fired by the gun.

5. The remaining 0.7% accounts for *wild shots* whose trajectory is unusual for peculiar and exceptional reasons.

6. The concept of *theoretical* horizontal impact point pattern ('*theoretical*' because it refers to infinite shots) is particularly useful when it comes to the calculation of the hit probability of projectiles with not very flat trajectories and fired at surface targets at medium or high distance. Other theoretical impact point patterns can be considered, among which is the 'vertical impact point pattern' lying in the vertical plane; it is concentric with the horizontal and shares with it the '*y*' value. The concept of vertical impact point pattern is applied in the calculation of the hit probability of projectiles with flat trajectories fired at short-distance surface targets.

7. By definition, the width of the *Striscie al 50%* is two times the probable error.

8. For naval low-angle guns the above elements are limited to the first elevation arc of the trajectory, i.e. from 0° to 45°.

9. It is worth mentioning that the first digital computing machines (the Mk 1 developed by MIT (Massachusetts Institute of Technology) in 1944 and based on electro-mechanical relay technology, and the subsequent ENIAC fitted with 18,000 thermionic valves and built in the USA in 1946) were initially employed for the preparation of range tables.

10. This interference was studied by Gen. Pellegrini of the *Regia Marina*.

11. The probable errors in range and in deflection reported in the range table are '$\varepsilon pxRT$' and '$\varepsilon pyRT$'.

12. The probable error (εp) and the standard deviation (σ) are connected with the mathematical equation $\sigma = 1.4826 * \varepsilon p$.

13. Obviously, this error could occur only when the ordnance was not fitted with automatic aiming servo systems, thus requiring the manual intervention of operators.

14. For the sake of simplicity, the same theoretical impact pattern dimensions for each gun of the battery will be assumed, i.e. the same gun dispersion for each gun.

15. Considering the results of the tests carried out by the French Navy on the battleship FS *Richelieu* in 1948, and the power of the French 381/44.9 guns (380/45 before the *Richelieu*'s refitting in the USA in 1943) as well as that of the German 380/47 ones, we can reasonably estimate the variation of range impact points caused by muzzle blast interference from guns of the same turret to be of the same order as the 'm' discrepancy, while the variation of deflection (*y* axis) can be estimated to be half as much.

16. See J. R. Taylor, *An Introduction to Error Analysis, The Study of Uncertainties in Physical Measurements* (Mill Valley CA, 1982) pp. 76-77.

17. The function of the distribution is tri-dimensional and depends on two statistical variables, each one characterised by a specific standard deviation value: σx sea battery and σy sea battery.

18. This deduction requires that the values given by the range tables for variations in the mentioned ballistic quantities are known. Unfortunately, these values were not available; hence on first approximation use was made of the values contained in the range tables for the Italian Ansaldo-OTO 381/50 Model 1934 gun, thus acknowledging the related inaccuracies.

19. The 1.5 ratio of standard deviation of actual firing dispersion to the standard deviation values of the range tables is considered appropriate by Italian regulations for a modern low-angle weapon fitted

with servo systems for automatic aiming, while the *Bismarck*'s guns were aimed by operators.
20. In fact, a sensible modification of the errors estimate appears unrealistic within the battle's short time frame.
21. *Historisches Archiv Krupp* (HA Krupp), WA 52-429-0, WA 52-429-1, WA 52-429-2, WA 52-429-3. The necessary elements are indicated in the following graphs: '3AkB 2721' dated 27 April 1939 for lateral dispersion; '5AkB 2663' (date illegible) for longitudinal and lateral dispersion.
22. See ref. 24, p. 52.
23. See ref. 20, p. 31.
24. See ref. 3, p. 229.

Appendix D

1. Karl Pearson (1857–1936), an English scientist and statistician, was an academic of eclectic interests ranging from mathematics to philosophy, law and eugenics. Pearson's contribution to statistics includes the development of many statistical methods.
2. Sir Ronald Aylmer Fisher (1890–1962) was an English statistician and biologist. He made important contributions to both genetics and statistics, the latter including his studies of analysis of variance and of the statistics of small samples.
3. Each salvo can be considered a statistical sample made up of the fired shots.
4. This correction is usually applied because the chi-square test makes use of discrete data to estimate a continuous distribution.

Appendix E

1. APCBC = Armour Piercing Capped with Ballistic Cap.
2. Explosive shells were yellow with a black nose and a white band around the mass centre.
3. '*The bursting charge was TNT desensitized with beeswax, the amount of the latter decreasing from head to base of the cavity.*' See ref. 3, p. 221.
4. RPC/38 powder was made up of 69.45% nitrocellulose (12.2% nitrogen); 25.3% diethylene glycol dinitrate; 5% centralite; 0.15% magnesium oxide; 0.1% graphite. Calorific value was 810 Kcal/kg and the uncooled explosion temperature was 2495 °K. See ref. 3, p. 221.
5. If this figure is compared with the actual rate of fire sustained during the battle we can see that the time taken by the observation of the falling points and the possible corrections did substantially slow down the actual rate of fire.
6. There were two individual cradles coupled together for elevation. Each cradle was connected to a recuperator above the barrel (absorbing a portion of the recoil energy to return the barrel to its firing position) and two counter-recoil brakes below the barrel. An opening in the lower rear part of the turret allowed the ejection of spent cartridge cases.
7. *Training* of each turret was by means of an electric motor, and the auxiliary gears for elevation and loading were also electric.

    Elevation was by means of a Siemens electro-hydraulic system. A hydraulic piston was connected to a rack and pinion converting the linear motion of the piston into rotary motion driving the toothed elevating arc. The pressure medium was 50% water and 50% glycerine pressurised by an electrically driven pump. The electric motor driving the latter was controlled by a thyratron valve. Control was non-linear and depended on acceleration and on the pressure in the hydraulic circuit. This circuit comprised an accumulator providing the energy needed to start the system.

    Loading was normally driven by an electro-hydraulic system. The main and fore charges (the first in a brass case and the second in a fully combustible container) were end to end on one tray in a cage. The shell cage was below the charge case. Both cages were transferred together (one picking up the other on ascent) by the hoists coming up between the guns, from the shell rooms to the gunhouse. The shells were then transferred by rammers to loading trays that moved laterally into position behind each barrel while the charges were transferred to waiting cages. After firing, with the breech open the case of the main charge was ejected and moved out by a mechanical tray. Then extendable chain rammers thrust the shells into the breech until the copper bands bit into the start of the rifling. When the chain rammers retracted, the waiting cages with the charges moved down and the latter rolled into the loading tray by means of a ramp. The charges were rammed together and the rammers quickly retracted, allowing the breech to close. Two fans extracted exhaust fumes.

8. Whenever the vertical angle ω between the shell longitudinal axis and the horizontal plane is 0° the shell impacts at a right angle on the vertical armour plate.

9. The energy absorbed by shattering substantially reduces the level of penetration. The breakage of the projectile usually occurs when the armour thickness is nearly the same as the calibre and when the ω and/or β angles are not close to 90°.

10. The plate aspect angle is the horizontal angle between the shell longitudinal axis and the armour plane.

11. RPC/32 powder was made up of 66.6% nitrocellulose (11.5% nitrogen), 25.9% nitroglycerine, 7.25% centralite, 0.15% magnesium oxide and 0.1% graphite. Calorific value was 830 Kcal/kg and the uncooled explosion temperature was 2630 °K. See ref. 3, p. 221.

Appendix F

1. In particular see B. A. Fiske, *The Navy as a Fighting Machine* (Annapolis, 1988), Chapter 3 and Appendix C; and W. P. Hughes, *Fleet Tactics: theory and practice* (Annapolis, 1986), Chapter 4.

Sources and Bibliography

Historical and technical – general

Bekker, C. D., *The German Navy* (London: Chancellor Press, 1997).

Breyer, S., *Battleships and Battle Cruisers 1905–1970* (London: Macdonald, 1973).

Campbell, J., *Naval Weapons of World War Two* (London: Conway Maritime Press, 1985).

Creswell, J., *Sea Warfare 1939–1945: A Short History* (London: Longmans, Green and Co, 1950).

Dumas, R., *La cuirassé Richelieu 1935–1968* (Bourg-en-Bresse: Marines Editions et Réalisations, 1992).

Friedman, N., *Naval Firepower: Battleship guns and gunnery in the Dreadnought era* (Annapolis: Naval Institute Press, 2008).

Hodges, P., *The Big Gun: Battleship Main Armament 1860–1945* (London: Conway Maritime Press, 1981).

Konstam, A., *British Battlecruisers 1939–1945* (Oxford: Osprey Publishing, 2003).

Lacroix, E. and L. Wells, *Japanese Cruisers of the Pacific War* (London: Chatham Publishing, 1987).

Middlebrook, M. and O. Mahoney, *The Sinking of the Prince of Wales & Repulse: The End of the Battleship Era* (Barnsley: Leo Cooper, Pen & Sword, 2004).

Peillard, L., *La Battaglia dell'Atlantico* (Verona: Mondadori, 1976).

Raeder, E., *La Mia Vita* (Milan: Baldini & Castoldi, 1960).

Rastelli, A., *Le Grandi Battaglie Navali del XX Secolo* (Venice: Mondadori, 1996).

Raven, A., *Ensign 1: King George the Fifth Class Battleships*, (London: Bivouac Books Ltd, 1972).

Raven, A. and J. Roberts, *British Battleships of World War Two* (Annapolis: Naval Institute Press, 1988).

Roskill, S. W., *The War at Sea 1939–1945* (London: HMSO, 1954).

Roskill, S. W., *The Navy at War 1939–1945* (London: Collins, 1960).

Rowe, A., *Illustrated Record of German Army Equipment 1939–1945 Part 2* (Uckfield: Naval & Military Press Ltd, 2004).

Ruge, F., *La Guerra Sul Mare 1939–45* (Milan: Garzanti, 1961).

Skwiot, M., *German Naval Artillery* (Gdańsk: AJ Press, 2004).

Stephen, M., *Sea Battles in close-up: World War 2* (Runnymede: Ian Allan, 1988).

Tarrant, V. E., *King George V Class Battleships* (London: Arms and Armour Press, 1985).

Warner, O., *Great Sea Battles* (Verona: Mondadori, 1963).

Whitley, M. J., *German Capital Ships of World War Two* (London: Arms and Armour Press, 1989).

Historical and technical – specific

Ballard, R. D., *Il Ritrovamento della Bismarck* (Verona: Mondadori, 1990).

Breyer, S. and G. Koop, 'Schlachtschiff Bismarck', *Die Deutsche Kriegsmarine 1935–1945* No. 6 (Friedberg: Podzun Pallas Verlag, 1990).

Brower, J., *The Battleship Bismarck* (London: Conway Maritime Press, 2005).

Caresse, P., *Le Bismarck: Un cuirassé à détruire* (Outreau: Lela Presse, 2004).

Chesneau, R., *Hood: Life and Death of a Battlecruiser* (London: Cassell, 2002).

Elfrath, U., 'Schlachtschiff Bismarck', *Waffen Arsenal* No. 75 (Friedberg: Podzun Pallas Verlag, 1982).

Kennedy, L., *Pursuit: The Chase and Sinking of the Bismarck* (London: William Collins Sons & Co., 1974).

Koop, G. and K.-P. Schmolke, *Battleships of the Bismarck Class* (Annapolis: Naval Institute Press, 1998).

Mearns, D. and R. White, *Hood and Bismarck* (London: Channel 4 Books, 2001).

von Müllenheim-Rechberg, B., *Battleship Bismarck: A Survivor's Story*, (Annapolis: Naval Institute Press, 1980).

Roberts, J., *The Battlecruiser Hood* (London, Conway Maritime Press, 1982).

Robertson, R. G., 'Hood', *Profile Warship* No. 19 (Windsor: Profile Publications Ltd, 1971).

Schmalenbach, P., 'Bismarck', *Profile Warship* No. 18 (Windsor: Profile Publications Ltd, 1971).

Schofield, B. B., *Loss of the Bismarck* (Annapolis: Naval Institute Press, 1972).

Skwiot, M. and E. T. Prusinowska, *Operacja Rheinübung Polowanie na Bismarcka* (Gdańsk: AJ Press, 2004).

Taylor, B., *The Battlecruiser HMS Hood: An Illustrated Biography 1916–1941* (Annapolis: Naval Institute Press, 2008).

Specialist sources

Burul, S. and P. G. Fedeli, *Balistica Sperimentale: Applicata Terminale* (Turin: Scuola di Applicazione, 1985).

Cenni sulle Dispersioni del Tiro, Gruppo Insegnamento Artiglieria (Livorno: Ed. Accademia Navale, 1975).

Cipollini, G., *Tiro* (Livorno: Regia Accademia Navale, 1943).

Farina, B., *Tiro* (Livorno: Ed. Accademia Navale, 1950).

Farina, B., *Appunti sull'impiego delle artiglierie* (Livorno: Accademia Navale, 1948).

Fea, L., 'A proposito del tiro a grandissime distanze', *Rivista Marittima* (Rome, 1914).

Fioravanzo, G., *Manuale Teorico-pratico di Cinematica Aeronavale* (Livorno: Regia Accademia Navale, 1930).

Giannattasio, Ronca, *Elementi di Balistica Esterna* (Livorno: Regia Accademia Navale, 1937).

Gigantesco, C., *Nozioni di calcolo delle probabilità e statistica* (Livorno: Ed. Accademia Navale, 1973).

Gigantesco, C., *Nozioni di impiego delle armi* (Livorno: Ed. Accademia Navale, 1979).

Giorio, C., *I sistemi d'arma – analisi funzionale ed elementi di impiego* (Livorno: Ed. Accademia Navale, 1990).

Helgert, H. J., *A statistical treatment of various classes of gunnery errors and the calculation of hit probability* (Dahlgren: US Naval Weapons Laboratory, 1969).

Hughes, W. P., *Fleet Tactics: theory and practice* (Annapolis: Naval Institute Press, 1986).

Mongiardini, G., 'Sulle cause di dispersione nelle salve in mare', *Rivista Marittima* (Rome, 1915).

Pignone, R. and U. R. Vercelli, *Appunti di Balistica* (Florence: Olimpia, 1987).

Re, V., *Balistica Esterna* (Livorno: Ed. Accademia Navale, 1952).

Reilly, J. C., *Operational Experience of Fast Battleships; WWII, Korea, Vietnam* (Washington: Naval Historical Center, Department of the Navy, 1989).

Spiegel, M. R., *Statistica* (Milan: McGraw-Hill, 1994).

Ventsel, E. S., *Teoria delle probabilità* (Moscow: Edizioni MIR, 1969).

Vettori, F., *Elementi di Probabilità e Statistica*, (Livorno: Ed. Accademia Navale, 1992).

Articles

Bonomi, A., 'Stretto di Danimarca, 24 maggio 1941', *Storia Militare*, December 2005.

Caresse, P., 'Le Croiseur de Bataille HMS Hood', *Navires & Histoire*, August 2004.

Cernuschi, E., 'Bismarck', *Storia Militare*, December 2004.

Colliva, G., 'Le Artiglierie Navali nella Guerra del Mediterraneo', *Bollettino dell'Archivio Storico*, September 2003, December 2003, March 2004.

Cosentino, M., 'Caccia alla Bismarck', *Tecnologia & Difesa*, June 2005.

da Fré, G., 'La fine dell'Hood (24 maggio 1941)', *Rivista Marittima*, March 2001.

da Fré, G., 'Affondate la Bismarck', *Rivista Marittima*, May 2001.

Gilbertini, G., 'Caccia alla Bismarck', *Eserciti nella Storia*, November 1999.

Mazza, V., Modellismo 3D: 'La Corazzata tedesca Bismarck in 3 milioni di poligoni', *3D Professional*, January-February 2003.

Sgarlato, N., 'Le Navi da Battaglia del III Reich', *War Set*, October-November 2004.

Toussaint, P., 'Le poste principal de Direction de Tir du cuirassé Bismarck', *Marines & Forces Navales*, December 1998-January 1999.

Toussaint, P., 'Le Bismarck: Gloire et Défaite', *Histoire de Guerre*, July-August 2001.

Toussaint, P., 'Le Croiseur de Bataille Hood', *Histoire de Guerre*, April 2003.

Archival documents

HM Ships Damaged or Sunk by Enemy Action (3rd Sept. 1939 to 2nd Sept. 1945), ADM 234/444 (London: The National Archives, 1952).

HA Krupp, WA 52-429-0, WA 52-429-1, WA 52-429-2, WA 52-429-3 (Essen: *Historisches Archiv Krupp*, unpublished, 1930-1940).

Tavola di Tiro (Firing Table) No. 1 cannoni da 381/50 Ansaldo e O.T.O. Modello 1934 (proietto tipo 'palla'), Regio Balipedio Gregorio Ronca (Viareggio, 1939).

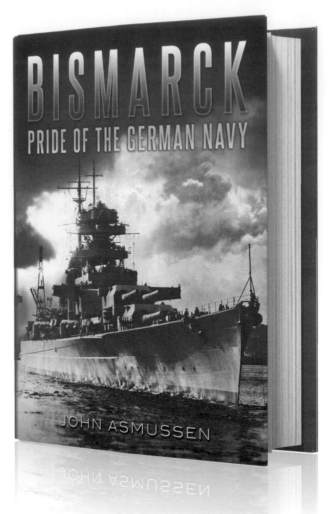

Bismarck: Pride of the German Navy

ISBN 978-1-78155-039-7   £50.00   Hardback 310 x 240mm 240pp

330 illustrations, 50 in colour

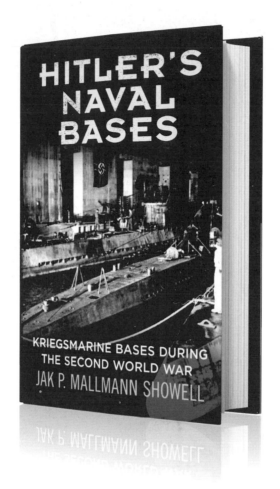

Hitler's Naval Bases:
Kriegsmarine Bases During the Second World War
ISBN 978-1-78155-198-1 £20.00 Hardback 248 x 172mm 256pp
200 illustrations

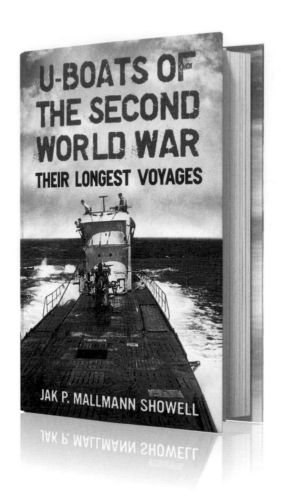

U-Boats of the Second World War:
Their Longest Voyages

ISBN 978-1-78155-102-8 £18.99 Hardback 234 x 156mm 240pp
98 illustrations

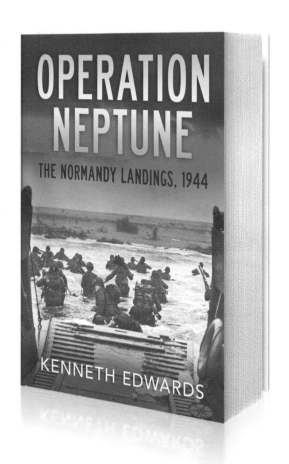

Operation Neptune:
The Normandy Landings, 1944

ISBN 978-1-78155-127-1 £16.99 Paperback 234 x 156mm 352pp

147 illustrations